Praise for
ALL ABOUT Y

'*All About Yves* is one of those books that will stay with you—a smart, intimate and generous memoir of coming-of-age that is always keenly aware of the historical context and lineage, so often hidden, of which it is a part. Rees has a wonderful ability to speak plainly—and engagingly—about complex ideas, and the ways in which much larger forces make their marks on all of our lives. Above all, it is a book of great heart and gentle intelligence, and one that will mean a great deal to many people.'

Fiona Wright, author of *The World Was Whole*

'Rees has given us a gift. Here, they give us euphoria. Their writing is a balm for anyone who has lived on the margins. Rees takes this experience and gives it breath so that we might better understand the essential humanity of our own project; that we are here to love whoever is around to be loved. In the detail, they give us knowledge. In the story, hope.'

Rick Morton, author of *My Year of Living Vulnerably*

'A wondrous and searingly honest story of becoming and being trans. A must read for us all. A remarkable memoir that gives readers the space to imagine the other possibilities outside of the gender binary. *All About Yves* is a powerful act of resistance that will open up new possibilities for readers.'

Mandy Beaumont, author of *Wild, Fearless Chests*

'With their winning combination of piercing intelligence, wry humour and raw emotion, Yves Rees has provided a touchstone for anyone who might know, deep down, that they are not living their truth—trans or otherwise. Ultimately, *All About Yves* reveals all about us: the messy, painful, hungry, joyful, complex condition of being human. Brilliant, brave and paradigm-shifting, this is the book we need now. This book will change—and quite possibly save—lives.'

Clare Wright, Stella Prize-winning author of *The Forgotten Rebels of Eureka*

'This is the memoir we need right now: thoughtful and truthful, engaging and illuminating, sometimes vulnerable and often powerful, and above all, exquisitely written. Like all good memoirs, *All About Yves* tells one person's story and creates meaning and questions for us all.'

Dr Kelly Gardiner, writer, poet and academic

'*All About Yves* welcomes you into the anxiety and quest of finding one's path in a binary world: An utterly charming and deeply contextualising take on trans identity.'

Kaya Wilson, author of *As Beautiful As Any Other*

'Rees welcomes us into the intimate experience of transition by interweaving their coming out story with philosophy, academic thought, and recent politics. Writing with openness and wry honesty, Rees encourages us to embrace the expansiveness and contradictions of nonbinary gender. You'll never be prouder to attend the same gender clinic.'

Briar Rolfe, illustrator and comic artist

'*All About Yves* is a deep and messy journey of personal transformation, that sifts through the complexities and the contradictions of living honestly. Yves compels us to move outside stale binaries of thinking and being, that limit not only our imaginations and hearts, but also reproduce legacies of incredible harm and injustice. Reminding readers that we are always in flux, and the real value and richness of living the questions, and following them, wherever they lead.'

Sarah Firth, comic artist and writer

'We need more books like this in the world. *All About Yves* has fundamentally transformed how I think about gender. The best writers complicate things and their work is incredibly complex, filled with insight and power and vulnerability and in the end: hope. Should be compulsory reading.'

Katherine Collette, author of *The Helpline*

Dr Yves Rees (they/them) is a writer and historian living on unceded Wurundjeri land. At present, Yves is a lecturer in history at La Trobe University and co-host of the history podcast *Archive Fever*. Yves was a 2021 Varuna Residential Fellow and was awarded the 2020 ABR Calibre Essay Prize for their essay 'Reading the Mess Backwards'. Yves is a regular contributor to ABC radio and *The Conversation*, and their work has appeared in the *Australian Book Review*, *Meanjin*, *Sydney Review of Books*, *Overland*, *Inside Story* and *Archer Magazine*. Yves volunteers with Transgender Victoria and is the co-founder of trans writing collective Spilling the T. In 2021, they guest co-edited *Bent Street 5.1: Hard Borders, Soft Edges*. Yves' monograph *Travelling to Tomorrow: Australian Women and the American Century* is forthcoming with Nebraska University Press. *All About Yves* is their first book.

Twitter @YvesRees
Instagram @Yves_Rees

All About Yves

Notes from a Transition

Yves Rees

ALLEN&UNWIN
SYDNEY · MELBOURNE · AUCKLAND · LONDON

First published in 2021

Copyright © Yves Rees 2021

An abbreviated version of 'Blood Will Tell' was originally published by *Archer Magazine* #14 and online; an abbreviated version of 'Misadventures in Menswear' was originally published by *Archer Magazine*
'Blondie' was originally published by Darebin Council
'Reading the Mess Backwards' was originally published by the *Australian Book Review* and won the Calibre Essay Prize

All rights reserved. No part of this book may be reproduced or transmitted in any form or by any means, electronic or mechanical, including photocopying, recording or by any information storage and retrieval system, without prior permission in writing from the publisher. The Australian *Copyright Act 1968* (the Act) allows a maximum of one chapter or 10 per cent of this book, whichever is the greater, to be photocopied by any educational institution for its educational purposes provided that the educational institution (or body that administers it) has given a remuneration notice to the Copyright Agency (Australia) under the Act.

Allen & Unwin
83 Alexander Street
Crows Nest NSW 2065
Australia
Phone: (61 2) 8425 0100
Email: info@allenandunwin.com
Web: www.allenandunwin.com

A catalogue record for this book is available from the National Library of Australia

NATIONAL LIBRARY OF AUSTRALIA

ISBN 978 1 76087 931 0

Set in 12/17 pt Fairfield LT Light by Bookhouse, Sydney
Printed and bound in Australia by Griffin Press, part of Ovato

10 9 8 7 6 5 4 3 2 1

MIX
Paper from responsible sources
FSC
www.fsc.org   FSC® C009448

The paper in this book is FSC® certified. FSC® promotes environmentally responsible, socially beneficial and economically viable management of the world's forests.

To all the trans people who came before, who battled to exist and be seen, and whose efforts made space for me and others to breathe. Thank you for lighting the way.

CONTENTS

AUTHOR'S NOTE

THIS BOOK WAS WRITTEN IN NAARM, the place now known as Melbourne, on the stolen lands of the Wurundjeri people of the Kulin nation. Parts were also written on the stolen lands of the Dharug and Gundungurra people, in the place now called the Blue Mountains. I am an uninvited settler on these lands and I pay my respects to Elders past and present. Indigenous sovereignty was never ceded. This always was and always will be Aboriginal land. A proportion of royalties from this book will be donated to the Pay the Rent campaign. I encourage settler readers to also consider paying reparations.

I am indebted to First Peoples in Australia and around the world for opening my eyes to the possibilities of doing gender outside the binary enforced alongside European colonisation. When it comes to gender, as with so many things, First Nations cultures hold deep knowledge that has too often been ignored and violently suppressed.

This book tells one particular trans story—an account of a white professional transmasculine millennial, a settler in urban Australia.

This story is by no means 'normal' or typical; in many respects, it's atypical. With my well-paid job, white privilege and secure apartment, I am richer and safer than many trans people—a demographic that experiences disproportionate rates of discrimination, unemployment, homelessness, sexual assault and violence.

But averages only tell us so much. There are as many trans stories as there are trans people. There is no right way to be or do trans. It can involve countless surgeries or none at all. It can involve switching between sides of the gender binary or ditching the binary altogether. It can look high femme, androgynous, super butch, or plain nondescript. Some trans people come out at age six; others come out at sixty. Some are loud and proud, outspoken activists; others just want to quietly live under the radar. Trans is an identity that contains multitudes, resists prescriptions and blurs boundaries. That is its power.

Don't take my experience or opinions as representative. My perspective is no one's but my own. I cannot speak for anyone else. Like most communities, trans encompasses great diversity. It includes people of all ages, classes, races, religions, ethnicities, abilities and locations. Not all trans people will agree with my position. I encourage readers to seek out other trans voices—especially those of transfeminine people and trans people of colour, who are the most oppressed members of our community. You'll find some suggestions in the back of this book. I look forward to a future when we have great libraries overflowing with trans books, shelves stretching as far as the eye can see. We will all be the richer for the gift of these stories.

Finally, readers should be advised that this book contains discussion of anorexia, mental illness, suicide, self-harm, hate crimes and transphobia. Look after yourself as you read through its pages.

This is a true story but some names have been changed.

ANZAC DAY

ON 25 APRIL 2019, I WALKED up Swanston Street in a grey coat that matched the subdued skies. It had just gone 8 am, but already the pubs were teeming; uniformed men clutching pints of beer spilt onto the footpath. Along the street, the usual herd of trams was replaced by navy cadets marching in formation, pimpled and raw in their starched white uniforms. Anzac Day was here again.

I'd been up since 4 am, when my alarm shrieked through the pitch black. Barely awake, I'd leapt into the shower, inhaled toast, and thrown myself into the Uber waiting downstairs. The morning was frigid and the driver kept the heat on high as she sped through deserted streets.

I was going to my first Dawn Service—not to stand in sombre silence with the other pilgrims, but to provide commentary from the ABC radio booth set up next to the Shrine of Remembrance. The ABC needed a historian to join the regular morning host, and my media-savvy but over-committed colleague Clare had passed on the gig. I'd done radio before, but nothing of this magnitude.

Originally a day of military commemoration, Anzac Day has become a de facto birthday for Australia. According to popular mythology, 25 April marked the 'birth of the nation' on the Gallipoli Peninsula in 1915. It is a public holiday that arouses strong emotions, that has cultural warriors at loggerheads each year, and I'd been called upon to provide analysis for the national broadcaster. To put it mildly, I was shitting myself.

The broadcast passed in a blur, nearly three hours flying by as the host and I interviewed guests, talked history and passed commentary on the official proceedings. As I dispensed historical factoids about Black diggers and the Treaty of Versailles, the sky slowly lightened, fading from black to charcoal to oyster grey. All of a sudden, it was over. I had made it, without going blank live on air or otherwise humiliating myself. Job done. It was 7.30 am, and my work was over for the day.

I was ejected from the makeshift studio into the dewy Botanic Gardens, body flooded with adrenaline and relief. What now? Caffeine pulsed through my veins from the soy latte I'd downed on air. It was a public holiday, my time was my own, but I was too wired to go home and rest.

Looking for purpose, I drifted back towards the city, trailing the veterans and families who'd attended the service back up St Kilda Road. The air reeked of grilled meat and reverberated with military drums; the usual commuter frenzy of a weekday morning replaced by a strange cocktail of carnival and mourning. Sausage sizzles and death, pomp and ceremony.

As I weaved through the crowds assembling along Swanston Street, my mind replayed the radio broadcast. Like most historians, I had serious misgivings about Anzac Day's jingoism, but was pleased to have the opportunity to inject some honest history into the conversation. My performance wasn't perfect, but I'd made the key points from my notes. I'd even enjoyed bantering with the impish bald host, whose eyes shone with curiosity as we discussed World War I. Once again, the white-knuckle ride of live radio had lit up all my pleasure centres. Already I was hungry for more, looking for the next hit.

But something niggled.

On air they'd called me 'Anne', my legal name and the moniker I'd embraced without question for thirty years. Yet that wasn't my name anymore. Unbeknownst to almost everyone, I'd recently acquired a new identity, a new gender—even a new name. Few people knew the truth. I'd told my immediate family and a handful of close friends. But out in the world I continued to perform the identity on my birth certificate. At work, at the dentist, at my yoga studio, on my electricity bills—and now, today, on radio—I remained 'Anne', a lady historian who wrote about ladies in the past. A woman doing women's history. A girl, a chick, an 'F', a miss, a ma'am. Female.

Except it wasn't true. I was living two lives, and the strain was beginning to tell. The performance of 'Anne' consumed more energy than I had to spare. On radio that morning, I'd cringed and squirmed every time a *she* or *her* was lobbed in my direction. Each female pronoun was an accusation: you're a woman, and don't you dare try to pretend otherwise.

'Anne is joining us this morning, and she's a historian at La Trobe University,' the radio host reminded listeners every quarter hour. *She, she, she.*

'So, Anne, tell us about the nurses who served in World War I,' he'd prompt.

I'd smile and answer with pre-prepared soundbites. People pleasing, over-achieving, as always.

But the whole time, my soul was screaming: *I am not Anne. I am not a 'she'.* These were facts I knew to be incontrovertible, even as they defied all reason. Despite my breasts, despite my vagina, despite my high voice and menstrual cycle, 'woman' was not a container where I belonged.

Yet every single person told me otherwise. Every stranger somehow knew, incontrovertibly, within half a second, that I was female. They were all so sure, so confident in calling me *she* and *miss* and *ma'am*. Who was I to question that, to challenge the whole world?

Lost in these mental thickets, I'd reached the top of the city. From the concrete grid of the CBD, I emerged into the lurid green of Carlton Gardens. My feet took me up Nicholson Street, north towards Fitzroy. Perhaps I'd visit a friend who lived in the Cairo flats, an Art Deco complex opposite the gardens. Away from the beating drums of the CBD, the morning was still and deserted, shrouded by a mournful Melbourne sky. It was only my mind that was on fire. *Anne, she, woman, lady—don't try to deny it, you silly little girl. Who do you think you are?*

The phone in my pocket promised escape. Without interrupting my stride, I unlocked the screen for a hit of Twitter. There was the usual Anzac Day history wars, especially fierce this year as the federal government had announced a $500 million funding boost for the War Memorial in Canberra. Historians and shock jocks traded barbs back and forth. In my agitated state, the vitriol was almost soothing. Each lobbed grenade that condemned Anzackery or mocked political correctness gave my monkey mind something solid to grasp onto. Here was a battle I could apprehend with language and reason, a conflict that demanded only the measured analysis I'd honed over a dozen years in universities. Today, as on most days, critical thinking provided a safe space from myself.

But something else was trending on Twitter this morning. The cover of an interstate tabloid—let's call it DT—featured a hysterical attack on healthcare for trans kids. According to the paper, poor confused innocents were receiving 'unnecessary sex change procedures' due to a sinister left-wing 'gender agenda'. *Think of the children*, the article screeched. Never mind that all transgender healthcare—for kids or otherwise—was subject to strict gatekeeping procedures. Never mind that trans kids never receive irreversible medical intervention. The article was pure fiction masquerading as news.

As I scrolled through the hateful words, I stopped dead, fuming. Primed for a fight. Enough. This insult could not go unremarked.

Frozen on the footpath, as tram after tram clanged past, I composed a tweet that attempted to give voice to the pain inflicted by this poor excuse for journalism.

I am trans, I tapped out in a fury, adrenaline pumping for the second time that morning. *It took me 30 yrs to start coming out. For years I struggled with debilitating gender dysphoria in silence because I was terrified of the violent transphobia that pervades society. Many times I considered suicide. Headlines like this cause untold harm. Shame on you DT.*

By the time I'd finished, the sun had cracked open the clouds. Before I could second-guess the tweet, I sent my outrage into the Twittersphere. It wasn't a big deal. My Twitter following was minuscule. All my fellow-historian followers would be Anzac-focused today. I'd tweeted about transphobia before, and those words had sunk without a trace. Today, if I was lucky, I'd get five likes. I put the phone back in my pocket and continued walking, fury sated.

Twenty minutes later, I was curled up on my friend Sandro's couch, regaling him with a blow-by-blow account of the Anzac Day broadcast. Always the dapper gent, he'd opened the door in a pressed shirt at 9 am on a public holiday. He now poured steaming cups of tea as I narrated the morning's events.

'And then we interviewed this old dude from the RSL, who said that . . .'

Mid-sentence, my coat pocket began to vibrate. My phone was pulsing with notifications. What was going on?

I unlocked the screen. Turns out I'd been retweeted by a senior historian. That was unexpected. I put my phone back in my pocket and resumed the story.

'. . . and then another journo interviewed people in the crowd. Heaps of people had family connections to the war.'

Moments later, my phone started buzzing again. What now? Turns out I'd been retweeted by a local journalist. As I scrolled through the notifications, I was retweeted by an interstate journalist. Then a national media personality. What the hell? Turns out there was an appetite for something other than Anzac stories this morning.

Taking refuge in Sandro's bathroom, I stared at my phone in disbelief. The notifications kept coming. New likes, comments and retweets each minute. Soon I was up to a thousand likes. Did this mean I was going viral? Was I going to get trolled? Already there were a few haters in the comments, calling me an 'it', mocking my pain.

Turns out I'd accidentally announced myself as transgender to the entire internet. Without meaning to, I'd come screaming out of the closet, shrieking 'trans' to all and sundry. Some cock-tail of sleep deprivation and post-radio adrenaline had given my subconscious licence to broadcast the words I'd been swallowing for years. The dam of my silence had broken before I'd even realised it was starting to crack. By the time I arrive at work tomorrow, everyone—every colleague I hadn't told—would have seen or heard about this tweet. Maybe even my former PhD supervisor would find out. Already my old boss, a former student and an ex-boyfriend had responded. All three of them seeing my most raw and naked self.

I swallowed, took some shallow breaths. Maybe that coffee during the broadcast had been a mistake, giving me a buzz that destroyed my inhibitions. I've always been sensitive to caffeine.

Perched on Sandro's toilet, phone in hand, I could feel a vulnerability hangover coming on.

This Anzac Day was meant to be about performing a sleek professional self on radio. It was meant to be about public engagement, about building my profile—all those career goals I pursued to avoid thinking about my gender. But it turned out that 25 April 2019 actually marked the public implosion of Anne. Her time was over, ready or not. I'd finally stopped pretending I was female and named a truth that was as strange and terrifying as it was undeniable. I was not-woman, I was trans. It was one of those facts you know in your bones, however much you wish it wasn't true. I wasn't a man, but I most certainly was not female. I was trans. There was no going back, no un-knowing this fact. Now everyone else knew, too.

I only wished I knew what came next.

LIVE THE QUESTIONS

LOOKING BACK, YOU COULD SAY that it all began with the THC.

August 2018. Eight months before my Anzac Day revelation. It is high summer in British Columbia, Canada, where I am holidaying alone after a work trip to Vancouver. I have a week booked in an Airbnb in Victoria, the provincial capital on Vancouver Island, where queer, vegan cafes flourish alongside English rose gardens cultivated by retirees. Half the population sport tattoos and asymmetrical haircuts; the other half favour grey slacks and thick-soled shoes. It is a fantasy English village circa 1950 spliced with Melbourne's inner north, artfully composed against a wilderness backdrop. It is love at first sight. When the Vancouver ferry deposits me on the foreshore after three hours cruising the Georgia Strait, I swoon at the endless vistas of ocean and mountain.

The next day, I discover Victoria's other selling point: cannabis dispensaries. Marijuana had recently been legalised across the province. Now every second street corner in Victoria boasts a dispensary. Many are fitted out like high-end boutiques, complete with minimalist decor and black-clad staff offering mini-lectures on the artisanal product range—like some stoner version of Aesop.

As a lifelong 'good girl', I have almost no previous experience with cannabis. Apart from half a joint smoked in an Amsterdam park years earlier, I am a thirty-year-old weed virgin. But that is about to change. When in Rome, I've decided. Here, the drug is legal and regulated. I have the time and cash to experiment, and no other obligations for a full week. It is now or never.

I sniff around a few stores, trying to suss out what to buy without betraying my complete ignorance. Finally, in a downtown dispensary on Yates Street, I summon the nerve to ask for help. Over the next ten minutes, I learn a whole new vocabulary: edibles, tinctures, capsules, THC, CBD. Both THC and CBD are cannabinoids extracted from cannabis. THC is psychoactive; it's what causes the high from smoking weed. CBD is non-psychoactive. It won't get you stoned, but is widely used for treating pain, depression and other health conditions.

Standing at the counter, I focus on this new knowledge to distract from the anxious churning in my gut. The assistant has an otherworldly calm, lining up my options on the glass cabinet, their thin arms covered in abstract designs. I walk out with a handful of THC capsules, only two dollars a pop.

I stride the twenty minutes back to the Airbnb, impatient to begin but too timid to start doing drugs on the street. Back home, I arrange a capsule and glass of water on the coffee table. I double-check the dose. Then I google to check this is really legal. This is it, the big moment. Down the hatch it goes.

And then—nothing. It is as though I've taken a paracetamol or vitamin tablet. Functional, utilitarian. It has none of the pleasurable ritual of sipping a glass of wine or smoking a cigarette. I pick up a *New Yorker* and wait for the effects to kick in.

Over the next hour I stand up every ten minutes, pace the room, surveying body and mind, trying to gauge the effects of the drug. Is it working yet? In an apartment by myself it is hard to tell if I am giggly or disinhibited. Eventually I discern a mild buzz, the same mellow sensation produced by a glass of red. It is pleasant, but nothing to write home about. More than a little disappointed, I switch off the lights and go to sleep.

The next morning, I resolve to up my dose. I'd taken only 2.5 mg, the entry level dosage recommended by the dispensary assistant. The effects had been negligible. Time to try a little more. That afternoon, sunbaking on a pebbled beach, not one but two capsules go down my throat. As I wander home through the evening light, a golden glow saturates my limbs. This is more like it. Back at the Airbnb, I have a sudden urge to blast Americana, a band from childhood. Soon I am rocking out in the kitchen to the tinny iPhone speaker. Outside the glass French doors, the neighbour's cat stares at my antics.

Emboldened now, I resolve to try one more capsule. The mellowness deepens, grows thick, muffling the scolding voice in my brain. My gold sneakers become fascinating, the colour shimmering under the kitchen light. I'm entranced by the intricate loops of the laces, white cotton weaving back and forth between the metallic leather. Deep insight feels close at hand.

They need to make this shit legal in Australia, is my last thought before sleep pulls me under.

⌒

The next day, I wake early, mind sharp and clear. As the dawn light yanks me towards consciousness, an idea arrives in my brain, fully formed and indisputable: *Wearing women's clothes is drag. You're not really a woman.*

I'd been alive for thirty years. In all that time I'd never allowed myself to consider that the term 'woman' might not apply to me. I was a rule follower, a good girl, so I'd accepted the notion that my vagina and boobs made me a woman. But in that moment of waking, all my old certainty crumbles, replaced by a new conviction:

You're not really a woman.

Of course. In the moment, it makes perfect sense. *I'm not a woman.* This statement is so true, so obvious, it brooks no questioning. There's no room for doubt. If I were religious, I might have named it a message from God.

Time to get to work. Leaping out of bed, I bundle the skirts from my suitcase into a plastic bag, ready to drop in a charity bin. Femininity extinguished. There's no need for this costume anymore.

Outside, the day is a blank slate, a shimmering promise of late summer. It's Sunday, and only a handful of joggers and dog-walkers are awake this early. After discarding my bag of clothes in a charity bin around the corner, I stride the deserted streets, marvelling at my new knowledge, energised by sudden clarity.

There's no fear, not yet. Only conviction. *I'm not a woman, I'm not a woman.* The message beats out in time with my footsteps. Down at the harbour's edge, I grin at nothing, startling the seagulls bent over discarded fries.

By midday, I sport a new tattoo to mark the occasion. *Lebe die Fragen* inked into my inner left wrist, Baskerville font, just below the watch band.

'What does it mean?' drawls the tattooist as he disinfects the instruments.

'Live the questions,' I answer. 'It's German, from Rilke. The poet.'

'Cool.'

He's barely interested, quite possibly hungover, but nothing can touch me today. Live the questions. This is my promise to myself.

To take this new knowledge, this awareness of being not-woman, and follow it, wherever it leads.

⤙

Later, still pacing the streets, a wolf whistle jolts me from my reverie. There's a glimpse of male smirk, a face ogling from a truck window before it zooms through the intersection and out of sight. He thinks I'm a woman, I realise. This red-blooded Canadian truckie has mistaken me for a lady he might like to fuck.

I stifle a chuckle. How absurd. Doesn't he see me? Doesn't he realise he's catcalling a not-woman, something closer to a man? It's astonishing he can't see through the disguise. If only he knew. I feel a strange tenderness towards the half-glimpsed face, as though he'd been caught red-handed with closeted gay desires. He'd wolf-whistled at a quasi-man, after all.

That moment, at the traffic lights, was when it truly hit me that this was real. My subconscious mind knew with unshakeable certainty that, despite what my body might indicate, 'woman' was not a label that could be applied to me. It understood that a truckie mistaking me for a lady was laughable, a joke. Deep in my bones, beneath the noise of language and thought, my transness had made itself known.

After hours of walking, I install myself in a sidewalk cafe with free wi-fi. An overpriced latte, the coffee burnt and top-heavy with foam, justifies my presence for the next hour. I pull out my phone. All around me, white retirees flick through fat weekend papers, nibbling pastries in the lazy afternoon sun. Pedigree dogs loll beside every second table.

But I don't see any of that. Instead, I dive headfirst into Instagram. I need to find other people like me, other not-women born with vaginas. I guess at a hashtag—#transman—and I'm off and away, enraptured by the endless selfies, the before and after pics. I see puny girls flower into muscled men, torsos grow hard and lean. Beards sprouting. Breasts disappearing.

My coffee sits untouched as I scroll and scroll and scroll, squinting to see the screen through the afternoon glare, half-mad with desire. This. Yes, this. These are my people; this is my future. Here is what I've been hungering for. I discover transmasculine models, writers, bakers, students. There are so many of us. We're an invisible army, hidden in plain sight.

In jeans and T-shirt, blonde hair bobbed, I'm innocuous. Not yet a visible gender traitor. For all the world just a skinny white girl, melding into the cafe tableau of sun-drunk retirees. But I know better. It's all a disguise, a disguise I will soon discard.

After an hour inside my phone, I come up for air. My gaze lands on a grizzled boomer at the next table. His neck is sun-weathered above a faded navy polo. Between his khaki-clad legs sits a blonde poodle with doleful eyes, appraising the scene. The man frowns over an iPad, stabbing the screen with sausage fingers. On his wrist, I spy a Rolex. A rich old white man, lord of his domain. The type of man who's always known himself to be the protagonist of every story, the loudest voice in every room. The type of man I resent and fear and obey.

Is this what I want to become? I imagine myself, masculinised, thirty or so years down the track. I'd be a silver-haired white dude, swimming in privilege. I'd be a doppelgänger for this gent. Have I spent a decade studying and living feminism just to abandon ship and join Team Patriarchy?

Maybe I'm deluded. Maybe the THC has warped my brain. Maybe I've been spending too much time alone.

The man's poodle whines from beneath the table. He stretches down a hand of comfort, stroking the curls along its back. Eyes still fixed on the iPad, he soothes the dog back into surrender.

I look down. Beneath its protective plastic wrapping, my new tattoo winks up at me. *Lebe die Fragen*. Live the questions. No more pretending. I am not-woman, I am trans. Whatever that might mean.

⌐

Is that where it all began? With the THC and the tattoo on Vancouver Island? Yes, in a way. That was when I started naming myself as trans. I went to Canada, found myself, and came back a different person. It's a neat origin story, a turning point easy to mark.

But it's also not quite true, or not the only truth.

In truth, my transness had been bubbling towards the surface for years. It's easy, in retrospect, to see the signs, the building knowledge, the moments of rupture and recognition. The things I refused or was unable to see.

There was the day in 2016 when, huddled beneath the sheets with a UTI, I inhaled Maggie Nelson's *The Argonauts*. In a fevered delirium, my eyes raced over stories of queer sex, gender-conforming bodies, chosen families. As I read, there was a man perched outside on the balcony, a man who'd been in my bed. A man I'd sought to possess. But the ties between us snapped as I discovered my own queerness through Nelson's words.

Next morning, still drunk with fever, I told the man it was over. He vanished into the backstreets of Chippendale within ten minutes.

Back under clammy sheets, I cuddled up with Nelson and her gender-bending lover, Harry Dodge. Harry, who had a masculine name, a muscled chest, who'd rejected the identity of woman but refused to be labelled a man. Harry, who was always becoming, unwilling to be pinned down.

When the UTI retreated, I found myself single for the first time in six years. It seemed an appropriate moment to download Tinder. *Interested in?* the app demanded. *Men or Women?* I'd never been asked that question before. I'd never asked myself that question before. Raised in a world where everyone was assumed to be straight, I'd never had the chance to consider I might be anything other than a woman who dated men.

But now, faced with the question, I wasn't so sure. The straight world had become alien to me. Perhaps I was interested in women, I considered. Women and men. Perhaps it had been both all along.

I gave myself permission to start swiping right.

At that moment, I could name my queerness only as a matter of sexuality—not gender. Lesbians were a known commodity, after all. Feeling masculine? Interested in dating women? You must be a dyke! Other possibilities were yet to be imagined.

Was *that* the true beginning, the moment when my transness first reared its head? Or did it start even earlier, the year before, when I glimpsed my future in the pages of a magazine?

Canberra, 2015. I was staying with a friend, on the run from a picture-perfect relationship that overnight had become a straitjacket. My friend's housemate was travelling, and I was camped out in her vacant room, where I fermented in my own juices, deranged by questions that couldn't be articulated, let alone answered. For months I'd been screaming in bathrooms, raging at nothing. Then I'd blown up my own life, for reasons entirely unknown.

'I don't want to be with you anymore,' I'd told the man who was my partner, my best friend, my future husband.

'LOML' we'd called each other. Short for 'love of my life'. For five years, I'd nuzzled each night into the nape of his neck, lulled into slumber by the perfume of his skin.

Now I was offering my resignation from the life we'd built together. I'd cheated, lied, betrayed, rejected—the whole kit and caboodle. I was the Madonna remade as damned whore. It was a dumpster fire.

My partner demanded answers, determined that we'd find words to explain the inexplicable. Our daily meals became interrogations, a barrage of questions and shame flung across the stained wood of our IKEA dining table.

But I had nothing. I had no idea why I'd pulled the plug on our coupledom, only that it needed to be done. So I'd fled to my friend's share house in the next suburb. For weeks I slept in the sheets of her absent housemate, taking refuge in the empty burrow of a stranger's life.

Amid the books piled next to my borrowed bed, I found a fat magazine: *Archer*. The fourth issue. 'Sex, gender, identity', the masthead proclaimed. The cover showed an older couple embracing, their naked flesh wrinkled and beautiful.

I devoured the magazine's pages, swallowing paragraphs whole, stuffing myself with words about bisexuality, homophobia, porn, naturism, sex in aged care, gender transition.

Here was a portal into an unimagined world. Nothing in the long Canberra years of couple's dinner parties and overpriced brunches, public service ambitions and sipped shiraz had hinted at this utopia of gentle outlaws and fierce queers.

For the first time in months, the fog lifted, stupefaction replaced by a dull but unmistakable hunger. I still knew nothing, had nothing, that would explain the implosion of my life. But I did know this magazine was a signpost to my future. Within its pages I'd recognised something in myself. Within its pages lay glimpses of the life I must build.

It was a brief flame in a long trudge through the dark.

The true beginning, then?

The beginnings of transness are always contested. Were you born this way or were you made? Did you emerge from the womb in the 'wrong body'? Or did you just read too many books as an impression-able undergraduate?

Are you real, do you matter? Or are you just a fantasist looking for attention?

Each story of beginning is a weapon that can be used for or against you. Each life, a battleground.

The same battles rage over trans identities at large. *Where did you come from?* is another way to ask *Are you legitimate?* Origin stories shape how the world imagines trans bodies, trans lives.

Trans advocates know that we have always existed, part of the tapestry of humankind since time immemorial. Not a fad, a phase, a delusion, but an immutable part of the human condition. Immutable—and therefore legitimate.

Among reactionaries, trans gets dismissed as invention, a 'gender ideology' designed by contemporary deviants with a leftist agenda. Trans as a harmful fiction, a threat to the natural order of things. Trans as a latecomer, a trend that will pass.

For historians, trans dates back to the invention of sexology in the late 1800s. It was an idea that emerged alongside broader efforts to put people into boxes. The Victorian age was in love with classifi-cation, a time of proliferating categories designed to order humanity like butterflies on a pinboard. Black/white, normal/deviant, self/other, man/woman, primitive/civilised. 'Trans'—or, originally, the 'invert' or 'transvestite'—was a medical concept used to classify people so they could be known, ordered, controlled.

To be clear, this was not the beginning of gender non-conformity. It was just the moment when trans became the concept Western medicine used to understand those who coloured outside the lines of 'man' and 'woman'.

For historians, trans is not human nature nor fad-of-the-moment, but merely one way of understanding gender diversity. There have been others. Over the centuries, almost every culture has had names for people who don't fit within the gender binary—although many have been written out of history, lost to the germs and guns of colonisation. Doubtless there'll be more to come.

There are many stories of trans beginning. Always, the stories matter. They tell us how to see, who to see, whether to revere or revile this thing we call 'trans'. Stories make worlds, and the stories we tell about transness can be a matter of life or death.

My life, so often something I was tempted to throw away, was saved and remade by trans stories.

⌁

Another of my trans beginnings: the night I looked at my reflection and saw a man staring back at me. One wintry Saturday eve, 2017. A year after *The Argonauts*; the year before Vancouver.

I was slumped against the window of a swaying train, returning home to Melbourne's north after a night in the city. The reflective glass showed someone familiar. Strong jaw, sceptical gaze, broad cheekbones. Unquestionably male. A second later, he'd disappeared. I yearned to run after him, as you would dash after a childhood friend glimpsed in a crowd. In his place, I saw only a sad simulacrum of a woman, wonky lipstick and wig-like mane. She huddled into her coat, face pinched and hungry.

Months later, at an airport far from home, my Kindle suggested a novel: *Nevada*. On the plane, I raced through the virtual pages. It was a trans remake of the classic American road story. The hero was a trans woman on the run from New York who befriends a young man questioning his gender deep in the Wild West. The youth confesses to fantasies of having sex as a woman, known as autogynephilia. I paused, jolted into unwilling recognition. Squashed into my plane seat, I remembered all the times I'd imagined myself with a penis, penetrating a woman. Later, Google will tell me this is autoandrophilia, a condition controversially associated with 'transsexualism'.

Back home, I disintegrated into a 'major depressive episode'—a collapse that once would have been more poetically termed a nervous breakdown. One grey day, in the car with Mum, I stuttered a confession.

'I'm concerned about my gender. I read a book about trans people and I recognised some things.'

She's distracted, preoccupied by traffic, focused on the need to keep me alive until the depression abates.

'I wouldn't worry about that. Let's just get you home, have some lunch.'

My words have skated off the surface of the moment, as though they'd never been. Later, she'll have no memory of this conversation.

And that was the end of it.

Until a year later, when I flew to Canada as a woman and returned as something else. Until the northern summer of 2018, when I left my womanhood in a BC charity bin along with my skirts. You could say it was a bolt from the blue, a sudden insight or delusion triggered by mind-altering drugs. Or you could say the signs had been there all along, waiting for the right moment. Perhaps both are true. Perhaps neither is.

In 1903, the German poet Rainer Maria Rilke counselled a young protégé to welcome uncertainty. *I want to beg you . . . to be patient toward all that is unsolved in your heart and to try to love the questions themselves*, Rilke wrote. *Do not now seek the answers, which cannot be given you because you would not be able to live them. And the point is, to live everything. Live the questions now.*

Live the questions. Now. These were the words inked onto my wrist, a dictum etched into the tender spot where blood runs close to the skin. Black ink above blue veins. A reminder to exist with the unknown, the unknowable. Live the questions, wherever they lead.

READING THE MESS BACKWARDS

A TRANS BABY AT THIRTY, that was me. A laggard, a latecomer at the party, someone who'd sheltered inside my assigned role of woman for decades before finally coming to my senses. But although my transness only surfaced well into adulthood, this wasn't the beginning of my gender trouble. That had a far longer history. From the beginning, gender equalled heartache for me. It was the place where I was forever flailing, teetering on the edge of failure, a mess I carried around in my skin. Woman was an ill-fitting costume I hadn't yet realised could be removed.

Looking back, vision sharpened by new insight, you could say that the transness had been there all along. You could say I'd been born that way—only I didn't have the words to know it. Was I a woman for three decades or was I never a woman at all?

⤳

When I'm ten or so, my brother appears shirtless at the dinner table. Ever the eager disciple, I follow his example without a second thought. It is a sweltering January day, and our bodies are salt-crusted from the beach. Clothing seems cruel in these conditions.

As my brother tucks into his schnitzel, tanned chest gleaming, I grow conscious that the mood has become strained. Across the table, my parents exchange glances. The midsummer cheer of recent evenings is on hold.

I look down. Two small nubs peak from my ribcage, barely the beginnings of breasts. My torso is white and soft, a reptile's underbelly to my brother's hard brown exoskeleton. I realise: this chest of mine does not belong in public. It is somehow obscene, something to be hidden rather than flaunted. My brother and I differ in this crucial respect.

Excusing myself, I flee upstairs and don a T-shirt. Back at the table, there is a palpable sense of relief. Chatter resumes. All is well with the world.

When I am eleven, I cut my hair. The yellow river that poured down my back is snipped onto the white tiles of the David Jones salon. It's a massacre of blonde. In the mirror, a new person emerges. Strong jaw, sceptical gaze, broad cheekbones no longer softened by a golden mane. Nothing feminine to see here. Here I am, fresh from the chrysalis of girlhood.

On the way out of DJs, Mum and I browse the children's clothing department. In the boy's section, the racks of navy blazers speak of an entire world—a world where urbane flâneurs stroll through some nameless European metropolis. I want one. I fondle the silk lining, inhaling its promises. Here is all I cannot have.

That year, I graduate from family beach cricket to my very own team. Dad had been a star wicketkeeper before a car accident put paid to his dreams of a sporting career, while my brother is a Zeus on any sporting field. Now it's my turn. In the absence of a local girls' team, I join a boys' club. I acquire the regulation cricket whites, and the whole family sinks into the rhythm of mid-week training sessions and endless Saturday mornings beside a sun-bleached oval. I am bemused when the coach's wife, febrile with good intentions, assures me that I am accepted alongside the boys. Why wouldn't I be? I know where I belong.

It soon emerges that I'm an abysmal fielder (too afraid of the ball) and a middling-to-poor batsman but a dab hand as a bowler. Word gets round at school, and soon the Year Six boys allow me into their lunchtime matches. The day the invitation comes to open the bowling, I abandon my orange Sunnyboy and girl posse like so much trash. I'm one of the boys now.

One day after cricket training, I'm at the supermarket with Dad. We're playing our favourite game: a competition to greet the most people we know. Not surprisingly, my father—a middle-aged professor—always trounces me, the shy pre-pubescent. The contest is rigged, but I love it anyway. This afternoon, as we wheel the trolley to the car, Dad pauses to chat with a colleague.

'It's lovely to meet your son,' she says.

I see myself: cropped hair, blue shorts, white crewneck. My second skin. Does this equal boy?

Dad laughs awkwardly.

'This is Annie, she's going to high school next year.'

In the car going home, neither of us speaks.

⤻

That summer, my brother grows muscle, stubble, pimples. He starts sleeping 'til noon, and his sentences become barnacled with expletives. I am left behind. Frantic to catch up, I understudy his new role like a pro. I learn to make Warhammer sets, then listen to Jack Johnson on repeat. Next, I buy a skateboard, spending afternoons cruising the foreshore in my cargo pants. I never manage any tricks, but my first online handle is sk8ergirl88.

At high school, I learn that I am wrong.

'Why do you have a boy's haircut?' the Year Eight boys jeer.

A girls' cricket team starts, and I join, but soon miss the boys' easy camaraderie. Within a season, I abandon the sport for good.

The nubs on my chest turn into pillows, and overnight I become fat. My body is both too little and too much. Then I discover the answer: stop eating. My lunchtime sandwiches, oily with salami and Swiss cheese, are replaced by a green apple, consumed in birdlike mouthfuls. I jog to and from class. Sometimes, as a special treat, I nibble a single rye crispbread. By summer, my shoulder blades jut out sharp and proud, trophies that proclaim my labours to the world. I sunbake facedown at the ocean baths, revelling in the dull pain of hipbone against concrete. Breasts disappear and periods dry up. I am right again.

Or am I?

'She's disgusting,' mutter the boys clustered round the school gates.

'We're worried about you,' the year adviser says, her voice scolding.

Too much girl, not girl enough. I can't get it right. At a sleepover, when giggles and teases became tickles and wrestling, a cold voice rings through the darkness.

'Oh my God, you must be a lesbian!'

Hot with shame, I crawl back into my sleeping bag. Does tickling equal lesbian? I have no idea what lesbians do; I only know that they are wrong. Like me, again.

When Year Twelve comes around, I fall into friendship with a fey scamp of a girl. She's all freckles and puns, topped off with an encyclopaedic knowledge of Agatha Christie. During study periods, we walk, brazen, out the school gates and gorge on gelato at the Italian cafe down the road. On stormy afternoons the beach calls. We throw ourselves about in the rough surf for hours, then sit shivering over hot chocolates. I have never felt so right.

As final exams approach, we shop for formal dresses. Her choice is a cheongsam-inspired gown, black with red panelling, a daring creation found at the city's first designer store. I can't wait to be seen beside her on the night. Next week in class, a message is conveyed: Sam—charming Sam, secret crush of all the girls—wants her as his date. At the formal, I sit alone and miserable as Sam twirls her on the dance floor, black dress flaring just as I'd imagined. My friend is giddy with joy, but everything is wrong. Wrong casting, wrong lines, wrong me. With my strapless aqua gown, I am no match for besuited Sam. The blazer has won again.

↙

It's the early 2000s in an oversized town populated by redundant steelworkers and their surfer sons. The streets are dense with empty shopfronts, and a frothy cappuccino is the height of sophistication. 'Gay' is an accusation, not an identity. 'Trans' means only the drag queens teetering across the outback in *Priscilla, Queen of the Desert*. 'Diversity' is the occasional Greek surname, or the solitary pair of Hong Kong-born sisters at school. Beneath the vacant blue skies that keep us 'relaxed and comfortable', my unruly body has desires I cannot name. Only at the beach, where the world is water and light, do I slip free from the wrongness that stalks me into each new scene.

'How to explain, in a culture frantic for resolution, that sometimes the shit stays messy?' writes Maggie Nelson in *The Argonauts*. In her telling, the 'born in the wrong body' trans narrative obscures the fact that many belong in the messy middle, forever betwixt and between.

When your gender is a dog's breakfast, how do you know whether this is your own mess or the world's? Was I always trans, part boy beneath my skin, or did I land in a place where 'girl' was a container so small it could break your bones?

The pallid feminism dished up in the Howard era told us that 'girls can do anything'. They can be athletes, they can be doctors, they can run a business. They can even be prime minister. (That didn't work out so well.) To be a feminist, I learn, is to challenge and grow what 'woman' can contain. You want to skate like your brother? Great, you're a feminist. You want short hair? Feminist gold star for you.

But my guilty secret is that 'woman' never feels like home. I don't want to be a ball-breaking superwoman, smashing glass ceilings with my shoulder-pads while my husband tends the stove. I want that David Jones blazer and the body to fill it out.

Why, indeed, would any child embrace 'woman' when they are the seeming losers, the victims, the Penelopes who get left behind? The men in my life are the ones who jet off on international business trips, eat meals cooked by others, have their sexual currency increase with age. My father moves to a beachside apartment with his coiffed new wife, while my mother inflates with grief. She dishes up mid-week spag bol and watches re-runs of *The Bill*; he buys a Bose sound-system and quaffs pinot noir against a backdrop of eighties synth jazz and Japanese cologne. In the battle of the sexes, I know who will win every time.

Yet make no mistake: for all my cricketing exploits, I am no rough-and-tumble tomboy, running riot with the lads. That 'born in the wrong body' conviction is never mine. My shit is messier than that. For all that my aesthetic signals 'boy', I am the quiet child who gravitates towards books and make-believe—sedate, acceptably feminine pastimes. I have Barbies and I like them. Most days, it's not so hard to pass as female.

↵

Without a language to express this mess, I leave my body behind. I smother its unruly desires beneath textbooks, prizes, degrees.

Photographs are to be avoided at all costs. Shopping is an exercise in drag. I buy the dresses, the skirts. I go through the motions of performing 'girl'. I even go on dates when men ask me, half-amused they can't see through the farce. I learn that a ready smile and a sympathetic ear are the only props required to impersonate a woman. The performance becomes so familiar I almost forget that it's staged.

There are only occasional moments of rupture. Talk of marriage, breast fondling, beauty salons, being called 'Miss'—all induce revulsion and panic. At one big white wedding in Greece, I spend the reception shaking in the toilets while the other guests dance in raucous circles.

There's only one possible explanation: it must be all my mother's fault. Wasn't she supposed to have taught me how to be a woman? Her blunt style and aversion to fashion and make-up must be the reason why I lack some essential understanding of femaleness. If only I had a different mother, a mother who wore mascara and kitten heels, I would have learnt the passwords, the secret handshake. Or so I tell myself.

The day before my brother's wedding, Mum and I drive to a beauty salon for obligatory mani-pedis, a bonding exercise with the bride-to-be and the women of her clan.

'How does it work? I've never done this before,' Mum proclaims on arrival, announcing her ignorance for all to hear.

She doesn't even know to be ashamed, to see that she's failed femininity and failed me in the process. I turn to ice and refuse to look at her. In the car going home, arms crossed, I spit out her shortcomings, one by one. Anger provides a refuge from confusion and fear.

The next day, I watch my first YouTube make-up tutorial. Maybe I can acquire the secret handshake elsewhere. But I don't go back to a beauty salon for years. Without Mum on hand to play the naïf, surely my own ignorance would be obvious. I can't afford to be unmasked in the citadel of womanhood.

Through it all, I keep myself small and lean. No womanly curves, the merest hint of breasts, muscular quads—androgyny to the max. When I'm not studying, I'm exercising, either living in my mind or keeping my body under wraps. Cake, ice-cream, chocolate are all verboten. Even alcohol is suspect: too many empty calories. Feminism tells me this is patriarchy in action: women are not allowed to have large bodies that claim space. My body regulation is surely just another artefact of a sexist world. Yet it isn't size I fear so much as hips, buttocks and breasts, those expanses of flesh that scream 'woman' to the world. No J.Lo booty for me, however toned. Heroin chic is more my style.

↵

Deep into my twenties, the wrongness persists, unnamed and unnameable, my constant friend. Words are my instruments, language my drug of choice, but something festers beneath the surface of what can be seen and known. Unnamed, unnameable.

Until one day, I stumble upon a new vocabulary. Until one day, I see myself anew in the mirror. Until one day, I take THC and wake up remade.

Remade—or should I say awakened, able to see what was always there?

The 2018 Australian Trans and Gender Diverse Health Survey found that trans people take an average of eight years from first glimpsing their transness to telling anyone about it. For most people, transness takes almost a decade to bubble to the surface.

You could say I was typical in this respect. Not in the sense that I'd carried around my transness like a secret, a skeleton bundled in the closet. But rather that I'd long known something was askew and it took me years, decades even, to understand the shape and texture of the problem and announce it out loud.

Either way, I have the words now. The wrongness has a name. Language has made me real to myself—no longer a failed or faulty woman but something else altogether. Something beyond, outside, other. Not woman, but not quite man either. A mess, certainly. But a mess that can be mapped in words and sentences, a mess that demands to be seen. A mess with a beauty all its own.

YOUR DIAGNOSIS IS 58

I SINK ONTO THE RED couch, clutching myself tight. I cross my legs, instinctive self-protection, then think better of it. Too feminine. Better to manspread a little. Before me, a coffee table houses a water jug, two glasses and a box of tissues. Typical shrink set-up.

'Would you like some water?'

'Um, yes please.'

The gender psychologist bends his lanky frame to pour from the jug. After handing over a glass, he settles into the armchair opposite. He crosses his legs, I note, but in that loose male way—one foot resting on the opposite thigh, crotch wide open. Still taking up space.

I look down at my own legs, spread them a little further apart. It feels insolent, to be so cavalier with my limbs.

The psychologist studies me over the rim of his glasses. He sports a white shirt and dark jeans, business casual, the slim-cut fabric flattering his elegant lines. No matter what happens, I'll never achieve that lissom shape. I'll remain forever stuck at 5'7", with a pelvis built to accommodate a human skull.

The psychologist watches me and I squirm under his gaze. I don't know what to do with my hands. Without thinking, I re-cross my legs.

'So,' he begins. 'What brings you here?'

~

Five months earlier I'd returned from Canada a person in love. I'd fallen head over heels with the idea of my own transness. Like a long-lost dictionary, it explained all the wrongness. It provided a language to parse my difference.

Best of all, transness offered a roadmap away from the pit of the present. The never-ending play in which I'd been miscast as 'woman' had finally reached interval, and now I was fleeing through the side exit, making a mad dash out into the street. No longer would each day be spent trapped in a role that never suited me. I was my own casting manager and I could give myself whatever part I chose. Surgeries, hormones, clothes, names, haircuts—there were infinite costumes, infinite roles to play. Possibilities without end.

In the wake of that post-THC morning, when I'd woken to new knowledge about myself, I'd been punch-drunk, giddy, lunging into the future like a puppy straining on a lead. For the first time in forever, I wasn't trudging through life; I was skating across the surface of each day, blood pumping and wind in my hair.

I had it all planned out: I'd return home to Melbourne, announce my transness to my liberal family, who'd embrace this new part of me like the open-minded progressives they were. Then I would commence transition.

On the long plane trip back across the Pacific, squashed between dozing passengers, I fantasised about hosting my own gender reveal party. The conventional gender reveal is a bizarre heteronormative ritual that involves expectant parents (assumed to be a straight couple) popping a balloon or exploding fireworks to reveal the pink or blue of their child's supposed gender. In my imaginings, I'd subvert the genre by revealing my own gender at the tender age of thirty. The guests would assemble, wondering at my absence, and then I'd burst out from inside a giant cake, adorned in the pink, blue and white of the trans flag. *Surprise! I'm not a girl. Or a boy. I'm trans.* It would be a high-camp extravaganza, choreographed to the tunes of Diana Ross's queer anthem 'I'm Coming Out'.

As the Qantas Airbus sped above the clouds, carrying me back to Melbourne, I pictured the rainbow glitter raining down. Eyes closed, I curated a perfect playlist and planned my outfit.

One thing was for sure: there was no time to waste. I'd already languished in ill-fitting womanhood for thirty years. I knew myself, finally; knew what must be done. It was just a matter of spreading the news and getting on with the job.

Only, as it happened, things didn't turn out like that at all.

⤝

'Are you telling me you want to turn into a *man*?' Mum asked, a look of horror on her face. She said 'man' like it was something you'd find in the dirt.

We were eating at a Federation Square restaurant, winter coats draped over our chairs and bowls of ramen steaming on the table. Outside, the night was blue-black.

'Not exactly,' I replied. 'I don't want to turn into a man. But I do want to stop living as a woman. I want surgery and hormones that will masculinise my appearance. I don't feel like a man, exactly, but I feel more man than woman. It's called being transmasculine.'

I speak carefully, trying to salvage this conversation.

Mum's brow furrows. She's stopped eating.

'I don't know how I feel about that. I don't want you to become a man. You're my beautiful daughter.'

'I'd still be me,' I counter. 'I'd still be the same person. I'd just look different.'

'No, no, it wouldn't be the same at all,' she exclaims. 'I'd find it so confronting if you looked like a man. I always wanted a daughter. When I was pregnant, I was convinced you were going to be a girl. And I was right. You were my perfect little girl.'

This conversation is veering way off script. Where are the warm embraces? The declarations of love and support?

'Oh,' I say, voice small. My sad little girl voice. I cross my arms tight, eyes fixed on a slice of carrot floating in the soup.

'I thought you might be happy I've worked this out,' I attempt. 'You know I've always felt wrong in my body. You know, the eating disorder, the compulsive exercise, the depression? This is good news, I reckon. It explains a lot.'

'But it's all so sudden. I know you've had body issues, but do you really want to look like a man? Most men are awful. And you're such a beautiful woman.'

She's only seen me from the outside. She's only seen the woman costume and the never-ending performance, not the Munch-like scream within. For her, the performance was real. I'd played the part too well.

Mum takes a sip of wine, checks her watch.

'We'll have to hurry; the play is starting soon. And we still need to pick up the tickets.'

While Mum pays the bill, I retreat to the bathroom. I linger in the cubicle, head in my hands, a numb sack of flesh. I want to howl like a baby, to howl and keen and cry, and have my mother gather me up and dry my tears and whisper sweet nothings that would lull me into peace. Instead, I flush the toilet, wash my hands, and walk out into the restaurant. We shrug on our coats.

'We only have twenty minutes,' I say. 'We'll need to walk quickly.'

Outside, cold seeps from the pavement into my boots, ice creeping into bone.

↵

The months that followed were hazy. In my family, the mood was grim, as though I'd been handed a stage 4 cancer diagnosis with only months to live. My long-divorced parents met for an emergency summit, lunching at a cafe in the city.

Afterwards, Mum reported on the proceedings.

'Your dad is very concerned. This is all so sudden. We're worried about you. We don't want you to do something you might regret.'

My family circled me, funeral-sombre, wary of this sudden sickness, cautioning against action. Everyone wanted me to wake up and come to my senses. *Remain our daughter*, they willed me with fearful eyes. *Don't succumb to this delusion. Remain sister, remain aunt, remain woman.*

I would if I could, but it was too late. I'd already discovered the exit, realised I could simply walk off stage, so there was no keeping me in the performance.

'We need time,' my family said. 'This is all so sudden.'

Silences fell between us, thick emptiness that weighed on my heart.

I lowered my expectations, learnt to want less.

Later, I watched footage of an American father declaring pride in his trans child.

'If you have a transgender kid, you are living with a unicorn. An *amazing* human being,' he said to an audience of other parents, voice rich with love.

'To be next to someone so brave, so cool, so close to themselves . . .' The father shook his bearded head with awe.

I wept then, for what wasn't said to me.

Amid all the silences, doubt crept in. Shame, too. My transness was clearly a problem, or else everyone wouldn't be so solemn. A new kind of wrongness began to gnaw at me—the wrongness of being the difficult person, the unsightly stain everyone pretends not to see. I'd become the elephant in the room.

As I realised there'd be no cake or balloons, only silences, I retreated into myself, mulish and wary, forever flinching at anything that resembled a blow.

Mum was bemused.

'You keep telling us that being trans is a good thing. But how can we believe that when you're so tortured all the time? You don't seem happier now than before. If anything, you seem miserable.'

I didn't have the words to explain I was tortured because I was in the grip of a dramatic, often painful, metamorphosis, turning from solid to liquid back to flesh in my too-public cocoon. I didn't know how to tell her I was miserable because I'd never felt so alone. I didn't know how to say that, despite all this, still I knew, in the deepest pit of my gut, that I was moving in the right direction—that already I felt a rightness I'd never known before.

Instead I snarled, '*I'm* not miserable. *You're* just so anxious about transition and it makes me stressed.'

Our miseries fed off each other, becoming fat and bloated, poisoning the air with noxious gases, crowding out the possibility of grace.

The joyful conviction I'd brought home from Canada evaporated. I was no longer a person in love but a troublesome teenager undergoing second puberty, more disruptive than the first. My transness had become a problem that needed to be solved, a disease to be cured. It was time to call in the doctors. I needed experts to explain me to myself.

ᘐ

'Let's talk about your childhood,' the gender psychologist began.

It was our second session. I was here to submit myself to science, to have my gender trouble diagnosed.

The psychologist was accredited with the World Professional Association for Transgender Health (WPATH), the global body that oversees trans medicine. Since 1979, WPATH has published Standards of Care to guide the treatment of trans and gender-non-conforming people. By using WPATH Standards, the psych would determine whether I was suffering from gender dysphoria, the medical term for the 'discomfort or distress that is caused by a discrepancy between a person's gender identity and that person's sex assigned at birth (and the associated gender role and/or primary and secondary sex characteristics).'

In other words, gender dysphoria was the wrongness associated with my assigned role of woman. I'd been born with female genitals, the world pronounced me woman, and now I was convinced there'd been a terrible mistake. That was dysphoria.

The psychologist's role was to shine the light of science on my distress. If I was found to have sufficient gender dysphoria, I would be officially transgender. With that diagnosis, I could get the green light for hormone replacement therapy and gender-affirmation surgery. I could carry my transness around like a certified document, awash with red wax seals and weighty signatures. The world would have to believe me. I'd be a legit member of Club Trans. Without the gender dysphoria diagnosis, I could get nothing. No surgery, no legit-imacy. No hormones, unless I could find someone who prescribed testosterone via informed consent. Without the diagnosis, I'd be just a fucked-up woman, a lady with issues—disturbed, perhaps, but not trans. Or not, at least, according to the medical profession.

'So, what do you remember of early childhood?' the psych asks. 'What kind of toys did you like to play with?'

He's in a blue shirt today, a lanyard draped around his neck. I feel like an insect under a magnifying glass, a strange specimen ripe for classification.

'Um . . . well, I liked playing with my older brother,' I begin. 'I idolised him. I always admired his clothes and wanted to look like him.'

'Hmmm, okay.' The psych scribbles a few notes. 'And what were your favourite toys? What games did you play with your friends?'

I make some quick calculations. The true answer is that I played with Barbies. Doll's houses. Dress-ups. I read fairytales. All the classic girl stuff. But that's not the answer the psych's looking for. I'm supposed to say that I rolled around in the dirt with trucks and climbed trees with my catapult and always, always refused to wear pink. That's what female-to-male gender dysphoria is meant to look like. That's the trans script I'm meant to follow.

Only why is this new script as dull and narrow as the one I left behind?

'Well, I played with a mix of toys, I guess. I had Barbies but also played heaps of cricket. We had Lego. I loved doing Warhammer with my brother.'

I'm spinning a story, telling neat tales of a tomboy childhood, once again inhabiting the character I've been assigned: the trans person, born in the wrong body, a sick person looking for a cure. This is today's role. I must pull off the performance to get the diagnosis I need.

None of it's a lie, not exactly—just a question of emphasis. I mention the skateboard; omit the pink T-shirts and fairy wings. The full truth is so messy, too messy to fit inside this antiseptic office. The full truth is not woman, but not man either. Rather it's something else altogether, something outside the stale binary that limits our imagination.

The psych pauses to take notes, re-crosses his legs. I sip water to fill the space.

'And how did you feel about your body during childhood?'

'Well, I had an eating disorder as a teenager.'

'An eating disorder? Really? Tell me about that.' He's excited now, pen flying, on the trail of some solid dysphoria points. I can see my tally rising.

This is all a game, I realise, not a quest for truth. The rules are obvious: love everything 'masculine', disdain everything 'feminine'. Hate your body. Share trauma. Be a fuck-up, but not too much— psychosis is a disqualification. If you tick all the boxes, accumulate enough points, you'll win the grand prize: gender dysphoria diagnosis, the golden ticket that opens all the doors.

The whole farce would be amusing if the stakes weren't so high.

'Simply put, diagnosis wields immense power,' writes trans and disability activist Eli Clare. 'It can provide us access to vital medical technology or shame us, reveal a path toward less pain or get us locked up. It opens doors and slams them shut.'

I would play along with the diagnosis game because I needed doors to open.

᠆

When you visit a doctor, you're there to be fixed. You're there for a cure. To seek medical aid is to admit there's a problem, something broken or defective or unnatural, something that science and medicine promise to take in hand.

For a long time, transness itself was a sickness that demanded treatment. The first edition of the *Diagnostic and Statistical Manual of Mental Disorders* (DSM), released in 1952, classified the experiences of trans and gender nonconforming people within 'Sexual Deviations'—a catch-all that included homosexuality, transvestism, paedophilia, fetishism and sexual sadism. To be trans was to be disturbed in mind, a 'deviant' akin to a child molester.

Things changed in 1973, when the *DSM* belatedly responded to the social changes of the sixties. After years of campaigning, homosexuality was finally removed from its pages, no longer classified as a mental disorder. Yet transness remained on the books. In the *DSM-3*, which came out in 1980, trans assumed the new labels 'Transsexualism', 'Gender Identity Disorder of Childhood' and 'Psychosexual Disorder Not Elsewhere Classified'. In the eighties, the decade of my birth, the gay and lesbian community were no longer subject to the humiliation of medical diagnosis (though homophobia remained rampant, fuelled by the AIDS crisis), but trans folks were still deemed sick in the head.

In 1994, the *DSM* evolved again. 'Transsexualism' was out; 'Gender Identity Disorder' and 'Transvestic Fetishism (with Gender Dysphoria)' were in. Trans people were no longer deviant, but we were still disordered or fetishists—hardly a great improvement.

As Eli Clare reminds us: '*disorder* means not only dis-ordered but also wrong, broken, in need of repair. *Disorder* is used to constrict and confine, devalue and pathologize.'

Since the 2010s, there's been another paradigm shift. Today, doctors are careful to distinguish between the state of being trans and the mental distress it can cause. Transness itself, they say, is not a sickness. The fifth iteration of the *DSM*, released in 2013, ditched 'Gender Identity Disorder' to avoid the stigma of implying trans people are 'disordered'. In announcing the change, the American Psychiatric Association stressed that 'gender nonconformity is not in itself a mental disorder'. But while 'Gender Identity Disorder' was out, *DSM-5* included a new diagnosis: 'Gender Dysphoria', or the 'clinically significant distress' associated with gender trouble. In 2018, the WHO's own disease compendium, known as ICD-11, also made efforts to destigmatise transness by renaming it 'Gender Incongruence' and removing it from the chapter on mental disorders.

In this new model, transness itself isn't pathological, but the sense of wrongness that haunts trans experience is a medical condition that can be diagnosed and treated.

Being trans isn't sick, but feeling trans is.

If you're confused, you're in good company. It's a subtle distinction, a shift in emphasis so technical it can easily get lost. In practice, not all that much has changed. Trans people still feature in the *DSM*, that notorious encyclopaedia of problem minds. The WHO continues to categorise transness as a disease. Trans people still require psychiatric diagnosis to undergo gender-affirmation surgery and—in most cases—hormone replacement therapy. Transness is still colonised by the medical profession, still located within the domain of sickness and cure. We still have a diagnosis, which, while no longer technically a 'disorder', is nonetheless listed within the official *Manual of Mental Disorders*. No matter the words used, so long as transness remains within the *DSM*, it will remain a problem to be fixed.

'There is nothing neutral about the *DSM*,' Clare writes. It's a palace of sick and dangerous minds, a compendium of scourges to be eliminated.

All things considered, I would prefer not to be a scourge. I'd prefer to have my transness embraced rather than eliminated. To be sure, being trans is hard. It's painful, often lonely and sometimes brutal—but that doesn't mean it should be cured or corrected. Transness itself isn't the problem; the problem is the stigma and discrimination that make trans lives painful. It's the stigma we need to cure, not the transness. Transness itself is a natural variation, part of the texture of humanity, a source of insight and meaning, a place of aliveness inhabited by a tribe of fabulous unicorns. It should no more be eliminated than we should eliminate fat or ageing or red hair. They're all just part of the human condition.

But isn't gender dysphoria actually a problem? Surely that's why I was in the psychologist's office—to get access to surgeries and hormones that would alleviate my gender trouble.

After five sessions on the shrink's couch, I was no longer sure. True, I wanted access to things that would change my appearance to better match the image inside my head. But why was that process framed in the medical language of *diagnosis*, *treatment*, *cure*—especially when, given its frequent changes, the diagnosis seemed more than a little made up? Within my short lifetime it had transformed from Transsexualism, to Gender Identity Disorder, to Gender Dysphoria. Who knew what it would be a few years down the track? All the pivots didn't inspire faith that any of it was definitive. If the 'diagnosis' was just official-sounding weasel words, liable to be superseded within a few years, why situate trans bodily modification in a diagnostic framework at all?

There are many forms of bodily modification that require no diagnosis. Think of tattoos, piercings, plastic surgery. For all of them, you can just walk in off the street and order what you want, no questions asked.

Like gender-affirmation surgery, breast enhancement and face lifts are both procedures to modify appearance—major procedures that penetrate the flesh and carry risk. Yet unlike trans surgery, these 'cosmetic' procedures require no psychiatric assessment. Why was there one rule for boob enhancement and another for boob removal? Why was I the disordered one?

The diagnosis game was losing its charm. I began to suspect the whole thing was rigged. Win or lose, diagnosis or not—either way, I'd surrendered myself to the authority of a medical framework that diminished my agency, told me what I could and couldn't do to myself. Even if it gave me the green light, I'd still carry the sour taste of subordination in my mouth.

↳

'I've compiled your results,' the psych announces.

It is February, two months since I'd first walked into his office. Over five sessions, we've poked and pried into every aspect of my gender trouble. During my last visit, I'd completed an exhaustive questionnaire about my body, my childhood and my relationships. For forty minutes, I'd perched on a plastic-covered chair in the waiting room, answering pages of tick-box questions with a cheap biro. With every tick of blue ink, my innermost self was converted into numbers to be crunched.

Now the results are in.

'On the basis of this assessment, you have scored 58.' He peers at his computer screen to check the figure. 'Fifty-eight out of a maximum of 70.'

'Fifty-eight? What does that mean?'

'Anything above 28 is classed as diagnosable gender dysphoria. A score in the fifties is classed as severe. You've scored 58, which indicates you have severe gender dysphoria.'

He pauses, waiting for me to digest the news.

My first feeling is triumph. *A high score, I've aced the test!* Even well into adulthood, I'm still the perpetual straight-A student, always desperate to top the class and win the teacher's favour. A high score, no matter the metric, is cause for celebration. *A pity I didn't get into the 60s, though.* A flash of shame.

'Okay, I see,' I respond, attempting to arrange my face into an appropriate expression.

How is the patient meant to feel in this situation? Dismayed? Overjoyed? I've got the desired diagnosis, but also been told that I have a 'severe' problem. Perhaps the moment calls for some serious nodding, nothing too enthusiastic.

'In my opinion,' continues the psych, 'the only possible explanation for these results is that you are transgender. We've screened for comorbid conditions like autism. You don't have any of those. With gender dysphoria this severe, it's almost certain you're trans.'

It's almost certain you're trans. The words hit me like a dumper, a wall of water that appears without warning, throwing me off my feet into the roiling swell.

I am trans, for real. A shrink had said so. It's not just in my head; or, more precisely, it's in my head enough to be deemed legit. I'm not a deluded little girl; I have a verified diagnosis: severe gender dysphoria, officially trans. Science has spoken. Everyone will have to believe me now.

I walk home in a daze, oblivious to the besuited commuters sweating in the Melbourne afternoon glare, still mentally flailing in the surf. It was so big, too big to comprehend. With my diagnosis, I'd crossed a threshold. It was as though 'trans' had been carved in my flesh, turning an inner feeling into something official and irrevocable. I'd be no one's daughter, no one's sister, anymore. No one could argue with those numbers: 58, 58 out of 70. Fully 30 points above the diagnosable threshold. *Severe.* I savour the gravity of the word.

Back home, I scrounge a half-empty bottle of red, a long-open drop well on the road towards vinegar. With a full glass, I head up to the rooftop. The evening is hot, too hot for red, but the occasion requires a sacrament.

On the roof, I straddle a picnic table and sip the vinegary wine, staring at the city skyline fading into a blur of pink. *Trans. Severe gender dysphoria.* These are my words now. Nobody can question whether they belong to me.

Fifty-eight. I roll the number around in my mouth. So absurd, to be reduced to an arbitrary number, and yet that number carries so much consolation.

'At its best, diagnosis affirms our distress', Eli Care writes. Diagnosis 'legitimises some pain as real'.

After the months of doubt and distaste, this diagnosis is the affirmation I'd craved. For all my scepticism about the diagnostic process, for all my frustration over the medicalisation of transness, the diagnosis itself is a blessing. I'd been anointed, smeared with holy oil, and now drifted in a rarefied state, apart from the world.

This is my trans equivalent of a wedding, a birth, a christening: a life-changing moment, grave yet beautiful, that can only be metabolised via solemn ritual. Alone on the rooftop, surfaces still warm from the sun, I yearn for whispered prayers, rousing speeches, tables heaving with food, special garments, and even a dance or two to safely usher me from one life to the next. The gravity of the occasion demands nothing less. If I squint, I can almost picture a congregation of tipsy guests crowding the rooftop, tottering about in toe-pinching shoes with flutes of champagne.

But there is no ritual for this moment, no ceremony to fall back on. I am alone. The world goes on, an ordinary Tuesday eve in late summer, oblivious to my metamorphosis. Down on the street, the traffic lights change and a tram clangs past. A lone jogger runs by, moving along the footpath in great loping strides. I finger the phone in my pocket, thinking of all the people I need to tell.

There is no ritual, no ceremony for this moment, so, in the great trans tradition I improvise my own: bathing my veins in wine, marinating in the pink air, alone and awed with the bigness of it all.

I'm real now, so real it almost hurts.

MISADVENTURES
IN MENSWEAR

MY FIRST TIME, I'M TERRIFIED. I loiter around the edges, heart pounding. Sneaking furtive glances over my shoulder to check if anyone's watching. The store's near deserted, bar the occasional pensioner and teenage employee. It's late Friday evening and the masses have retreated home to their wine and Netflix. The Kmart Men's section is unguarded, ripe for the picking.

Time to take the plunge. I cross the threshold, feigning a casual stroll into forbidden territory. The land of blokes, guys, 'M'. Men. I'm soon deep in a khaki forest of shirts and slacks. My breath comes quick and shallow, stomach clenched, mind on high alert for the inevitable voice shooing me away.

Grabbing clothes at random, I scurry into the fluorescent change room like a criminal—only to discover that nothing fits my female frame. Even after months of push-ups, my shoulders are dwarfed by the wingspan of a men's XS shirt. I'm reduced to a child in his father's clothing. Absurd.

I walk out empty-handed.

A week later, I muster my courage once more and venture into Uniqlo in the CBD, a cathedral of normcore. In the acres of monochrome shirts and knits, tees and polos, surely there must be something that fits. Something that will remake me into the dapper gent of my imagination. But no. No luck. Shirts drape from my shoulders, pants fall to mid-thigh.

At H&M, Topman, Muji, Zara, Country Road—all the fast-fashion chains—the result is the same. Everywhere the cheap cotton makes a mockery of my attempted masculinity.

Op-shops are even worse. I browse through meagre racks of discarded men's shirts, finding little more than garish prints marked by sweat stains. Small sizes are rare as hen's teeth.

Where do the skinny cis men find clothes? Melbourne has no shortage of men with even less bulk than me. How do they source shirts that fit?

A quick google provides the answer: Asia, where menswear is tailored for smaller dimensions. In Singapore or Hong Kong you can get shirts in sizes near impossible to locate in Australia. Even Japanese brands like Uniqlo and Muji alter their sizing for different markets, and supersize their menswear for the imagined heftier blokes in Australia. A Uniqlo small in Sydney is not the same as a small in Tokyo. After absorbing these facts, I briefly ponder an overseas jaunt to furnish my new wardrobe.

Leaving the supermarket one afternoon, I spy a bearded person in a flared skirt. Diamante jewels sparkle from each ear. Neck long, back erect, refusing the hunched posture of shame. I seek eye contact, but they stride past like a queen, eyes fixed on the horizon, heedless of the gawping punters. In half a second, they're gone, a vision that might never have been.

For weeks afterwards, I scan the supermarket crowds for this human butterfly. *How did you find the strength to buy and wear the 'wrong' clothes?* I silently ask. *Can you teach me?* But I never see them again.

Internet research leads me to a chain that specialises in slim-fit menswear. In Sydney for work, I brave the tiny boutique. Upon entry, I'm assailed by a trio of shop assistants. No other customers in sight. The staff assess me with cold eyes, sizing up their prey. Avoiding their gaze, I sidle up to the racks.

'So, what can we help you with? Are you looking for a gift?'

'No, for me.'

'For *you*? A new look?' she asks, with thinly veiled scorn.

I nod inconclusively, mute, eyes fixed on the racks of clothes. Several minutes of searching rewards me with three shirts that might, just possibly, fit. Plain white, navy, checks. I can picture him, the man who sometimes flickers in the mirror, bringing them to life.

'Could I please try these on?' I whisper.

I'm shown to a cubicle in the middle of the store. It's a blank box, no mirror inside. Only a communal mirror next to the registers.

'Don't you have any other change rooms?' Of course, they don't.

My resolve wavers. I cannot stomach the humiliation of three assistants gawking as I don men's shirts—shirts that will, most likely, sit askew on my puny 'female' torso. I refuse to let them see my awkward, most intimate desires. I thrust the shirts at the closest assistant and flee into the roar of Broadway. Empty-handed, again.

These experiments confer hard lessons about bodies and gender. As a slim-hipped, flat-chested person, I'd long imagined myself an androgynous creature, barely woman at all. I thought remaking myself as a man would be as simple as donning a new shirt.

But now, confronted with men's tailoring, I must reckon with my 'female' architecture. It's in the small things: the curve of my thighs, the span of my shoulders, a swollen posterior. A subtle but undeniable waist. Together they scream 'female'. Together they refuse the strict geometry of a men's suit.

Body and cloth refuse to cooperate, straining in different directions.

The men's tailoring that runs counter to my 'female' physique becomes another form of gender policing, scolding me for daring to wear the wrong shirt, to enter the wrong store.

Tailoring, I discover, is a technology that enforces binary gender norms by dictating how 'male' and 'female' bodies should occupy space. Through the seams and darts of even the simplest shirt, we're taught how certain bodies must correspond to certain genders. Wide shoulders equals male. Waist equals female.

Any attempted transgression is punished with discomfort—both the physical unease of ill-fitting attire and the humiliation of being made ridiculous in change room mirrors. Any attempted transgression is punished by leaving stores empty-handed.

Only if you follow the rules can you find clothes that fit.

A transmasc blog suggests a solution for my fashion woes: boys' clothes. 'Male' clothes in smaller sizes, at half the price.

Back at my local Kmart, I investigate. The boys' section is tiny, less than half the size of the adjacent girls' range. The colour palette is muted, all blues and greys, sombre in comparison to the hot pink and sequins of the princess gear across the aisle. I edge in for a closer look. Robot underwear, dinosaur hoodies. T-shirts adorned with cars and skateboards and surfboards—all the trappings of the masculine privilege to roam and play. Here is patriarchy for sale at five dollars a pop. But there're also plain jeans and a blue shirt in what looks like a reasonable size.

I scour the selection, all the while trying to project the image of a mother shopping for her son. Totally normal, nothing to see here.

In the change rooms, the mirror reveals I'm a perfect boys' size 14. I approach the cash registers with shaking hands and walk out with my contraband. Not empty-handed this time.

Next morning, I test out my male disguise. In the bedroom mirror, the transformation is dramatic. No longer woman but not man either. Instead, a baby-faced boy stares back at me, neat in a collared shirt and fresh jeans beneath cropped hair and big eyes. A boy on his way to church or to visit grandparents. Wholesome, innocent, ripe for bruising.

I recognise him from somewhere. His earnest gaze and round cheeks are a Proustian madeleine from some forgotten past.

A memory rises to the surface: my school photo from Year Six, back in 1999. The year I cut my long mane. The year I wore a uniform of navy shorts and white tees. The year I played on a boys' cricket team and was mistaken for a boy at the supermarket. The year I wrote a story starring Sir-Lady Wufflesump, a gender-bending knight who lived out my own unarticulated genderqueer desires. The year before puberty set my body awry.

Now the boy of that year has returned to me. Thanks to the magic of a $14.99 shirt, I've lost twenty years. Two decades of faux womanhood erased.

Out on the street, I brace myself for stares, for derision, for standing out like a sore thumb. I walk fast, striding through the morning crowds towards a local cafe. A gender traitor on a reconnaissance mission.

Not that long ago, 'cross-dressers' like me risked arrest. Until the era of gay liberation, cross-dressing was illegal in many US states. Leslie Feinberg's autobiographical novel *Stone Butch Blues* recalls how butches were terrorised by police in 1960s New York. During regular raids on gay bars, the butches were arrested, beaten and even raped by police for daring to wear a suit and tie instead of skirts and heels. The law stipulated that female-assigned people needed to wear at least three items of women's clothing (and vice versa for male-assigned folk).

Australia was no less committed to policing gender deviance. Well into the twentieth century, besuited 'women' and 'men' in dresses were arrested in Sydney, Melbourne and other cities under state vagrancy laws.

One of these persecuted individuals was Neville McQuade, a male-assigned teenager arrested multiple times in Sydney during the 1940s for 'dressing as a girl'. In June 1942, McQuade appeared in North Sydney Court under vagrancy charges, and was released under bond. The following year, McQuade was again apprehended and sentenced to two months' hard labour. The charge? 'Impersonating a woman.' The sentence was suspended, but that didn't stop McQuade being arrested a third time, on New Year's Eve 1943, for stepping out in women's clothes on the arm of a male paramour. McQuade's NYE celebrations were brought to an abrupt halt when the happy couple were taken into custody by a passing cop. For no offence other than wearing dresses, McQuade was persecuted by the state and given a criminal record.

Braving the footpath in boys' clothes, I feel the full weight of that history. I know, all too keenly, that being a gender traitor in public rarely ends well. Of course, with my blonde hair and androgynous look, I'm less vulnerable than most, protected by the status attached to whiteness and masculinity. Even so, I'm afraid, and brace myself against the blows that discipline the different, panicked by the sirens in my brain that associate gender trans-gression with social death. After a lifetime of gender policing, I've learnt to police myself. *Abort! Abort!* screams my inner gender-cop as I step out onto the street.

But I walk one block, two, then three without incident. I cross the street and head towards the local shops. The anticipated wave of attention never arrives. In its place, there is a startling absence. Gone are the lustful glances, the wolf-whistles, the assessing eyes running up and down my frame. Now men and women alike stride past oblivious, paying me no heed. For the first time since puberty, I'm near invisible. A person walking down the street, neither competition nor prey. No longer a slut, goddess, bitch, whore, Madonna, princess, mother or virgin. Just a body, perhaps a boy, moving through space.

At first I'm disconcerted, even bereft, mourning the gaze of others—the gaze that 'women' are taught must define their meaning and worth.

But within minutes a new lightness enters my gait. Movement comes easy without the weight of so many eyes. Only now, as the world's attention recedes, can I measure what a burden it had been.

↵

As I start wearing this disguise full-time, my age warps and bends, detached from chronology. For the first time in years, I'm asked for ID at bottle shops. When I meet new people, they ask what I'm studying and are incredulous to learn I'm a teacher, not a student.

'I'm older than I look,' I assure them. They remain unconvinced.

At work, I position my forearm to conceal the 'Zara Boys' label adorning my shirt, trying to convey professional authority from within a child's blazer.

Each day I slip through time, both younger and older with every new wardrobe acquisition. Am I 32 or 19, 12 or 25?

My enthusiasm for the gym wanes, causing my shoulder span to contract even further. No longer swollen by weightlifting, my torso shrinks from a boys' size 14 to size 12. But I'm more at ease in my skin than ever—smaller, younger, but inflated with a new confidence. I'm falling back through the years as I grow into myself.

At my cousin's wedding, I turn up in Zara Boys slacks and shirt, a navy blazer from Myer Kids, with jaunty suspenders to add some flair. It's the first major outing in my new wardrobe. I stand tall, claiming space with squared shoulders, wending my way through the reception room with a swagger I'd like to bottle.

Later, I'm mailed an envelope of prints, the work of the official wedding photographer. One photo is a candid snap of Mum and me, heads bent together with her hand on my shoulder, my body towering above hers. We're both beaming, with matching smiles and crinkled eyes and blonde mops. In my size-12 blazer, I could pass for her teenage son, the two of us giggling at some private joke. The whole image has a golden tint, courtesy of the late afternoon light.

Since forever, I've recoiled from seeing myself in photos, always shocked to find a stranger inhabiting my flesh. *Who is that woman with a forced smile and anxious eyes, and what is she doing in my body?* The camera lied, again and again, for years, forever depicting me with a shape that wasn't my own.

This photograph is different, though. This wedding snap depicts me—actually me, in the form that I know myself. The boys' clothes allowed the camera to see me for the first time. I stare at the image for long minutes, savouring the unfamiliar pleasure of feeling real.

'This is the first time I've ever recognised myself in a photo,' I tell my cousin, more than a little awed.

For months afterwards, I keep the photo propped up on my bookshelf, a daily reminder that I'm going in the right direction. Backwards into boys' wear; forward towards myself.

⤻

Perhaps I'll never 'advance' from boys' clothes into menswear. Perhaps, in fact, I don't want to. Perhaps to be queer in gender is also to be queer in age, refusing the strictures of linear progress and growth that keep us in check. Perhaps to be trans is to scramble past and present, young and old, much as we scramble the binary of man and woman.

In the book *In a Queer Time and Place,* Jack Halberstam argues that queer and trans bodies make a mockery of normative temporalities. Trans folk like me are unwieldy beings that cannot or will not make an orderly progression through childhood, adolescence, careers, marriage, home ownership, parenthood and onwards towards death.

Instead, we invent our own dance through time. Trans folk might experience a second puberty as they take hormones to affirm their gender, queers may continue 'youthful' partying and play deep into adulthood, some will become parents to non-biological offspring or reject parenthood altogether.

To be queer or trans is, in one sense, to reject what Elizabeth Freeman calls chrononormativity—the dominant temporal order, structured around efficient production and reproduction. Chrononormativity is working 9–5 to save for a house in which to raise kids so they can grow up and repeat the cycle. By failing chrononormativity, queers and trans folk show that adulting can take many forms. It doesn't have to be about property and parenthood; instead, it can be wearing boys' clothes, living alone with cats, and reinventing oneself again and again. Time and age are remade anew when cishetero norms are abandoned.

As Halberstam puts it, queer time allows the 'potentiality of a life unscripted by the conventions of family, inheritance, and child rearing'. Alternative 'futures can be imagined according to logics that lie outside of those paradigmatic markers of life experience— namely, birth, marriage, reproduction, and death.'

It's disorienting but also profoundly liberating. When the temporal map of life is cast aside, there are no 'shoulds' anymore. It's all a blank page, yet to be filled.

In change rooms, in my bedroom, on the street, I discover these truths through my own march towards boyhood. Perhaps there are new possibilities to be found in temporal 'regression'. Perhaps there is no forward and back, no real march towards anywhere—just our stumbling, ever-hopeful present, shorn of expectations of how we should progress through life.

Perhaps, indeed, Kmart helped set me free.

TRAPPED IN A BODY

ONCE WE HAVE THE DIAGNOSIS, the gender psychologist is keen to get cracking. For him, gender dysphoria = transgender = hormone replacement therapy. Simple. Problem solved, fixed by the miracle of modern medicine.

'Transitioning to male is easy, really,' he tells me at our next appointment. 'The testosterone can work wonders and you just gain male privilege.'

He speaks as though it were akin to putting a cast on a broken leg or treating diabetes with insulin. A mere mechanical process to fix a diagnosed condition.

'Here, have a read of this.'

He hands me printout about the effects of testosterone.

It lists the expected changes: deeper voice, increased muscle bulk, facial hair, clitoral growth, increased libido, body fat redistribution. Male-pattern balding and the cessation of periods. Breast tissue atrophy. Everything, short of a new bone structure, needed to remake a female-assigned body into the shape we call 'man'. Side effects include acne, vaginal atrophy, reduced fertility, and increased risk of heart disease and high cholesterol. Most of the effects are reversible and will fade within a few months of suspending HRT.

'You should note there are a few irreversible changes,' the psych points out. 'These include lowered voice and facial hair. But you can always shave or laser the hair, if needed.'

I read on. Testosterone comes as a gel, cream or injections. The injections are popular because they are administered only once every three months. The gel or cream, by contrast, needs to be applied daily.

The final section outlines the option to freeze my eggs prior to starting testosterone. If desired, I could use them to become pregnant at a later date.

On the couch, I fold the paper into a neat square and look up at the psychologist, who is checking his watch.

It's true that I wanted this. Ever since I faced up to my transness, a persistent whisper in my ear told me testosterone, or 'T', would be the solution. My shape would change, the menswear would begin to fit, no one would mistake me for a woman. I'd seen it play out a hundred times on the internet. I knew that, with enough time and T, I could 'pass' as male. On the street, no one would ever guess I'd been born with a vagina.

But now I'm here, on the brink, I prevaricate. The psychologist's haste feels like an effort to tidy me away, to sort out the mess of my transness via a therapy that will re-insert me within the gender binary. 'Woman' was a failure, so now I'm being propelled over to 'man'.

Once again, it feels like transness is the problem.

'I'm a bit unsure, I guess,' I stutter, tucking away the info sheet in my pocket. 'I'm having some complex feelings I'd like to discuss before proceeding.'

'Hmmm, well okay. But we've covered all the relevant ground already. And your diagnosis was unambiguous—58, severe gender dysphoria.'

It's clear that the time for talk is over. The diagnosis is in, and I'm now supposed to grasp my cure.

If only it were so straightforward.

In truth, despite what the psychologist's questionnaires tell me, I'm no more M than F. I'm not a man trapped in a woman's body; I'm a trans person flailing around on this strange binary earth. Transmasculine, not male. Neither side of the gender binary feels like home.

My fear is that testosterone would merely transport me from the F camp into the M—which, from the outside, seems riven with random violence, all hard fists and swallowed tears. I couldn't survive there. After thirty-one years in a female body, fear of men is implanted deep in my cells.

In his 2018 memoir *Amateur*, New York trans man Thomas Page McBee relates how, once he started passing as male in everyday life, masculine violence began to rain down on him as it never had when he was 'female'. Random strangers would pick fights on the street, a stray glance could lead to raised fists. McBee responded by learning to box. As for me, I'd sooner eat dirt. I can't even bear to strike a punching bag in the gym.

More to the point, I just don't feel like a man. I can no longer live as a woman, but nor do I desire to enter the parallel universe of men. My shit will stay messy, I can tell.

According to the medical model of transness, my diagnosis of severe gender dysphoria renders me an obvious candidate for medical transition. I'm being funnelled into a predetermined pathway of gender-affirming therapies designed by experts invested in treating dysphoria within a medical framework structured around the gender binary. This is the right path for some people. It's not, however, the path for me.

My diagnosis was useful, enormously so. It provided the validation I sorely needed. It allowed me to take myself seriously. It compelled others to respect my transness as real. But, as Eli Clare reminds us, 'diagnosis is a tool rather than a fact, an action rather than a state of being, one story among many.'

Now this tool has served its purpose, and I want to tell different stories about my transness. Stories about being wild and unruly, beautiful in my strangeness, rather than stories about sickness and cure. 'Brilliant imperfection' is Clare's name for these counternarratives.

Brilliantly imperfect is how I'd like to proclaim myself.

↶

And yet. When I catch up with a transmasc acquaintance deep in the second puberty of transition, the whiff of their new teenage-boy sweat has me reeling, sucker-punched by envy. In that moment, I'm overcome by want, a raw desire for testosterone that annihilates all doubt. It lasts maybe twenty seconds, a minute at most.

It happens again on Instagram, when I see self-made men shed their female skins and sprout into sleek young bucks. Their metamorphoses have all the seductive pull of a fairytale: broken, then fixed; wrong, then right. That narrative tugs at my brain, tempting me with the prospect of an ending. What a comfort it would be, to have a destination.

For the most part, though, I belong not in the M camp or the F camp but in the murky middle—or more accurately, on a different plane altogether, one where we're all just bodies, living and dying, in infinite marvellous configurations.

The struggle is to craft that gender in embodied form, to somehow fashion flesh and blood that confound the gender binary, that refuse to be categorised as F or M. Most days, that task seems impossible.

In her poem 'vague', the trans poet Alex Gallagher writes:

people assume my problem
is that i'm woman trapped in a man's body
when the problem is more like
i'm trapped in a body

I too am trapped in a body, trapped in a world that sees only two genders. The problem is not me, nor is it transness, nor even gender dysphoria—the problem is the gender binary that insists upon reading all bodies as either 'man' or 'woman'. Every time I'm perceived as a woman it's a small death, a grief that gets added to the pile festering in my belly. Yet I don't want to be perceived as a man, for the simple reason that I'm not one. All I want is to be seen for who I am: a transmasculine person, part of the mighty non-binary or genderqueer universe, neither man nor woman but trans. For that to happen, what needs to change is not me but the world.

'The real crisis is not that gender non-conforming people exist, it's that we have been taught to believe in only two genders in the first place,' explains Alok Vaid-Menon (also known as ALOK) in their 2020 book *Beyond the Gender Binary*.

ALOK is a gender non-conforming artist, based in New York, who adorns their hirsute brown body in a technicolour array of dresses, jewellery and make-up. The finished product explodes our assumptions of what 'masculine' and 'feminine' can be. On any given day, ALOK might step out in blood-red lipstick that pops against their beard, alongside dangly gold earrings and a floor-length gown with plunging neckline that reveals a hairy chest. They're a living work of art, celebrated worldwide as a gender provocateur carving out new possibilities for living in a body. Although unable to walk down the street without facing harassment, ALOK is leading the charge against the gender binary.

If the true crisis is binary gender, the solution is not to assimilate trans and gender diverse (TGD) people back into the categories M and F. The solution is to expand our imaginations of what gender can be. In truth, people who are neither men nor women are not deluded or sick or dangerous; we're part of the glorious variation of humanity.

Make no mistake: people who aren't men or women are not some invention of woke millennials who've spent too much time on the internet. Gender diversity was not born on Tumblr. The words *non-binary* and *trans* and *genderqueer* and *agender* might be new, but the ideas behind them are not. People who are not simply F or M have existed in some form or another since ancient times. They're found in Indigenous cultures worldwide.

In Turtle Island, or North America, First Nations gender systems include the category Two-Spirit. As the Two-Spirit researcher Margaret Robinson explains, Two-Spirit is an umbrella term, first coined in 1990, for the numerous pre-colonial gender categories that combined masculine and feminine energies. Indeed, an estimated 168 Indigenous languages in the United States have terms to describe someone who is neither a man nor a woman. For example, the A:shwi have a gender called *lhamana*, translated as man-woman. The Lakȟóta (also known as the Dakota, or the Sioux) use the word *wíŋtke* to refer to male-assigned people who combine masculine and feminine traits. The Diné or Navajo Nation recognise people called *nádleehí*, a term meaning 'constant state of change', a category that can include feminine men, masculine women or intersex people. The Ojibwe (Chippewa) even have four genders: *inini* (masculine male), *okwe* (feminine female), *agokwe* (feminine male), and *agowinini* (masculine female).

Diverse genders are also widespread elsewhere, including *hijra* in India, *basaja* in the Indonesian island of Sulawesi, and *ogbanje* among the Igbo people of Nigeria. Tibetan Buddhist culture includes a 'third sex' known as *paṇḍaka*. Maori language includes the term *Whakawahine* to denote trans people. In Samoa, *Fa'afafine* is a third gender, a femme non-binary space. There's also the related term *Fa'afatama*, for transmasculine people. Amao Leota Lu, a *Fa'afafine* living in Sydney, explains that Samoan ideas of gender easily accommodate someone like her. Amao is neither man nor woman, and that's no problem. 'Binaries are such a colonial way of thinking,' Amao notes.

In the continent now known as Australia, First Nations cultures also allow for genders beyond the binary. Brotherboys and Sistergirls are flexible identities that allow for a mix of masculine and feminine energies. Indigenous researcher Madi Day explains that these terms can 'refer to transgender women and men, but they can also be used to refer to people of varying genders and sexualities'. For Indigenous Australians, the idea that F and M are the only possible genders was an import of colonisation. 'The gender binary arrived with the boats,' explains the Wiradjuri Brotherboy Hayden Moon, citing the words of a Bunjalung Elder who has passed away.

As Europe colonised the world, the binary came to dominate our imaginations. 'These binaries of male and female reflect the colonial project and invader stereotypes imposed through religion and cultural annihilation,' Wiradjuri trans researcher Sandy O'Sullivan tells us. In settler colonies like the United States, First Nations gender diversity was held as evidence of Indigenous inferiority and used to justify colonial conquest. Gender diversity was suppressed, its history ignored—a process in which I, as a white settler, am complicit. But gender diversity has always been here—called different things, understood in different ways, cropping up again and again wherever there are people. It's part of our humanity.

Out in public, the binary is nigh impossible to avoid. Each day, strangers make assumptions about our gender, slotting us all into one of two boxes. Girl, lady, woman—these are the assumptions that cling to me no matter how much I masc up my hairstyle and wardrobe.

At the drycleaners, I wait at the counter to pick up some blazers. The owner is distracted by an evening dress he's trying to arrange on a hanger.

'You girls!' he exclaims in my direction. 'You have such complicated clothes.'

At the cafe, the waiter walks up to my table.

'Now, what can I get you ladies? Would you like some coffees to start?'

On the street, a parent shoos their child out of my way.

'Careful, watch out for the lady!'

Our everyday speech is peppered with assumptions about the gender of the people we encounter. Within half a second, without any conscious effort, our brains sort the bodies in our vicinity: M or F, lady or male, he or she.

Out in the world, non-binary people like me are erased, wiped off the domain of the possible. This is a form of epistemic domination—Kate Manne's term for one world view silencing another. Non-binary people know ourselves to be neither men nor women, but the world refuses to acknowledge that people like us can even exist. Our self-knowledge is dismissed. Through the architecture of daily life, we are made inconceivable. There's literally no space for us.

This was brought into stark relief in early 2021, when the non-binary singer Sam Smith was excluded from the gendered categories at the Brit Awards. Smith, who came out as non-binary in 2019, is ineligible for both the solo male and solo female artist awards. Despite being one of the most successful British pop artists of the past decade, there is simply no solo artist award for which Smith could be nominated. The categories exclude them from the whole endeavour.

In everyday life, nowhere is this exclusion more obvious than in public bathrooms. Whenever I need to pee—which, given my copious tea consumption, is often—I'm confronted with the bathroom dilemma. Which one: M or F? Sometimes, if I'm lucky, there's a gender-neutral toilet, usually a disabled bathroom repurposed for this additional function. More often though, there's the old binary choice: M or F. Neither is accurate. Forced to choose, my preference is generally for F—not because I'm a woman, but because women's bathrooms tend to be cleaner and boast the privacy of individual stalls. I have no desire to see strange men with their cocks out, pissing in a chorus line. Unless the ladies is packed to the gills with a queue out front, I'll steer clear of the gents.

But once inside the female bathroom, I'm on edge. I'm hyper-aware of each stranger's assessment of my gender, each woman's analysis of whether my boyish body belongs or not. Even though I scuttle into a stall, eyes down, I feel each curious look, each hostile glare, each double take. They burn hot on my skin.

This is what Jack Halberstam calls 'the Bathroom Problem'. In the book *Female Masculinity*, Halberstam notes that humans 'who present in some ambiguous way are routinely questioned and challenged about our presence in the "wrong" bathroom.' Halberstam, who is non-binary, knows this problem all too well. As a female-assigned person with a masculine aesthetic, Halberstam experiences regular hostility within women's bathrooms. Once, he was inside a stall at Chicago's O'Hare airport, en route to Minneapolis, when he was interrupted by a knock on the door.

'Open up, security here!' Halberstam heard.

A fellow bathroom user had deemed him a threat and called security to have Halberstam removed.

In one view, this gender policing is absurd. If someone is minding their own business, and just wants to pee in a private cubicle, why should it matter how feminine or masculine they appear?

The fact that it does matter is evidence of the enduring power of the gender binary. Not only are we presented with only two bathroom options, but we scrutinise the gender of everyone who enters these spaces. Whenever someone's gender is ambiguous—*is that a man or a woman?* —they're met with hostility and suspicion. Anyone who can't be slotted within the binary is categorised as deviant. Gender rebellion is punished, leaving the binary strong enough to live another day.

I'm one of the lucky ones: I haven't been verbally or physically abused in public toilets, unlike so many trans people. No one has ever called security on me. Even so, peeing in public toilets has become an ordeal. No matter which bathroom I choose, I'm all too conscious of entering foreign territory, penetrating a space not made for me, where any moment I'm liable to be asked to explain myself. My heart rate spikes. Sweat dampens my armpits. I turn into a frightened animal, hyper-alert to anything that resembles a predator, ever ready to flee into the undergrowth. My hands shake at the basin. It's another reason it's tempting to stay home.

I'm far from the only one who feels this way. A recent US survey of 28,000 trans people found that almost sixty per cent avoided public bathrooms in the previous year due to fear of confrontation. So many of us are unable to participate fully in civic life because we can't safely urinate outside our own homes.

My dilemma is this: in a world that recognises only man or woman, one that struggles to imagine other possibilities, I'm forced to choose between two bad options. At the moment, in the absence of a medical transition, the world treats me as a woman. That's an endless sequence of slaps.

But in this binary world, it's near impossible to escape one gender container without being lumped into another. If I was to masculinise my appearance via hormones and surgery, the talk of *lady* and *girl* would cease, but new misidentifications would spring up in their place. Instead of being mistaken for a woman, I'd be mistaken for a man—in effect, swapping one ill-fitting costume for another.

My dilemma, the non-binary dilemma, is to make my gender legible in a world that refuses to see it. Each day, we must choose anew: which is the lesser of two evils? Is it better to be misread as man or woman?

Imagine, for a moment, you only drink tea. It's the only beverage you can stomach, and you drink gallons of the stuff at home. Whenever you go out, however, to a cafe or restaurant or friend's house, they only serve coffee or hot chocolate.

'I'll have a tea, please,' you say, each time.

'Tea? No, we don't have that,' you're informed with raised eyebrows. 'Would you like coffee or a hot chocolate?'

The truth is you can't stand either. Both coffee and hot chocolate make you nauseous; you might even be allergic. But still, you order one or the other, because you have to order something. You can't just sit at the cafe with a complimentary glass of water. You'd be asked to leave. So each day you sip the coffee or the hot chocolate, the rich liquid causing uproar in your guts, a bit sicker each time, slowly poisoning yourself. Eventually this sickness becomes your baseline.

The absence of tea is perplexing. You drink tea at home, after all; it's a beverage that exists and is drunk worldwide. If the customer is always right, and you're a customer asking for tea, why not start offering tea as a third option? It would be such a straightforward solution. When this doesn't happen, when years pass and still you must choose between coffee and hot chocolate, leaving you forever queasy, the world begins to feel hostile. No one cares whether you're sick, you realise. No one cares whether you're welcomed or excluded. You can't change yourself, and the world will not bend to accommodate you, so you start to regard yourself as an alien being. A freak who cannot belong.

It becomes easier to stay home, where tea is on tap, rather than go outside and drink the liquids that poison you by degrees. Still, it's lonely. More than anything, you'd love to savour a brew in a cafe while your friends drink their flat whites.

This, more or less, is how it feels to be non-binary in a binary world. Except it's worse, because in this case it's your own identity that's not on the menu. As a non-binary person, you're given the impossible task of trying to thrive in a world that denies you basic succour and force-feeds alternatives you cannot stomach. To add insult to injury, it all seems so gratuitous. Like adding tea to a menu, there's no reason why non-binary couldn't be recognised as a third gender.

This everyday erasure translates into discrimination and distress. All TGD peoples face stigma and prejudice, but it's easier for our binary world to understand and accommodate those who transition from one side to the other. A male-assigned person who becomes a woman, or a female-assigned person who becomes a man, doesn't fundamentally threaten the gender binary. They're changing teams, not refusing the game altogether. By contrast, non-binary people are sitting on the sidelines, thumbing their nose at the whole endeavour.

In practice, this makes daily life an uphill battle. A British study of trans youth, published in 2019, found that non-binary participants 'experienced significantly more anxiety and depression and had significantly lower self-esteem than the binary group'. The study concluded that being non-binary in a binary world comes with 'greater barriers and feelings of discrimination'. Non-binary genders are also associated with higher rates of self-harm and substance abuse relative to binary trans people. Australian research from 2020 replicates these conclusions, finding that non-binary people have significantly higher rates of mental illness and addiction. According to this study, seventy per cent of non-binary people experience depression, compared to fifty-two per cent of binary trans people.

The National LGBTQ Task Force, a US non-profit, made similar findings in a 2012 study called 'A Gender Not Listed Here', based on data from the 2008 National Transgender Discrimination Survey. The study found that compared to binary trans people, genderqueer respondents were more likely to be unemployed, suffer physical assault, experience harassment by law enforcement, and forgo health treatment due to fear of discrimination.

On almost every measure, non-binary people have a rough ride. This is not to minimise or dismiss the struggles of binary trans people, but rather to acknowledge that non-binary folk experience unique challenges that stem from being fundamentally at odds with the gender system that organises our world.

Often, I yearn to be a trans man. The incomprehension of the world is wearying, an endless swim against the current just to stay afloat. Even leaving the house can be a trial. *What to wear? How will I be perceived? How to exist as something deemed impossible?* Every day is a marathon of being gaslit by a world that tells me I can't be real. Deep in the marrow, my body aches for reprieve.

A binary identity would make life more straightforward. As a trans man, I could use the male bathroom, change my ID from F to M, wear adult menswear, tick M on every form. I'd have a slot to fit into. I would be a known commodity. Best of all, if I slipped back into the binary, I wouldn't have to out myself as trans every single day.

The problem is that I'm not a man. Gender is fluid, and some days I'm more masculine than others, but never do I belong in the world of men. Not-woman, not-man, transmasculine. There's no point escaping one ill-fitting costume just to adorn myself in another. No matter how much I hunger to belong, to be some semblance of 'normal', normality at the cost of self-erasure is no prize worth having.

The Brisbane band Cub Sport puts it best in their 2020 song 'Confessions'. The lead singer, Tim Nelson, who has a golden mane and identifies as gender-free, belts out lyrics that contain a lifetime of frustration with the gender binary. Bound with chains, writhing on the floor, Nelson sings:

> The truth is I don't wanna be one of the boys
> The truth is living by a gender makes me feel annoyed
> The truth is I still don't feel like I fit in anywhere
> The truth is I love staying home with you in underwear

Like all powerful lyrics, this stanza contains simple words arranged to hit on a little-spoken truth: gender *is* annoying. Bloody annoying, in fact. It's arbitrary rules and 'shoulds' and toxic oceans of shame. It boxes all of us in, even or especially cisgender people.

Women must be thin but not too thin; pretty but not airheads, but not so smart they intimidate men. They must be sexy and sexually available but not a slut. Confident but not aggressive, maternal yet not mumsy.

These are not voluntary prescriptions. As philosopher Kate Manne outlines in her work on misogyny, women who flout these oppressive norms experience fierce reprisals—punishment that discourages other women from stepping outside the lines.

Nor do cisgender men get a free pass. Although beneficiaries of male privilege and entitlement, cis men are also stifled by their own set of suffocating gender norms. Men must be tough and strong and protective but not remote or aggressive; they should be a 'good guy' but not a wimp who cries. A family man, but not a doormat. Softness equals weakness; femininity is discouraged.

For everyone, men and women, the standards are impossible and impossibly narrow. Every day is a new test, an endless gender exam in front of a thousand judging eyes.

'The gender binary is set up for us to fail. For us all to fail,' Vaid-Menon explains. We've all been sold a pup.

Faced with this broken gender system, living outside the gender binary is a political act. An act of resistance.

'To be nonbinary is to set one's existence in opposition to this [gender] system at its conceptual core,' writes Robin Dembroff, a philosopher at Yale. In their pioneering study of non-binary genders, Dembroff argues that 'nonbinary' (or 'genderqueer') is not defined by a particular aesthetic or behaviour. Non-binary is not androgyny, as non-binary people can be high femme or super butch or anything in-between. Nor is non-binary just a matter of *they* pronouns or 'space switching' (moving between male and female spaces). Rather non-binary is a rejection of the very idea of the gender binary. As Dembroff puts it, it's 'resistance to the binary assumption'. Non-binary (or genderqueer) is 'a category whose members collectively resist the binary assumption, or the assumption that the only possible genders are the exclusive and exhaustive kinds *men* and *women*.'

This collective resistance opens up a playground of new possibilities. Without rules, without predetermined gender scripts, the sky is the limit. Every person has the potential to do gender exactly as they wish. A tradie with pink nails, winged eyeliner and bulging biceps? Sure. A corporate exec in a lace sundress floating around their hairy calves? Knock yourself out.

On good days, the collective energy of this resistance fizzes in my veins, propelling me headlong into a future where the binary assumption begins to crumble. This future can be glimpsed on my university campus, or around the local high school, where young bodies peacock in gaudy feathers of their own choosing.

Like all utopian visions, this gender rebellion will fall short of expectations. It will promise emancipatory horizons that don't eventuate and even breed new oppressions. But even so, it's preferable to what we have now. I'd rather gender to be a playground than a pair of cages, even if that playground might give rise to bruised knees, wounded feelings and the occasional broken arm. Better the freedom to stumble and fall than a life spent bound and yearning.

BABY NAMES

THE SUMMER OF 2019 WAS a season of foreboding. Temperatures hovered in the mid-40s for days on end, wilting plants and humans alike. Burning air slipped beneath doors and assaulted window-panes, waging war against air-conditioning units and fans. Each sun-bleached noon was a missive from the future: this is what a changing climate feels like, this is how it will leach moisture from your organs and scorch your skin. This is only the beginning.

During desiccated January days, when all of Melbourne languished in a stupor, I fled the city for cyberspace. Sheltering behind drawn blinds, prostrate beneath a ceiling fan, I fell down an internet rabbit hole: baby name websites. For me, it was the season of BabyNames.com.

Each day, I lost myself in pink-and-blue websites that formed a shrine to heteronormative reproduction. At BabyNames.com, or over at close rival TheBump.com, you could learn what names were trending in the last twenty-four hours. You could learn which celeb-rities were breeding. I discovered the top names for 2018: Sophia for a girl and Jackson for a boy. Isla and Leo were climbing in the charts. Zoe and Logan were going in the opposite direction. Every day, I returned to the home page and was greeted with updates. Archie was rising; so too were Ocean and Peace.

Inside the name database, my tongue tripped over letters in constellations beyond imagining: Alohilani, Jajly, Katriel, Waldemar. There was an entire galaxy of names that began with K: Kalb, Kale, Kal-el, Keb. Who was naming their baby Kees? It was Dutch for 'horn'. At R, I discovered that Raputo was a Romansh name meaning 'counsel bold'. At W, I encountered Winaugusconey—a Native American name meaning 'not afraid to travel'.

All through January I ploughed through the alphabet, compiling lists of possibilities. Alex, Morgan, Noel, Sam. Maybe Axel? Or too automotive? Each day I revised the shortlist, culling names and adding others.

But I wasn't on BabyNames.com to name an infant. There was no foetus in my womb, and I hoped there never would be. Parenthood didn't feature in my imagined future. I wasn't scrutinising name databases for my future son or daughter—or anyone's son or daughter.

I was there to name myself.

↳

I never thought I'd change my name. Since childhood, I was convinced Anne Rees would be my moniker until the grave. I'd grown up amid the daughters of Women's Liberation, permed supermoms who wielded shoulder pads and retained 'maiden' names after marriage. My own mother had kept her family name after wedding my dad. She wouldn't be anyone's Mrs.

Why would I do any different? When I married—*if* I married—my surname would remain untouched. It was the only conceivable option for the modern, emancipated career woman of the new millennium—the woman I was meant to become.

As for changing my first name, that was unthinkable. Anne was simple, minimalist, classic. It suited me, everyone said. I was only too happy to believe them. My parents had never seriously considered other options.

'When I was pregnant, I was convinced you'd be a girl, so we only discussed female names,' Mum told me.

'We started at the beginning of the alphabet, and never got further than A,' Dad joked. 'We both liked Anne. It was an easy choice.'

Anne meant grace, I learnt. It was the name of queens, a name that evoked history.

At primary school, I started off as Annie. By the time Year Two rolled around, I felt myself too old for such diminutives. I had matured to Anne now, I informed the teachers, aged seven.

I loved the efficient one-two punch of Anne Rees. Two syllables, one each. Contained, a neat little box to shelter inside. No messy edges.

In Year Six, I spent months perfecting a signature. Should I sign as Anne Rees? A. Rees? Anne L. Rees? A.L. Rees? Then there was the matter of handwriting. Cursive or printed? Endless scraps of paper around the house recorded my draft attempts. I'd have this name until death, so it was worth investing the time to get it right.

Then, when I was in high school, Dad remarried. Her name was Anne and she would take his surname. She would become another Anne Rees. Another *blonde* Anne Rees, to boot.

'Do you mind?' Dad asked, as I munched Vegemite toast in his new apartment after school.

'Yes, I do. I don't want her to have the same name as me. It's my name.'

I didn't realise, then, that it wasn't a question. They weren't asking my permission; they were telling me. I would have to share my name with a stepmother. It was a fait accompli.

After that, Anne Rees lost some of its lustre. It was no longer mine alone but a name that could be worn en masse, like some fast-fashion frock of the season, sported by multiple guests at the same party. I'd shown up dressed in Anne Rees only to find my stepmother wearing the identical gown. Who knew how many others were out there, similarly adorned? A parade of Anne Reeses, all dressed alike. We, none of us, were the original article. We were all just another replica off the assembly line.

Nothing sacred, nothing immutable about these words: Anne Rees. Just a mass-produced name-garment, one liable to fray and fade with the passing years.

꒦

When trans people rename themselves, it's common to seek out a moniker that resembles one's birthname. It's convenient, especially if the first letter remains the same. John might become Jill; Stephanie might become Steve. A new person, but with the same initials. It's less of a hassle, easier to negotiate the thickets of law and state bureaucracy. It's easier for others to get right.

On BabyNames.com, I zero in on the listings under A. Albert, Arthur, Andrew, Artemis. I'm on the hunt for a name that will allow me to remain A. Rees. Those long hours perfecting my signature can't go to waste.

But the right name is elusive. The options are all too archaic, too pompous, too modern. Too male. I try on these various name-garments, one after another, only to find that the seams pull, my breathing is constricted, the tailoring is designed for someone else. Nothing sits right on my strange not-woman, not-man frame.

How to know when I've found a name that fits? We might expect to name a child or a pet, but nobody teaches you how to name yourself.

The only thing I've named to date was a tropical fish for my childhood home aquarium. Getaway was a rainbow shark named after my favourite TV show, the 1990s travel program on Channel Nine. Our relationship was short-lived, as Getaway was soon eaten by my brother's fish Sharkie—an incident that proved beyond doubt the fallacy of nominative determinism. Getaway had spectacularly failed to get away. (Although, on the other hand, Sharkie certainly did live up to his name.)

Naming a doomed fish has in no way prepared me to name myself. This is a far more high-stakes business. This time around, lifestyle television is definitely not a legitimate source of inspiration. Even more daunting, the decision needs to last a lifetime—a life-time that could last another five decades or more. You can't adopt and discard names each season like a new pair of jeans or fresh sneakers. I need to get this right.

But my self-knowledge is crumbling, just when I need it most. If I was content with Anne two years ago, who knows how I'll feel two years into the future?

The more I hunt for a stable self to guide my naming quest, the more I feel myself dissolve into sand. Formless and infinitely malleable. A pile of grains that could be shaped into any name—or none at all.

↘

Within the list of A names, Alex jumps out. It's a classic, with a pleasing androgyny. Alex Rees. I can see that. Alex Rees could be a man, a woman—or something else entirely.

But no. I already have four friends named some variety of Alex. Alexandra times two, Alexis, Alessandro. There's no room for another Alex in this overcrowded field.

Adam, Alfred, Allen. There are too many names and not enough guideposts to navigate the maze. My brain reverberates with the music of a thousand potential future selves. Alistair, Altan, Anton? Each name has its own rhythm, its own song. Together, they beat out a discordant symphony that follows me onto trams, down supermarket aisles, deep into the chlorinated blue of the council pool.

Perhaps I should choose a name that nods to my family's heritage. Like many white Australians, I'm mainly English and Welsh, with a sprinkling of Russian. But I also have Norwegian ancestors. My father's great-great-grandmother Inga migrated from Norway as a teenager. We still use her Christmas cake recipe. Each year we dig out her faded handwriting to recall exactly how many raisins to soak in how much brandy. Perhaps a Scandinavian name to honour those northern roots? It's almost a family tradition. My father was named after Inga's brother, who died as a teenager back in Norway after a skiing accident. Dad's cousin is also called Inga, the latest in a long line of fearsome Ingas descending from the original matriarch.

Back on BabyNames.com, I filter by national origin. The Scandinavian names are blunt, misshapen, as though stunted by Arctic winds. Algot, Alrik, Arvard, Ask. Ask? Anders, Esben, Elof, Ingo, Odd. I certainly feel Odd. If the hat fits, so to speak.

I pause at Anders. On the surface, it ticks a lot of boxes. It's Norwegian and starts with A. Better yet, it is an 'An' name; phonic kin to 'Anne'—just with an extra syllable at the end. But when I hear 'Anders', all I can see is Anders Breivik slaughtering teenage campers on Utøya back in 2011. White-supremacist terrorism is really not the vibe I'm after—especially since my blonde Scando looks can already give off unfortunate Aryan overtones. I can't discard my white privilege or absolve the sins of white forebears, but I can avoid naming myself after a white supremacist. Anders gets the chop.

What about Ansel, then? It's got the same attractions as Anders without the whole terrorism issue. Ansel. It sounds like Mum's pet name for me: Anso.

'Hey Anso, do ya want a cup of tea?'

'Anso, are you ready to go?'

I've heard these sentences my whole life. I'm used to answering to that name. Anso could become Ansel. Ansel Rees. There's nothing wrong with it. It fits all my criteria.

Yet something about Ansel sticks in my throat. It's perfect on paper but has no fizz, an eligible bachelor with all the wrong pheromones. In my mind, Ansel conjures a hulking middle manager, a baby-faced giant in a crumpled suit, with a nascent paunch and straw-coloured hair, thinning at the temples. Ansel would speak in monosyllables and he'd wear a yellowed singlet under his business shirt. Inoffensive but ineffective. Ansel is not who I want to be.

～

In mid-January, the proofs for my latest article arrive for checking and approval. Hunched over my desk, I mechanically review each paragraph before coming to a halt at the author bio.

'Dr Anne Rees is a historian at La Trobe University.'

Anne Rees. Here is yet another document that yokes my identity to Anne, about to appear in the world. It's a name that won't be easy to discard. It adorns nine years' worth of publications—a list of articles that form the bedrock of a hard-won academic career.

As I gaze out the window above my desk, another option presents itself: do I even, in fact, need to discard Anne at all? For many trans people, their birthname is their 'deadname'—a hated moniker they seek to bury under thick layers of earth. Once killed off, the deadname should never be mentioned again. To do so is an act of violence, equivalent to summoning a malevolent ghost. 'Deadnaming' is one of the worst things you can do to a trans person. A good deadname stays dead and buried, ignored and forgotten by all.

Anne will never be dead to me, though. It's a name that's served me well for three decades, a name that always felt right. It's a 'female' name, no doubt, but it doesn't scream 'girl' like a flowery epithet such as Lily or Rose.

Does it really need to go?

Some transgender people, especially non-binary folk, retain their birth name. Jeffrey Marsh is an American non-binary 'influencer', assigned male at birth (AMAB), with a penchant for dresses, heels and eyeshadow. Marsh has a femme presentation and uses they/them pronouns, but still goes by their conventionally masculine birthname. In the process, Marsh is enacting a quiet revolution. By waltzing out in fabulous lipstick and pearls, then introducing themselves as Jeffrey, Marsh is challenging the idea that masculine name = masculine self. Just by existing, Marsh explodes assumptions of how a 'Jeffrey' can appear and act.

Could I do the same with Anne? Perhaps I could be a trans person, a not-woman, a non-binary transmasculine creature called Anne. If I'm not a 'man', maybe I don't really need a 'male' name.

More to the point, does 'Anne' have to be a 'woman's' name? It's only female because we humans imagine it to be so. We could always imagine otherwise. If Marsh can remake Jeffrey into a non-binary name, surely Anne could be likewise repurposed. There's no law that prohibits Anne being assigned to any gender. Only convention prevents us from doing so, and convention is always evolving. Hypothetically, we could have male Annes, non-binary Annes, genderqueer Annes. Annes of every gender and none at all. (Indeed, in the Netherlands, Anne is already sometimes used as a male name.)

There's no reason why I couldn't lead the charge here. I could be a transgender, not-woman Anne—different gender but same name.

It would certainly involve less paperwork. By remaining Anne, I could avoid the exhausting prospect of changing my name on bank accounts, credit cards, driver's licence, passport, utility bills, tax file number, ABN, Medicare card, library cards, yoga studio membership and a dozen other things besides. Everything could just carry on as before. There's always a certain ease in accepting the status quo, in swimming with the tide.

ᒧ

On a day ravaged by a fierce northerly, I cycle down to the bay to visit an old childhood friend. We're at a local cafe, feasting on smashed avo and flat whites, when an athletic figure in Patagonia approaches our table.

'Hey Steve, great to see you!' my friend exclaims. 'How are the kids?'

'Great, great,' Steve replies. 'They're at swimming this morning. I'm just picking up some bread, then later we're all headin' down to the beach.'

'Nice! We might see you there.'

I'm mute, wearing a painted-on smile, as pleasantries flow over my head. Then my friend remembers me.

'Steve, this is my old friend Annie. She's like an auntie to my kids.'

Auntie, Annie, she. Each feminine descriptor is a heavy boot on the tender seedlings of my trans self. This friend has known for months that I'm not-woman, trans, but the old names prove hard to dislodge. For her, I'm still the same Annie I always was.

I nod a polite greeting to Steve and feel myself vanquished from this sunlit cafe.

It's strange how easy it is to be erased by grammar, how a single pronoun can stomp my green shoots back into the dirt.

That afternoon, on the long cycle back up the bay, I make a decision. Anne must go. As long as that name persists, so too will my female identity. Without a new name, my transness will not fully register with the world. Anne served me well, but her time is up. Anne was the name of someone convinced she was cisgender, someone who accepted that her female anatomy equalled womanhood.

That person no longer exists. Anne has become someone else altogether. That new person demands a new name, a name of their own that will force the world to pay attention. To acknowledge them as real. A name to shield green shoots as they reach towards the sun.

As I peddle through bayside suburbs, inching towards the skyscrapers on the horizon, Anne falls into my slipstream and twirls away on the salt breeze. I last see her somewhere in Brighton.

⌐

The following week, I'm drinking tea at my mother's dining table, its surface piled high with old newspapers and dog paraphernalia, while she unpacks groceries to the tune of ABC Classic. Her new puppy deconstructs an abandoned sneaker by the kitchen door.

'So, Mum . . .' I begin, hesitant, tongue-tied.

'Hmmm?' She's got her head deep in the pantry. 'Hey, do you want any of these chocolates leftover from Christmas? Or some mince tarts?'

'No, thanks.' I try again. 'Mum, I've got something important to tell you.'

She emerges from the kitchen, bearing two cans of chickpeas and a questioning look.

'So, Mum, I'm thinking of changing my name, changing Anne to something else. You know, as part of my transition.'

She nods, serious now, and takes a seat.

I continue, heart hammering.

'But I'm worried getting rid of Anne might seem like a rejection. Because, you know, it was the name you gave me. I don't want to upset you.'

The words spill out, a panicked confession. Ever since she recoiled from the idea of transition, I'm wary of her reactions.

'Oh, my love.' Mum reaches for my hand. 'It's fine with me if you want to change your name. I won't feel rejected at all. I always disliked my name; it's so suburban. I always wanted a classic name like Elizabeth or Katherine. So I completely understand your desire to change.'

I take my first deep breath in hours, days. The puppy nuzzles my leg, determined to join the action.

'You know,' I say as I lift the bundle of fur onto my lap, 'you could still change your name, if you wanted. You could become Elizabeth. We could both get new names.'

Her lips curl in amusement, contemplating a new name at sixty-five.

'Hmph. Maybe I will do that.' She chuckles. 'Maybe I will.'

～

In the oven of mid-afternoon, I'm at a tram stop on St Georges Road, waiting for a tram that refuses to arrive. The scene is deserted, apocalyptic, save for an elderly gent in khakis clutching a calico shopping bag to his chest.

Beneath the mean shade of a solitary palm, yellowed grass scratching my haunches, my fingers swipe and poke at the iPhone until we land back at BabyNames.com. The name of the day is Tylie, a hybrid of Ty and Kylie.

A quick dive into M, a peak into R, a dash through T, idly hunting for inspiration. There's no system, no logic anymore. My fingers take me to the back end of alphabet, to the barren wilds of X, Y, Z. Yaholo, Yanni, Yogi, Yuri, Yves.

Yves. It's a name from childhood, the French name given to the brother of my best friend from primary school. Yves. One syllable, opening with a vowel sound, like Anne. Yves Rees. The same one-two punch as Anne Rees. Yves. A 'male' name, but redolent of an elegant European masculinity, all black turtlenecks and book-shops, cobblestones and espresso—a world away from the muscle, grunts and beer of a sunburnt Shane or Dave. Yves. A male name, but indistinguishable to the ear from Eve, its female twin. A name that floats between genders, shapeshifting to fit the context.

The tram finally makes an appearance. The old gent boards, and I'm close behind, Yves tucked snug in my back pocket, secreted next to my phone.

As the tram drags itself north up the hill, the clamour of names in my mind recedes, replaced by a single melody: Yves. Yves Rees.

ALL ABOUT YVES

CHOOSING A NAME IS THE easy part, I discover. What comes next is the kicker: birthing a new name into the world. Much like an actual birth, this stage takes things from the soothingly hypothetical to the all too real. Suddenly, other people are involved. You lose control over the process. Things get messy. There might be blood and shit. The name, like a bawling infant, takes on a life of its own.

Changing your name is an iterative process. Yves is born in increments, unfurling in quiet moments that slowly add up to something more. As with 'coming out', there's no grand announcement that sets off fireworks and immediately alerts everybody who needs to know. Instead, there are a thousand small actions, endlessly repeated, until they harden into something that might be real.

'My name isn't Anne anymore; I'm changing it to Yves.'

You tell people again, and again, and again, and again—hoping that, at some point, you'll start believing yourself.

I start small: close friends, immediate family. Gradually, the circle of trust widens, expanding out to colleagues, old high school mates, doctors. There are so many people who need to be told.

Yves Rees. It's a new identity, conjured from thin air. Audacious, an insurrection. Anne would never be so bold. After a lifetime of following the rules, freedom on this level feels illicit. Surely someone official, wearing a uniform and government lanyard, will arrive to stamp out my fantasy before too long.

'You silly little girl, how dare you think you can just invent a new name,' the red-faced official would scold. 'You're a woman called Anne. How absurd to think otherwise. You're clearly deluded. You're fortunate we haven't locked you up. Count this as a warning. Next time, you might not be so lucky.'

Surely this humiliation will be the inevitable end to my insurrection. Surely I can't keep getting away with it. But the official never arrives. Perhaps they have the wrong address.

In the meantime, I keep making my strange pronouncement. Again, and again, and again—all the while expecting the gender police to turn up at any moment.

'So I've changed my name. I'm Yves now.'

At first, I stumble over the words. At an event I'm hosting in Sydney, I introduce myself to the audience.

'Hi, my name is An—I mean, Yves. my name is Yves. Yves.'

I'm met with a sea of baffled faces, a roomful of people wondering why I don't know my own name. My cheeks burn red as I plough on with the introductions. My mouth needs to learn new shapes to talk about itself.

It's a peculiar transformation, devoid of the rituals that cushion our path through the world. We expect people—by which I mean women—to change their surname upon marriage. We have systems, conventions, words to manage that process. We know what it means when Miss Robertson becomes Mrs Lee. No explanation required.

But who changes their first name? How does that even work? Perhaps I could mail out a printed announcement with a gold border and fancy lettering. Or perhaps I should hold a party, send a circular email, ask friends to spread the word, post something on Twitter—or all of the above? (Does Twitter even allow users to change their name?) There's no handbook, no precedent here. I yearn for the reassurance of rules that don't exist.

'I'm not Anne anymore. My name's Yves now.'

It's a proclamation of strangeness, a moment of exposure. It forces intimacy with medical receptionists, IT support, dentists, editors, call-centre workers and long-lost second cousins, National Parks rangers, psychologists, librarians, conference organisers, yoga teachers, physiotherapists, parents' colleagues, dog breeders, volunteer coordinators and cops.

Everyday encounters become confessions.

It never gets easier.

Until it does.

⌁

Yves comes to life amid mishaps and confusion. Over weeks and months, this strange creature stumbles into the world.

At the cafe on campus, I hand over my keep-cup.

'A soy latte, please.'

'Your name?'

I swallow. Today is the day for the big reveal.

'Yves,' is my whispered reply.

I brace myself for fireworks, expecting applause or stares at the very least. This is a momentous occasion, after all. Yves is being born. But the barista doesn't even blink. She scrawls on a scrap of paper: 'S L, Eve.'

'That'll be $4.20, thanks.'

She's already looking over my shoulder at the next customer.

Eve. This is the first time, but it won't be the last. I say 'Yves', the listener hears 'Eve' and I am remade into woman. The original woman, in fact. Eve, from Adam's rib. The irony is not lost on me.

My seven-year-old niece wants to know why I've taken her middle name.

'Why are you called Eve now, like me?' she asks with big eyes.

Is Eve to be my third name, my third self? Anne, Yves, Eve—like babushka dolls, they jostle inside me, layered selves in uneasy coexistence.

Eve follows me as both blessing and curse.

Yves, Eve—indistinguishable to the ear. When you hear that name attached to my high-pitched voice, what are you going to think? *Woman here*, our unconscious brain decides. *Must be Eve*, is the conclusion reached in a millisecond.

Our human brains are so quick to put people into boxes. We order and label and categorise without even thinking. It's adaptive, a shortcut that helps our brain parse the mountains of data flying at us every second. We'd be paralysed by information overload without taxonomies to make sense of all the stuff in the world.

Yet these shortcuts lead us astray. We make assumptions, we make mistakes. We assume that high voice equals woman. We assume that Yves is Eve.

↵

At work, walking down the corridor or in the tearoom, colleagues beam with good intentions.

'Hi, Eves!'

'How's it going, Eves?'

'Have a good weekend, Eves.'

Eves, Eves, Evezzzzzz.

I smile, grateful for the effort, wishing the mispronunciation didn't grate. I hadn't realised so few people would know how to pronounce 'Yves'. Do I correct them, tell them the 's' is silent? That it sounds like 'Eve', not 'Eves'? This is new terrain for me; nobody struggled to pronounce 'Anne'. I don't want to tarnish their kindness, to nitpick over the details.

There's class politics embedded in all this. Yves is French and learning the language—or at least knowing how to pronounce key words—has long been a marker of status in Anglophone countries like Australia. Francophilia was and remains a way for social elites to perform their elite-ness.

I only have basic high school French, long rusted from lack of use. But I did grow up around French speakers and texts. I first visited Paris aged fourteen. My art history major at university was dense with names like Courbet, Delacroix, Manet. When living in London in my early twenties, I popped over to Paris every month or so. After a lifetime surrounded by French words, it didn't seem so strange to choose a French name.

But all this is a product of my affluence and privilege—a by-product of being the child of two white Anglo lawyers with postgraduate degrees. I was immersed in Frenchness because of my family's affluence and cultural capital. I don't want to flaunt this fact by quibbling over pronunciation.

But maybe Yves is already a flaunting of sorts. During my long trawls through baby name websites, I'd given short shrift to anything remotely 'working class', like Barry or Darren or Shane. I told myself these names were too 'masculine' for me. But maybe I really meant they were too 'coarse'—a euphemism for blue collar, rough. Poor. The masculinity I aspired to was an elite version—some rose-tinted fantasy of a Wildean dandy in a cravat and three-piece suit. Gentleman, not manual labourer.

Transition was meant to be about gender; I hadn't counted on the class issues that would crop up. Just as white people have the luxury of being oblivious to race, I—as an affluent person—had always found it too easy to be oblivious to class. As Zadie Smith

writes, 'Class is a bubble, formed by privilege, shaping and manip-
ulating your conception of reality.'

In my class bubble, everyone knew how to pronounce French
words. In this vision of reality, everyone knew how to say 'Yves'.
A naive fantasy, it turns out.

I don't know how to broach this topic, and so I say nothing at
all. I smile when I'm greeted as 'Eves' and continue down the office
corridor. The effort to say my name trumps the accuracy of the
execution. I'll take kindness over flawless pronunciation, any day.

⤙

At the electronics store, I order new headphones. They're out of
stock and the assistant takes my details for later. My name is Yves,
I say. Spelt Y, V, E, S.

The pimpled teenage assistant smiles in recognition.

'Yves! Like the colour,' he exclaims.

'Yes, like Yves Klein Blue.'

'That's great. What a cool name. But I guess you didn't actually
choose it. I mean, your parents did.'

'Well, actually . . .'

I pause, eyes wandering to the wall of yellow sale stickers. Is it
safe to acknowledge the truth? How will he react? I decide to risk it.

'Well, in fact, I did choose it. I chose it for myself.'

The assistant smiles even wider. 'Cool!'

I feel Yves grow a few inches under the warmth of his gaze.
Unfurling, little by little. Precious moments of becoming under the
fluorescent lights of a discount chain store.

⤙

At yoga, I queue to sign in for class.

'Hi, I'm Yves, I've already checked in online.'

'Really? I can't see you listed here.' The muscled teacher frowns, peering at the screen.

'I have. It's Yves, spelt Y, V, E, S.'

'Hmmm, can't see anything.'

His tanned face scans up and down, while I stare at the crystal display on the wooden counter.

The female assistant, standing alongside him, interjects.

'There, down the bottom.' She points at the computer. 'There she is.'

She. I swallow the hated word, feel it sit heavy in my guts.

'Ohhh, yes!' the teacher exclaims. 'There she is. Y, V, E . . . But I thought you said your name was Eve?'

Before he can finish, I'm gone, darting into the change room, eager to escape his incomprehension.

After class, the teacher buttonholes me at the exit. His tattooed biceps gleam with sweat. A Sanskrit pendant dangles above a hair-less chest.

'Tell me again, how do you say your name?'

'Yves.'

'But it's spelt Y, V, E—' he corrects me.

'Yes, I know. It's French.'

'Oh.' He pauses, thoughtful, dubious. 'But how do the French people say it?'

'Yves.'

He knows that can't possibly be true. He knows my pronunci-ation is all wrong. But he's prepared to indulge me, to let this slide. He prides himself on being magnanimous, on being the kind of guy to let women think they're right. It's part of his yoga practice.

He issues his most beatific smile and wishes me good day.

'Namaste!' he calls to my retreating back, hands in prayer posi-tion at his heart.

I don't go back to his class again.

At a transgender clothing swap, we're given stickers for our names and pronouns.

Yves, they/them. I craft the words in purple ink.

Outside the changing room, the femme attendant asks how to pronounce my name.

'Is it Ives? Or Eves?'

Another femme chimes in, all red lips and white teeth.

'I love it, it's the perfect gender-neutral name, it gives nothing away. You have no idea whether it refers to a man or woman.'

Here, at least, they understand. Here, they have an appetite for the not-knowing, the in-between. We trans folk are all so different, a whole ecosystem of bodies and genders, yet through it all runs a relish for the queer and uncategorisable. We're all driven to fuck with gender. To challenge its arbitrary rules.

This makes us one magnificent tribe. My tribe, at last. Forget footy clubs—a Melbourne obsession I've always found incomprehensible. I don't care for the crows or the dogs or the hawks or the saints—or even the AFLW. Sporting clubs have never been my thing. Here, in the badlands of gender, is my real team.

In the classic 1950 film *All About Eve*, the ageing Broadway star Margo Channing is gradually usurped by the younger Eve Harrington. At first, Eve is merely Margo's assistant, an indispensable maker-of-calls and hanger-of-coats. But soon she insinuates herself into all facets of Margo's life. After manoeuvring to be appointed Margo's understudy, Eve threatens to take over the star's theatrical roles, appropriate her favoured director, and even steal her husband. By the film's end, Eve is the new queen of Broadway, bound for Hollywood stardom. Margo has accepted her fate. She retreats into marriage and domesticity, defeated by the younger woman.

All About Eve is dripping with misogyny and homophobia (the villainous Eve is a lesbian), but it's nonetheless an apt metaphor for the story of Anne and Yves. Like Eve Harrington, Yves creeps onto the scene, the new kid on the block, easy to ignore. Anne, like Margo, is the reigning power, the diva who relishes the role of protagonist. It's only in increments, small enough to miss, that the balance of power begins to shift. Yves pops up their head in all sorts of places, appropriating fragments of Anne's life—a friend here, a job there. Yves turns up wherever Anne is expected.

'Anne is sadly indisposed,' Yves announces. 'I'll be standing in for her, for the foreseeable future.'

The audience is surprised, often bemused, but they're quick to accept the new reality. Yves wants everything Anne had, only more. Before you know it, Anne has been banished, made redundant at not quite thirty-one. She'd expected many more years in the limelight. Now she glowers in the corner, a character usurped before her time.

The story of my life is no longer the story of Anne; it's all about Yves, now.

↳

I've bought a new wallet online to celebrate my transition. It's a neat square of brown leather—a classic men's wallet, replacing the bloated purse that's carried my cards, cash and receipts for the past decade.

The package arrives when I'm at work. That night, there's an Australia Post collection slip waiting in the mailbox.

At the post office, the queue snakes out the door. Saturday morning, and the hordes have descended to collect their bounty from Amazon and ASOS.

I'm clutching a collection slip addressed to Yves Rees. It's the first time I've seen the words in a stranger's handwriting. The postie's scrawl is almost enough to convince me that Yves Rees might be real. They're a person who receives mail, after all. They're recognised by an instrument of the state.

As the queue inches forward, I open my purse to extract the ID required for collection. Then the mistake hits me: all my ID is listed under Anne. Apart from this collection slip, I don't have a single scrap of evidence to link this purported 'Yves Rees' chap to my personage. How will I collect the wallet? Surely they won't let me have it without ID. I curse myself for shopping online in the name of this character who doesn't exist. Yves is pure fiction, except in my mind.

There are only two people ahead of me now. Behind the counter, a grim-faced employee frowns and sighs over collection slips, glasses perched low on her nose. She's a volcano of irritation on the brink of explosion. This is not a woman to trifle with. I need a strategy. Fast.

I rack my brains. Maybe I could say Yves is my brother? Or my husband? We share a surname, after all. Yes, my husband. In a panic, I mentally concoct a spouse called Yves, busy at work at the real estate business, sending his wife Anne (me!) to collect the mail. It's such a bother that Yves always works Saturday mornings; he can never manage to run errands. He's probably doing an open-for-inspection right this moment, maybe at one of the renovated cottages in Northcote's back streets that sell for a million bucks. I can see Yves greeting the hopeful young couples who walk through the gate. He hands them a glossy floorplan, talks up the local schools.

'Real village atmosphere, great cafes,' he chirps. 'Fabulous transport connections.'

He's wearing a navy suit with a slight sheen, leather shoes that taper to a point. A hint of a French accent and the ghost of stubble.

Yves is looking forward to his new wallet. In my mind, he blossoms into life, so credible I almost start to believe in him myself.

Does Yves need to give Anne permission to collect his parcel? I can't recall the rules. To be on the safe side, I scramble in my bag for a pen. Resting the slip against my thigh, I scrawl a vague signature on the shiny card. To all appearances, Yves has now endorsed Anne collecting his parcel. Thankfully, the towering bloke ahead in the queue conceals my manoeuvrings from the Australia Post staff.

Done. Pen back in bag, ID out, signed collection slip at the ready. Game on. I'm sweating now, face hot and armpits damp despite the cool morning. I stare at a display of discounted back scratchers, my foot tapping with nerves against the brown-checked carpet.

Yves better be grateful for my efforts. The stress he's caused! He's ruined my morning, really—quite a feat for an invented estate-agent husband. I can just imagine the complacent smile and sweet nothings that will accompany his return from the office, a charm offensive to smooth away my irritation. Always such a charmer, the French bastard. No wonder he went into real estate. He'd better bring home some brie for lunch.

I'm front of the queue now, called up to the counter. With damp palms, I hand over my collection slip and ID. My mouth opens to start spinning the story of husband Yves.

But before I can utter a sound, the frowning woman grabs my slip and stalks off into the back room. A moment later, she's back, shoving a parcel across the counter.

'Next!' she barks.

The transaction is over, and we've not exchanged a word. The Australia Post employee didn't even appear to notice that Anne was collecting a parcel for Yves. Poor chap, he never got his moment in the sun. Yves, that slick real-estate mogul, has been made redundant before he had a chance to shine. Though I have, at least, got a smart new wallet for him. Or should I say, a wallet for me?

Like an undercover spy with multiple identities, forever slipping between characters, I've lost track of where Anne ends and Yves begins. Is Yves the invention and Anne the reality—or is it the other way around?

Back home, with the parcel unwrapped, I stuff the stiff new leather of Yves' wallet with bank cards and ID belonging to Anne Rees. The legal remnants of Anne tucked safe within the masculine trappings of Yves. The two characters will have to co-exist within their fractious marriage, for the time being at least.

⌣

That year, my birthday coincides with the Labour Day long weekend. My friends stuff a sedan full of hiking packs, muesli bars, water bladders, puffer jackets and our sleep-stiff bodies. With a full tank of petrol, we flee the city's embrace, speeding northwest up the National Highway towards the Grampians. Four hours later, we arrive to sharp mountain air and skies of Yves Klein Blue. Skies made for someone like me. It's heaven—or it would have been, if only thousands of other Melburnians hadn't arrived first and claimed all the parking spots. The city has beaten us here, a shadow we can't dodge.

Our hike begins as a gruelling ascent along naked rock, near-vertical steps carved into sandstone that almost kisses the sky. Our packs, bloated with three days' supplies, threaten to send us toppling back down to earth. We climb, hunched forward like prehistoric beetles to counteract the weight on our backs. Mouths parched, feet sore, muscles already aching from the load, we're overtaken by scores of day-walkers who amble up the mountain in jeans and thongs. These tourists gape at our elaborate get-up. Within an hour, I've burned through two litres of water and can sense the tingle of an approaching blister. We still have ten kilometres to climb and only a few more hours of light. We have two more days of the same, with rain forecast tomorrow. We will shiver, sweat, ache, stumble and curse.

I can't think of a better way to spend my birthday.

When we finally reach the first summit, we fling down our sweat-stained packs and inhale handfuls of dried apricots. We're silent, blank-eyed, chewing, waiting for the sugar to bring us back to life.

A welcome breeze carries the chatter of voices from behind a boulder. Alex, the boldest of us, heads over to investigate. Moments later she's back with an invitation to tea. Behind the boulder we find a crew of inner-north millennials, a tableau of tattoos and undercuts, merrily brewing Earl Grey and snacking on vegan chocolate.

'Welcome!' the tea-maker cries. 'Do you have a mug? I can pour you some tea.'

We join their circle, an impromptu cafe towering above Falls Gap. The strong black tea warms our bellies as the summit winds dry the sweat on our skin. The day-walkers have vanished now, and the world is ours alone.

Alex takes charge of introductions.

'I'm Alex, this is Anna. And this is Yves.'

Yves. Only six weeks ago I was Anne to her. Anne was the name she'd called me for the five years of our friendship. But she'd made the change to Yves without skipping a beat, without once forgetting or stumbling.

'Hi Alex, hi Anna, hi Yves.'

The two groups exchange smiles, swapping job titles and post-codes. Brunswick, Brunswick, Brunswick, almost without exception.

'Hey Yves, do you want some more tea?' the tea-maker asks.

I startle, look up from the dregs in my mug. Something about that question sends a jolt up my spine. With this most innocuous of requests, I feel my soul enter new territory.

Then I realise: it was the way he said 'Yves'.

'Yves, do you want some more tea?'

He said 'Yves' like it was my name—my true name, not some quaint fiction he was indulging to be polite or politically correct. And it was real to him. He didn't know Anne; he'd only met Yves.

'Or would you like some chocolate, Yves?'

This request comes from a green-eyed woman, holding out a bag of ginger cloaked in dark chocolate. She says 'Yves' with the same casual conviction. The conviction that this person called Yves actually exists. Because here I am, cross-legged on the rock in dusty shorts and a sweat-crusted shirt. Why would I give a false name? She takes me on face value.

These are the first people to know me only as Yves. It's delicious, how Yves trips off the tongue when it's not papering over something else. The rightness of it swells my chest with a warmth that might be joy.

Until now, everyone has known me as 'Anne-who-decided-to-become-Yves', and their knowledge of that history has manifested as invisible quotation marks around the name. They say 'Yves' like they're handing me a present. Like I should be grateful. Like they're playing along with a game of make-believe that will end before bedtime. 'Yves' has been a character I've been performing, a provisional identity, a rebranding of Anne—not a person in their own right.

But now here, on this wind-carved sandstone, malodorous and about to turn thirty-one, I'm just Yves for the first time. Nothing more, nothing less. Yves. One syllable, rolls off the tongue, no big deal.

And I don't owe them anything. They haven't done me a favour, haven't performed a kindness by calling me Yves instead of Anne. They don't know any different. What a relief to not feel indebted for hearing my name. What a relief to feel like any other person, just a person with a name.

'Yes, some more tea would be great, thanks. And I'd love some chocolate. Ginger's my favourite.'

'No worries, Yves. Here you are. Enjoy.'

It's not bad, as birthday presents go.

⌣

A few months later, I fly to Sydney for a workshop, two days of work interstate. The organiser has booked me into a hotel amid the concrete wastelands around Central Station. I catch the train in from the airport, then wheel my purple suitcase across endless lanes of traffic. I brace against the wind that whips around street corners, check Google Maps again and again, before finally plunging through the glass doors of the hotel lobby. The lobby is hushed, a sanctuary from the irate city, and the receptionists smile as I walk over smooth tiles towards the counter. A saxophone oozes from a distant speaker.

'I have a reservation,' I say. 'For Rees.'

I scramble for the printout of the booking confirmation, dogeared from the depths of my bag.

'Thank you. We'll just need some ID and a credit card.'

I reach for my wallet, unthinking. Then I remember. The two names, the issue with ID. Yves, Anne—the actual and legal selves that don't match. What name is the room booked under? I can't remember. Please, please, let it be Anne, the name still on my ID. Today's travel has sapped my resources. I just want to be ordinary this afternoon. To be an unremarkable person with one name, printed on my driver's licence. Not a living babushka doll, a composite of names and personae, an oddity that requires explanation.

I check the booking confirmation. One standard queen room, booked for two nights for Dr Yves Rees. Yves, that person who doesn't legally exist, who has no ID whatsoever. I swallow, conscious of the receptionist's stare.

My colleague, the person who arranged this booking, has known me as Yves for many months now. Of course she booked under this name. But now, in this polite lobby, I would do anything to scrub out Yves from the paper in my hand.

I take a deep breath, look up at the receptionist.

'Look. So, ah, there's a small issue here. The booking has been made for Yves. But my legal name is Anne.'

She blinks, uncomprehending.

I continue, rushing to get the words out, to clean up this mess.

'Yes, so all my ID says Anne Rees. Not Yves. See, here?'

I push my licence and credit card across the counter.

'Same surname—Rees—but different first name,' I say.

I offer no explanation and pray she won't ask for one.

She picks up the cards, brow furrowed in confusion.

'So, the booking should be under Anne?' the receptionist asks slowly.

'Yes, yes, under Anne. Please.'

Without a word, she turns to consult a colleague. The pair exchange urgent whispers, pointing at my ID and gesturing in my direction. My bladder strains against the fly of my jeans. I tap my boot on the floor tiles. I should have used the toilet at the airport. I should have polished my boots. I should've changed the name on my ID. Most of all, I should've remained a woman. I should have stayed in my box, not caused any trouble.

The second receptionist returns to the counter with a tentative smile. He's wearing a manager badge, pinned at a slight angle.

'Hello,' he begins. 'So, this booking should be under Anne, not . . .' He frowns at the computer. 'Not as Ivez?'

'Yes, yes, not as Yves. Under Anne instead. Please.'

My face grows hot from the burn of their confusion. There's a standoff, we lock eyes, before finally the manager concedes.

'Okay, I will have to change the booking in the computer.'

He pecks at the keyboard.

By now, there's a queue developing behind me. At my back stand grey nomads with supersized suitcases and the stale whiff of a long-haul flight. Behind them, a suited exec, suit bag flung over one arm, staring at his phone.

The manager continues pecking. The minutes pass. I hear audible sighs behind me. I will myself to disappear. The manager scratches his nose, frowns at the screen, and taps the keyboard some more.

Finally, the whirr of the printer announces the end to this purgatory. With pursed lips, the manager hands me a new booking confirmation, addressed to Anne Rees. Next, a room key. The mess of me has been tidied up. For the moment, at least.

THE X FILES

WHY DON'T I JUST CHANGE my name? This would solve my ID woes. I could be Yves in daily life and under law. The names would match. No more minor crises in post offices and hotel lobbies. It's been two years of Yves now, and my ID still says Anne. What's stopping me?

I ask myself this question every day. At first, I hesitated out of caution. Yves was brand new, straight off the assembly line. What if it wasn't, after all, quite the thing? It might fit all wrong, like coveted shoes that rub at the heel. I wanted to test the waters in everyday life before making Yves official under law.

Later, I was daunted by bureaucracy. Yves was a goer, no doubt—despite its confusing resemblance to Eve and the ongoing issues with mispronunciation. It just felt right. From the start, Yves made me feel like myself. It was a name that prodded me to stand up straight and walk with shoulders back.

But the logistics of changing my ID sent me into a cold sweat. There's no one form that will remake your legal self. Instead, there are countless bureaucracies to negotiate: VicRoads, banks, electricity companies, Medicare, the tax office, the passport office. Each with their own rules and procedures. Each requiring me to interact with staff who may be ignorant or transphobic—or both.

Then there was the issue with gender categories. If I was going to brave the bureaucratic nightmare of a legal name change, it made sense to change my gender marker at the same time. Do it all in one fell swoop. At present, all my IDs listed me as F. A woman. That was, undoubtedly, incorrect. Despite my vagina, I was no woman at all. Anne was wrong; F was wrong—the logical response was to change both at once.

In Australia, anyone can change their legal name, if they're so inclined. Both given name and surname are up for grabs. You don't have to be trans or get married. You just need a 'clear reason', which can presumably be almost anything. The only limits are time-based: in Victoria, you can only change your name once in twelve months and three times per lifetime.

It's harder to change your gender marker. You can't do it on a whim; you need endorsement from medical gatekeepers. You need to be 'officially' transgender. But I'd ticked this box. I'd been given a formal diagnosis of 'gender dysphoria', so it was well within my rights to get the F scrubbed out. There's no requirement to have gender affirmation surgery or other medical intervention. In most cases, to change the gender on ID like a driver's licence and pass-port, all that's required is a letter from a doctor testifying to your transgender status.

Birth certificates can also be modified. In 2019, Victoria passed legislation to make it easier for trans and gender-diverse people to amend the gender on their birth certificate. Previously, this was allowed only after gender affirmation surgery; now, it was available to any individual. For an adult born in Victoria, all they needed was a statutory declaration and a supporting statement from another adult.

As a diagnosed trans adult living in Melbourne in the 2010s, I could change my legal name and gender at any point. It would be bothersome, yes. Stressful? Quite likely. But not impossible. Countless trans people before me had done so. After completing the forms, they'd show off their new ID on social media, beaming next to a laminated card with the address blurred out. It was a trans rite of passage. A key step on the path to forging a new self.

In my case, however, progress was stalled by the dilemma: what gender marker to choose? F was, of course, wrong. But what was right? My only other options were M or X—the latter being the new symbol to denote intersex or 'other'. M was not strictly accurate. I was transmasculine, not male. A trans person, not a man trapped in a woman's body.

M also jarred with my physical appearance. I hadn't undergone medical transition, so the world still perceived me as female. My cropped hair and wardrobe of men's shirts could not conceal the curve of my hips or my vocal fry. As far as I could tell, any casual observer would assume my ID read F. What if an airport official, believing me to be F, found an M on my passport instead? Would I be mocked, interrogated, detained, harassed, strip-searched? All quite possible. All that and more has happened to trans people in airports. In the closely surveilled twilight zone of international travel, there's scant tolerance for people whose perceived gender doesn't match their ID.

In the 2015 US Transgender Survey, conducted by the National Center for Transgender Equality, nearly half of the twenty-eight thousand respondents reported negative experiences with airport security, such as invasive pat-downs or questioning. Similar findings were reported by researchers at Utrecht University, who in 2016–17 conducted an international study of 340 trans and gender diverse travellers. This research found that one-third had experienced trouble at airports, 'including being questioned, body searched, and verbally abused or humiliated'. Many others used careful strategies, such as 'putting on a drag show for security personnel', to pre-empt such problems. Others again had strong fears of airport transphobia, which, in some cases, led them to cease travelling altogether.

Among the third who had experienced trouble while travelling, this was most often connected to perceived discrepancies between their physical appearance and the sex marker on their ID. Typical was the case of trans woman Shadi Petosky, who ran into difficulties at Orlando International Airport in 2015. The body scanner, which had been programmed to read her as 'female', judged Petosky's penis an 'anomaly'. She was detained and instructed to re-enter the scanner as a 'male'. When she refused, police officers and an explosives specialist were called in. When finally released, some time later, she'd missed her flight.

Petosky's experience, which she reported on Twitter, inspired a new hashtag: #TravelingWhileTrans. A quick perusal of tagged posts makes it clear Petosky's ordeal is replicated on a daily basis. As Dan Waters tweeted in March 2019, '#travelingwhiletrans is basically always having to do the pat-down after an X-ray thing.' That November, author Sasha Costanza-Chock was bound for Barcelona when, at Boston Logan airport, her 'groin got flagged' by the body scanner. She was pulled aside and 'treated to one of the most invasive backhand groin searches I've ever had'. She continued: 'This happens all the time to me, so usually I just shrug and move on. But for some reason this time I feel gross. It was just . . . Really really really invasive.'

Given how common such incidents are, I quailed at the prospect of negotiating international airports with my lady voice and an M passport. Once or twice a year, I visit the United States for work. Although my whiteness shields me from the worst excesses of border surveillance, US border control could still be a nightmare, even without the spectre of gender deviance. Imagine if, in the future, I turned up at LAX with an M passport? Perhaps I'd end up in a windowless backroom, suspected of terrorism or fraud, with a grim-faced official examining my genitals.

One day, I might start taking testosterone. Then I'd grow muscles, stubble. My skin would coarsen and my voice would drop. At some point, almost inevitably, the world would begin to perceive me as M. In that scenario, M would surely be the best gender marker—even if I still knew myself to be more transmasculine than man. M in the eyes of others; M under law. I'd match, things would be straightforward. But would that ever happen? I wasn't yet ready to go on T. Perhaps I never would. Until the day I was sure, it would be premature to change my legal gender to M.

⌐

My other option was X. This third gender marker was created by the International Civil Aviation Organization (ICAO) in the aftermath of World War II. The war had resulted in a flood of refugees and stateless people. Millions were on the move, leaving Europe for Canada, the United States, Australia, New Zealand and elsewhere. They needed passports without delay, but aid workers struggled to parse the gender of names from different languages. Vytautas, Rasa, Ahti, Pipene—were these names M or F? How to know? And so the X was born—a third gender marker, connoting Other, invented by ICAO to use as a stopgap in situations when the actual gender was unknown.

After postwar migration died down, the X fell from use. But it remained a (theoretically) legitimate option, recognised by ICAO. Its next iteration was to denote people with intersex variations. In 2003, intersex person Alex MacFarlane became the first Australian to be issued a passport that specified gender as X rather than F or M.

More recently, the use of X has expanded to encompass people living outside the gender binary. For me, then, the X was undeniably the most accurate option. It captured the state of being somewhere between or beyond M or F—some capacious and uncategorisable 'other'. Yet the X also has troubling negative connotations. In everyday life, we use X to indicate a mistake, an error. We give Xs for incorrect answers on exams. We cross out the messy and wrong. Could I consent to reducing myself to this symbol?

Few trans and gender diverse people have opted to do so. Since 2011, when the X first became an option for gender diverse Australians, only 110 X passports have been issued nationwide. C.L. Quinan, a researcher studying the X marker, found that many non-binary people are deterred by its associations with wrongness. Often, non-binary people feared using the X could make them a target of surveillance—a registered gender deviant. They didn't fit in F or M, but couldn't stomach X. They said things like 'the X marker is dangerous because it identifies me as "other"' or 'X is as stigmatising and discriminatory as a gold star or pink triangle'—a reference to the symbols used to mark out Jews or gay men during the Holocaust.

I could relate. After being made to feel wrong our whole lives, why would we then choose to brand ourselves with the universal marker for 'incorrect'?

The X also presents practical challenges. As of early 2020, it's only used by twelve countries worldwide. This list includes New Zealand, Canada, Germany, Nepal, Pakistan, Bangladesh, India and Malta, but it excludes the United States and Britain—the two countries I visit most often. In the US and UK, not to mention most of the world, gender-neutral passports are unknown and likely to cause befuddlement. Border officials may not comprehend the X. It will prompt awkward questions, spark delays. It might even prohibit entry. As Quinlan writes, 'the X is recognized in Australia, but it remains unknown what will happen when a person with an X on their passport moves through other national and international spaces where this designation is unintelligible.'

The person travelling on an X passport is a body that doesn't fit in the rigid infrastructure of border control. Bodies that don't fit are suspect. Deviant. It's one thing to flaunt deviance while knocking back flat whites in Brunswick; it's quite another to do so when transiting through Singapore or Heathrow or Dubai. In those fluorescent spaces, where terrorism fears have officials on a hair trigger, there's zero tolerance for deviant bodies.

Even the Australian Passport Office acknowledges this danger. As of late 2020, its website notes that 'people travelling on passports showing "X" in the sex field may, for various reasons, encounter difficulties when crossing international borders. The Department of Foreign Affairs and Trade can't guarantee that a passport showing "X" in the sex field will be accepted for entry or transit by another country.' In other words: we can give you an X passport, but at high risk of low functionality. An X passport may not operate as a passport at all.

Having surveyed the gender options, I was left with nothing viable. M was out—at least until or if I started testosterone. X was out—too likely to get me stuck in legal limbo at an airport far from home. Meanwhile, F was just plain wrong. The sight of it on my ID prompted the sick, scratchy feeling that doctors call gender dysphoria. F was shame and panic, like being stuck in an airless animal costume with no one to hear you scream. But F was, at least, familiar. I already knew its capacity for harm. No surprises here. Better the devil you know, as they say.

F also allowed me to pass as cisgender, if required—no small consideration. With an F on my licence and passport, I could still perform the role of nice white lady on occasion. Hassles could be avoided, if at the cost of internal pain. F was a safety net, allowing me to keep one foot in the cisgender world. All in all, it seemed advisable to stick with F for the time being.

But where did this leave me with my legal name change? The plan had been to change my name and gender in one procedure. Get it done together. I doubted it was worth enduring the bureaucratic rigmarole for a name change alone.

Then there was the issue that Yves was a 'male' name. Although it was heard as 'Eve', the written version was less ambiguous. In its original French context, Yves was attached to penis people, as resolutely masculine as Brian or Craig. I was not a penis person. If my ID read Yves, but specified my gender as F, there'd be yet another mismatch. An M with an F, so to speak. That could cause problems of its own.

There were problems, in short, everywhere I looked. 'Yves + M', 'Yves + X', 'Yves + F'—these were my alternatives and none seemed worth the effort. So I did nothing. I sat, paralysed, at the crossroads, unable to choose between three bad options.

⌐

The ideal would be to simply dispense with the gender marker. To exist under law free from the labels and boxes. To be just a person, rather than a man or woman or other. There's no reason why this couldn't happen.

Of course, there are some legitimate medical reasons for knowing an individual's biological sex. Only people with ovaries get ovarian cancer, for instance. Penis people have a higher incidence of heart disease. Only uterus-owning people can give birth. Given these realities, Medicare and similar institutions have reasonable cause to record sex data.

But why is gender (not biological sex) recorded on non-medical ID like passports? To my mind, there's no good reason to include gender on documents designed to regulate movement across borders or permit use of a motor vehicle. Passports don't list profession or religion or marital status; how is gender any more relevant? It's convention, nothing more.

Until this convention evolves, I'm stuck with an impossible choice. Faced with three bad options, I follow the path of least resistance: inertia. The status quo. I am Yves the trans person in daily life but remain, under law, 'Anne + F'. Forever switching between two identities. I publish under Yves but am paid as Anne. I'm Anne at the voting booth; Yves on the radio. Yves in the class-room; Anne on the gas bill. I receive mail addressed to both names. The postie must think there are two of us jammed in my tiny apartment—though, strangely, he's yet to spot my other half. (Yves does work very long hours in the real-estate business.)

The two names cause no end of problems. Quite apart from the administrative bother, the mismatch between my legal and chosen names requires me to 'out' myself as transgender on a regular basis. With every new contract, medical appointment or financial transaction, the name issue presents itself. Again and again, I'm compelled to disclose: *You've met me as Yves, but I'm a trans person with a different legal name, so this document will need to list me as Anne.* It's exhausting, this incessant exposure to strangers.

Even if I change my legal name, Anne will continue to dog me, whether I like it or not. She'll never be banished from my life. The reason? Anne Rees did the research that forms the foundation of my hard-won career.

Since Year 10, when I was handed a shiny history prize at Parliament House, my heart was set on being a historian. After high school that sense of vocation translated into steely-eyed focus. I started uni before my eighteenth birthday and studied hard from day one. While other undergrads were sinking pots of Carlton at Naughto's or The Clyde, I was furiously highlighting journal arti-cles and scrawling red pen over essay drafts. Bachelor of Arts with Honours, Masters in History, then PhD in History: all ticked off in quick succession, no pauses in between. My eyes on the prize of an academic career. 'Publish or perish' was the motto we lived by, so I published my damn heart out. My first article, based on my Honours thesis, came out in 2010. Others soon followed. By 2019, when Yves was born, I had a tidy pile of publications to my name. These articles won me fellowships, awards, a coveted three-year postdoc. These articles were my passport to a brutal academic world. I needed them to be read, cited and quoted as much as possible. My whole career hinged on their visibility.

Herein lies the rub: Anne, my 'deadname', was the listed author of those articles. To disown Anne would require me to disown the articles as well, turning my back on more than a decade of dogged effort. My entire professional identity was tied to my birthname. Anne was not going anywhere anytime soon. Bloody obstinate little tacker.

This was the hard truth: Yves' career relied on Anne sticking around, on the page at least. So the duo embarked on a fractious professional marriage, giving my CV a bad case of multiple personality disorder. From 2019, new publications were authored by Yves, but there was a whole decade's worth of articles listed under Anne. One person, two names: on full display for all to read. The university database that records publications didn't know how to cope. Even after Yves had an established publication track-record, 'Y Rees' remained 'unknown' in the online system.

Colleagues are unsure how to proceed. Often, they cite Anne-authored articles under 'Yves', re-writing history to avoid offence. Suddenly a book co-edited by Anne in 2017 would appear, in a footnote, with Yves as the editor. Eager to respect my new identity, fellow historians project Yves back into the past. Anne has been magically erased. I appreciated the sentiment, truly. But I also feared that these inaccurate references would be missed by the systems that track all-important citation metrics. In the neoliberal university, where quantification is god, these numbers can make or break an academic career. Your H-index, as it's known, becomes a shorthand for your worth. This is a mad and toxic system, but one I couldn't afford to disregard. If I did, my citation metrics would flatline, threatening to take my career with them.

Fear of this outcome led me to a strange place: fighting for Anne's survival. *Please cite my old articles exactly as published,* I urged via email and social media. *Please attribute them to Anne to ensure the citation gets tracked.* Here I was, pleading to keep my deadname alive, brushing off well-meaning onlookers who assumed she should be dead and buried.

Most transgender academics struggle with these issues. US scholar Deidre N. McCloskey transitioned late in her career, with hundreds of publications under her former name.

'There wasn't much she could do to conceal her transition,' *The Chronicle of Higher Education* reports. 'She thinks that, at least in academe, changing genders can't be a private act.'

Genny Beemyn, meanwhile, wrestles with the complex feelings aroused by birthname publications. 'You love seeing your name in print. It's like, "Wow, I got this book published or this article in this really prestigious journal,"' says the University of Massachusetts academic. 'But it takes a lot away when you subsequently change your name and can finally be who you are and then see that book spine or that article with that name that isn't you.'

As yet, there's no established convention for citing transgender authors, nor any standard procedures for changing names on publications. In the absence of professional standards, individuals muddle along alone. Often, transgender scholars find themselves saddled with the labour of educating their colleagues.

If I had my druthers, Anne would be better off six feet under. It'd be easier to exist only as Yves, one straightforward professional self. It'd be a relief to stop hauling Anne around like a pet zombie, not alive but not fully dead either. I'd welcome a reprieve from disclosing my trans status—an experience not unlike disrobing in a room full of strangers. Sometimes, you just want to keep your clothes on.

But I've never had this option. As long as I remain a historian, Anne will stay with me. In the meantime, Yves and zombie Anne will continue their double act, the latter growing ever more malodorous with the passing years. It's gruesome, absurd and often humiliating. It's the price of doing business.

∽

And yet. For all the inconvenience, part of me revels in the contortions of two selves. There's a glorious theatre, a strange kind of liberty, in having multiple identities at my disposal. Yves, Anne—like a spy with two personae, I can switch between them to suit my purposes.

Whenever the phone rings, I answer with a tentative 'Hello?', waiting to see if the caller is after Anne or Yves. Both exist within me. It's a thrill, every time, like the moment before striding onstage to perform. Which character will I inhabit in the next breath? 'Yes, this is Anne,' I may say. Or perhaps: 'Yep, Yves speaking.'

These performances are a reminder I'm living undercover. A reminder you can't quite pin me down. A small yet delicious subversion of the surveillance of the state. The world, in its desire to categorise, tries to know me as one thing or another. To put me in a narrow box. My response is to be everything, all at once. Yves or Anne? F or M or X? All, or none, of the above. I stay slippery, a spy without a mission. To be unknowable, perhaps, is to taste something close to freedom.

∽

'I've decided,' Mum says. 'I'm going to do it.'

We're sprawled on her couch, honey-coloured cavoodle squeezed between us, chatting in a post-lunch stupor. Afternoon sun filters through the venetian blinds, making patterns on a rumpled newspaper.

'Do what?'

'Change my name. I've decided on Grace. It's a name to aspire to.'

'Grace.' I roll the word around in my mouth. 'Grace. It's perfect. I love it.'

'Grace' is also the meaning of Anne, I recall.

'Are you going to tell people? Change it legally?' I ask, sipping milky tea.

'I don't think so,' she answers. 'It's too late, for me. But we can use it between us. Instead of calling me "Mum"' you can use "Grace". It's the person I want to be: graceful, gracious. Less reactive.'

She's sixty-five, about to retire, décolletage wrinkled like paper, blonde hair almost faded to white, and she's still in the process of becoming. Still unfurling, refusing to wither or desiccate.

'It's too late, for me,' she says, but her actions prove the opposite. Her mind is wide open and her light grows brighter each day. She reminds me it's never too late, not for anyone.

The cavoodle snorts in her sleep and rolls over, angling for belly rubs.

'Grace,' I say, scratching the exposed flesh. 'Grace, let's take this dog for a walk.'

We stride out together into the golden afternoon, the dog shielded from chill breezes by a forest-green coat. Grace and Yves, shrugging off the skins of our old selves.

SCREEN TIME

IN THE NINETIES, THE DECADE of my childhood, *Ace Ventura: Pet Detective* was hard to avoid. The Jim Carrey comedy was released in 1994, when I was six. Over the next few years, I saw the film a dozen or so times. It made recurring appearances on commercial television, a reliable family favourite for the 8.30 pm movie slot on Friday or Saturday night. I watched and re-watched *Ace Ventura* with my brother, who revelled in the slapstick excesses of Carrey's pet detective.

I even have dim memories of watching it at school. It was the kind of film guaranteed to keep a classroom of restless kids entertained for ninety minutes on a sun-baked December afternoon. The teacher would dim the lights, set the overhead fans whirring, then insert the VHS tape into a huge black box wheeled in for the occasion. The boys would guffaw at Carrey's antics, slapping their desks in glee. We girls would titter politely. Everyone agreed: the film was hilarious. What a treat to get *Ace Ventura* instead of revising our times tables.

The climax of *Ace Ventura* involves the exposure of a trans woman. She's stripped in public, revealing the bulge of a penis concealed within feminine underwear. Cue mass shock and disgust. Carrey's character, who'd kissed this woman when she 'passed' as cisgender, has a violent bodily reaction. Upon realising he'd exchanged fluids with a trans woman, Ace Ventura races to the toilet. There, he projectile vomits, emptying his stomach again and again until nothing is left. He brushes his teeth in a frenzy, squeezing toothpaste down his throat. Eventually, he takes the toilet plunger to his mouth, sucking out any lingering remnants of trans contamination.

The message is clear: transgender people are—quite literally— sickening. They are abhorrent. They are deceitful freaks who inspire revulsion. They deserve to be shamed and exposed. This was the film's 'hilarious' punchline.

You make me sick, Ace Ventura told trans people. And audience after audience laughed in uproarious agreement.

This was my earliest lesson about transness. Aged only six, when I barely understood this thing called 'gender', I learnt that being transgender was the most disgusting thing you could possibly be. We were punchlines, not people. We were a fate to be avoided at all costs.

↜

I'd suppressed my memories of *Ace Ventura* until June 2020. Deep in the pit of that interminable lockdown winter, I spent a Saturday evening watching *Disclosure*, a Netflix documentary about the history of trans representation on screen.

That history is a long one, dating back to the birth of cinema. From the 1910s onwards, film and later television have been engaged in acts of representation that taught society what it means to be transgender. The power of this messaging is enormous. Even today, eighty per cent of Americans don't know an actual trans person. In Australia, only one in ten know a trans person well or have a trans family member. This means that the vast majority of people—including closeted trans people—are reliant on the media to understand 'transness'.

More often than not, the media paints a pejorative picture. Ever since pioneering director D.W. Griffith included a male crossdresser in the early feature film *Judith of Bethulia* (1914), trans women on screen have largely been a joke. They are portrayed as men in dresses. Grotesque parodies of womanhood rolled out for an easy laugh. If they're not a joke, they're a victim: sex workers and murder victims on crime dramas like *Law & Order: Special Victims Unit*, or cancer patients on *ER* and *Grey's Anatomy*. They're also apt to be psychopathic, like the serial killer Buffalo Bill in *Silence of the Lambs* (1991) or the knife-wielding crossdressers in *Psycho* (1960) and *Dressed to Kill* (1980).

Transmasculine people, by contrast, are largely invisible. We barely exist within film and television. Instead of being the butt of jokes, we're just erased. When we do make a rare appearance, we're also cast as victims. The most iconic depiction of transmasculinity on screen is *Boys Don't Cry*, the 1999 film about the 1993 rape and murder of real-life Nebraskan trans man Brandon Teena—a critically acclaimed drama that saw cisgender actress Hilary Swank win an Oscar for Best Actress.

And whether sinister or pitiful, trans people on screen are almost always disgusting. Midway through *Disclosure*, the documentary revisited the vomiting scene from *Ace Ventura*, playing a clip from the film.

'Einhorn is a man!' Jim Carrey exclaims in shocked realisation, face contorted in disgust. He sprints to the toilet, where he heaves his guts out.

On the couch, I sat transfixed, eyes widening, brain joining the dots. I'd watched this scene countless times as a child. I'd erased all conscious memory of it until this point. But, seeing it again as an adult, overcome by déjà vu, I realised its meaning had imprinted itself on my developing brain. I was suddenly six again, a child learning shame and disgust. The scene was a piece of shrapnel buried deep in my flesh, now rising to the surface.

This was what the world taught me about transness: it's puke worthy. Vomitous.

And make no mistake, *Ace Ventura* was no outlier. On the contrary, Carrey's disgust was all too typical of the transphobic 'humour' ubiquitous during the 1990s and into the 2000s. *Ace Ventura* was only one of many films that employed the 'trans-woman-inspires-vomiting' trope. It all started with *The Crying Game*, a 1992 film in which the protagonist Fergus takes home a beautiful woman called Dil. In the bedroom, they undress. The camera pans down Dil's naked body, all breasts and curves, only to land on a penis. Fergus recoils, shocked.

'You did know, didn't you?' asks Dil.

Fergus doesn't answer, instead slapping away her hand.

'Jesus, I feel sick,' he finally responds.

Fergus slams Dil to ground and runs to the bathroom, where he pukes into the sink, overcome by revulsion. Dil listens, crumpled on the ground, her face resigned.

The same scenario then reappeared in *Naked Gun* 33⅓ (1994), *Family Guy* (2010) and *The Hangover Part II* (2011). Again and again, transness acts as an emetic. It's a pathogen that needs to be expunged. In the process, cis and trans audiences alike were taught that, in the words of trans actor Zeke Smith, 'trans people make people physically ill'.

What an education. Like Smith, I'm still living with the scars. I'm still learning not to be disgusted by myself.

⤙

For me, being trans is inseparable from seeing trans. By which I mean: the representation of trans people in film, television and other media defined my understanding of what trans was and whether being trans was thinkable for me. *You can't be what you can't see*, so the saying goes.

For most of my life, I couldn't be trans because I couldn't see any trans people. There were only the freaks depicted in *Ace Ventura* and the like. Those trans characters were not really people. They were laughable deviants, not fully-fledged members of the human race.

I, however, was human. I was a human person who wished to be accepted and loved by other humans. So I couldn't possibly be trans. End of story.

A common misconception is that 'real' trans people insist upon their transness from earliest childhood. If I was *really* trans, so the logic goes, I would have refused dresses at three years old. I would have screamed whenever the Christmas wrapping paper revealed a Barbie or Baby Born. I would have demanded short hair and refused to answer to Annie. I didn't do any of those things, so my transness becomes suspect. *Surely if it was real it would have shown up long before adulthood? Surely you would've told your parents you weren't a girl. You didn't, so are you actually trans at all?*

But the truth is, for me, as a child, being trans simply wasn't thinkable because transness equalled sub-humanity. Children are wily creatures who'll go to great lengths to survive, even if it means denying their true nature. I learnt young that transness was a fate worse than death. The logical next step was to banish transness from the realm of what was possible. There was no conscious act of repression; I was simply unable to associate my own humanity with the supposed inhumanity of trans bodies. The two just couldn't go together. It was as unimaginable as calling myself a tree or a teapot.

This is cisnormativity or what could be called 'compulsory cisness'—the assumption that every normal and natural human is cisgender (or non-trans). It's akin to compulsory heterosexuality, a term popularised by lesbian poet Adrienne Rich to describe the assumption that heterosexual orientation is the human default, the only normal state of affairs. Just as compulsory heterosexuality implies that anyone with same-sex desires is wrong or deviant, compulsory cisness pathologises trans people as freaks who've strayed from the norm. The upshot of this ideology is that it becomes difficult to imagine oneself as trans. Because who wants to willingly cast themselves out from society?

It is no accident that everything changed for me in the wake of the so-called 'trans tipping point'. In May 2014, *Time* magazine put Black trans actress Laverne Cox on its cover. Cox had recently shot to stardom through playing an incarcerated trans woman in the Netflix prison drama *Orange is the New Black* (2013–19). Now she was the face of a movement. On the *Time* cover, Cox was queenly in black stilettos and a navy cocktail dress, honey-coloured curls spilling over her breasts, unapologetic gaze directed straight at the camera. Next to her photograph was the headline 'The Transgender Tipping Point: America's Next Civil Rights Frontier'. *Time* had spoken: trans people had hit the mainstream. We were normal now. We had our own celebrities. We were poised to overcome.

This narrative needs to be taken with a generous grain of salt. Transphobia did not magically evaporate in 2014. Getting a few trans people on screen is not the same as trans liberation. Visibility alone is not an inherent good. On the contrary, the visibility of oppressed peoples can in fact make them more vulnerable to harm. As critic Anne Boyer explains, 'Visibility doesn't reliably change the relations of power to who or what is visible except insofar as visible prey are easier to hunt.'

There's no doubt that cultural visibility has turned ordinary trans people into prey. In the years since 2014's 'tipping point', we've witnessed a global transphobic backlash, characterised by anti-trans legislation, media commentary and violence. Trans hate crimes are higher than ever. In 2020, at least 350 trans people were killed worldwide—up from 331 in 2019. In Australia, the 2016 moral panic over Safe Schools was followed in 2019 by *The Australian*'s anti-trans campaign. That same year, legislative reform in Victoria inspired transphobic fearmongering by TERFs (trans-exclusionary radical feminists). In 2020, the Tavistock case in the UK rolled back access to gender-affirming healthcare for trans youth. In the United States, within only the first four months of 2021, thirty-three states had introduced more than a hundred bills that curb anti-trans rights. These include a law passed in Arkansas that outlaws gender-affirming treatment for minors. Closer to home, the University of Melbourne academic Holly Lawford-Smith launched a website in February 2021 to amplify the disproven transphobic trope that trans women act as predators in female bathrooms.

So much for the 'tipping point'.

But there's another side to the story. While new-found trans visibility has fuelled anti-trans sentiment, it's also allowed people like me to finally recognise ourselves. For the first time, we've had transness depicted as a legitimate way to be human. Compulsory cisness continues to rule our imaginations, but the cracks are beginning to show. For the first time, people uncomfortable with their assigned gender have seen their struggles and their humanity reflected on screen. We've had guides and examples of who we might become.

Alongside Cox, we've had Janet Mock, a Hawaiian-born journalist who came out as transgender in *Marie Claire* in 2011. Her 2014 memoir *Redefining Realness*, which documented Mock's adolescent transition, was a *New York Times* bestseller. We've had Caitlyn Jenner on the cover of *Vanity Fair*. We've had *Transparent*

(2014–19), the five-season TV drama about a Los Angeles family adjusting to the news that their parent is a trans woman called Maura. We've had *The Danish Girl* (2015), a biopic about real-life trans woman Lili Elbe, who in 1930 became one of the first people to receive gender affirmation surgery. We've had *POSE* (2018–21), a Fox drama about the ballroom scene in 1980s and 90s New York that boasts an unprecedented number of trans actors, writers, directors and producers—including many trans people of colour. We've had *Gentleman Jack* (2019), a period drama about nineteenth century gender-bender Anne Lister. We've had trans-acted transmasculine characters on the rebooted *Tales of the City* (2019) and *The L Word: Generation Q* (2019), as well as a trans-acted transfemme character in teen drama *Euphoria* (2019). We've even had a recurring trans character on *Neighbours*, that long-running stalwart of white-bread Australia. Since 2019, trans advocate Georgie Stone OAM has played Mackenzie Hargreaves, a teen making her way at Erinsborough High.

This representation matters. It changes lives. It saved mine.

When I saw *The Danish Girl* on a wet Friday eve in spring 2015, I had no inkling I was trans. I arrived at Canberra's Palace Electric cinema in skinny jeans and blue suede heels, the toe dampened by the downpour—just a normal cis lady going to a film with a friend. The topic had nothing to do with me; we chose the film simply because it was the kind of highbrow cinema our tertiary-educated milieu was meant to consume. Before the opening credits, I ducked into the ladies to brush my hair and reapply lipstick. In the circular mirror, a tanned woman with a blonde mane stared back at me.

Back home, after watching Lili Elbe's story, something came over me. Undressing for bed, I stood again before a mirror, this time in my own bathroom. Topless, angled to the side, arms shielding my breasts, I saw, for the first time, the androgyny of my collar bone and slender arms. I saw how easily my breasts could disappear. In the dim light of a bedside lamp, the mirror showed a body that could shapeshift. A body whose meaning was not fixed in stone. Just as Eddie Redmayne, the cis actor who plays Elbe, had remade his body to betoken 'woman', my body revealed it had the capacity to be masculine.

This was the first time it became thinkable to regard myself as having any connection to a trans character. Although *The Danish Girl* has attracted deserved critique for casting a cisgender man (rather than a trans woman) in the lead role, Redmayne's performance was a sensitive one that brought enchantment to the otherwise reviled transgender body. There was no sense of a 'man in a dress'. No mockery or humour. Instead, his performance was a metamorphosis, a slow unfurling of womanhood via gesture and posture and make-up that had all the wonder of a fairytale. It was a glimpse of the magic and artistry of reimaging a body; it enabled me to regard my own body as a potential canvas for that art.

That night, I stood for long minutes before my reflection, transfixed by the sharp angles that added up to a boyish shape. Taut sinews of the neck, the ship's bow of the shoulder blade. I saw a body whose future was not foreclosed, flesh with potential to be remade into something new. Something that could be beautiful.

The following week, over a Thai meal with an old uni friend, *The Danish Girl* came up in conversation. Liz had seen the film with her new girlfriend, but their date had ended in disaster.

'She's started thinking she might be trans,' Liz explained, 'so she found it really triggering. It brought up all her body issues and dysphoria. She was upset for days.'

Huh. There were trans people—or prospective trans people—in my circles? I had no idea. Turns out, they could be anywhere. Turns out, one of my oldest friends was sleeping with one. Liz wasn't repulsed by her girlfriend's possible transness; she wasn't vomiting in great body-shaking heaves. Instead, she was helping herself to salt-n-pepper tofu, scooping the brown cubes flecked with chilli onto the rice in her small white bowl.

Slowly, transness assumed new meanings. It could be ordinary; it could even, perhaps, be beautiful.

⌒

'Changing representation is not the goal; it's a means to an end,' explains trans historian Susan Stryker. That end is to bring trans people back into the tent of humanity. When we're inside, mingling with all the cis folks, it's harder to hate and fear us. We become knowable; we invite empathy. But just as importantly, trans people inside the tent makes it possible to imagine gender transition as a viable future for others. It becomes a thinkable proposition, not a living nightmare to be repressed at all costs.

There is this thing called 'trans' and it's a legitimate part of humanity: this is the message conveyed by the trans tipping point. *You can be trans and remain a person. You may struggle, but you can have a life. You won't be a monster or freak.*

This is what I'd been waiting a lifetime to hear. I needed to see trans characters who were people, not punchlines, for me to allow myself to consider I was one of them.

Without seeing versions of myself on screen, would I have come out at all?

Back in the twentieth century, long before the trans tipping point, many trans and gender non-conforming people were drawn to keep scrapbooks. They filled the pages with news clippings and photographs of cross-dressers, transvestites, drag queens, celebrity transsexuals and other gender benders, curating an archive of trans possibilities. They were searching for evidence of people like them. Looking for any hint that they weren't the only one. Trying to feel less alone.

Julie Peters, a pioneering Melbourne trans activist, began collecting trans news clippings and ephemera in the 1960s—two decades before she transitioned. Today, her collection fills no less than six filing cabinets. Not to be outdone, her friend and fellow trans advocate Katherine Cummings has nine.

Noah Riseman, a historian of transgender Australia, calls this record-keeping a means of 'finding evidence of me' through 'evidence of us'. By collecting depictions of people like them, TGD people sought to know themselves. Media representation facilitated identity formation. To be trans, they needed to see trans. *You can't be what you can't see.*

Monte Punshon was one of these scrapbookers. A Melbourne teacher born in 1882, Punshon loved women and favoured a masculine style. She wore suits and friends called her Mickey. In the 1980s, she was heralded as a lesbian. Today, Punshon might be understood as transgender or transmasculine. She didn't use any of these terms to describe herself. She was just Monte. However she's categorised, Punshon was undoubtedly a gender rebel. And for four decades, from the early 1920s until the late 1950s, she made scrapbooks that collated traces of gender non-conforming 'women' like her. Her eye was drawn to female-assigned people who claimed 'masculine' freedoms and dress. Aviators, motorists, jockeys, horse trainers. Tomboys in pants. Male impersonators. Women who passed as men. Her scrapbook also included a review of Radclyffe Hall's *The Well of Loneliness*, the infamous 1928 novel about Stephen Gordon, a female-assigned person who loves women and adopts a masculine identity.

We can't know for sure why Punshon made these scrapbooks. But historian Ruth Ford speculates that they were connected to Punshon's own gender non-conformity. Perhaps, Ford suggests, Punshon was 'affirming her identification of self' by building an archive of fellow gender rebels.

It's not hard to imagine Punshon, an unwomanly woman trying to understand her difference, leaping on any hint of female masculinity encountered in a newspaper or magazine. *Here is someone like me*, she may have thought while leafing through the morning paper over tea and toast, eyes drawn to a slim-hipped figure in slacks. We can imagine her taking the scissors from the kitchen drawer and clipping the grainy photograph, pasting it into her book of treasures. *Others are rejecting womanhood, so I can too*, she may have whispered to herself. *Here is permission to break the rules.*

In the twenty-first century, the scrapbook was usurped by the internet. In Riseman's research on trans people in the military, he found that people questioning their gender in the 2000s looked for answers online. Blogs and chatrooms were where gender rebels now sought 'evidence of me' through 'evidence of us'. One of these was a transgender woman called Bridget, who'd been a member of the Army since 1999 and served as a peacekeeper in East Timor. In 2008, then living the life of a married man who competed in triathlons, Bridget started questioning her gender. She turned to the internet, where—like Punshon with her scrapbooks—she found people like her. Medical and government websites had little relevant information, but blogs were a revelation. She read transition blogs from people around the world and learnt a new vocabulary. It was 'scary' yet 'enlightening'. She'd found models of what she could become.

The internet served a similar function for Caspar Baldwin. In late 2011, then studying for a PhD in Sheffield, Baldwin hit rock bottom. He'd spent his whole life trying to be a girl, yet the performance always remained a 'costume based on a lie'. Aged only twenty-two, he was exhausted by life. One night, sobbing alone in his share house, he finally googled 'girl who feels like a boy'. The search results took him to videos of children assigned female at birth (AFAB) now living as boys. Within minutes, he'd found other people like him. He'd discovered the terms 'transgender' and 'gender dysphoria'. 'I fixated on these videos,' Baldwin later wrote, 'playing them again and again.' That night, pouring over the screen, he began to understand himself. 'Every word I read was as if it was written just for me. There was a name for the feelings I had fought all my days, a real, actual, name!' He'd found himself. '*I was a boy. I am a man. I am transgender,*' Baldwin said to himself for the first time. The relief was profound. It was an 'extraordinary emotional release after all those years of confusion, melancholy and pain'. He hardly slept that night, instead gorging on videos, websites and online support forums. He couldn't devour the information fast enough. Nearly a century after Punshon began curating an archive of female masculinity, Baldwin was creating his own scrapbook of gender possibilities. We were all looking for guides of what we could become.

⌣

Instagram was my scrapbook. The pink icon on the phone screen was my portal to a parallel universe of gender rebels who could teach me about myself. The selfies of strangers would furnish the blank box of my trans imagination. Instead of cutting and pasting like Monte Punshon, I curated my archive of transmasculinity through follows and likes. By scrolling and searching, tracking strangers across time, deep diving into hashtags, pouring over selfies and heartfelt captions, I built a mental library of all the different ways it was possible to be trans.

Transmasc folk in gyms, at the beach, embracing their wives, posing in new outfits. Recording audio of their lowered voices. Trans men with beards, bald heads, broad shoulders, stubble, dreadlocks, wrinkles around the eyes. There were so many who passed. So many who you'd assume were cisgender men. These men may not have penises, but who would know? They're fully clothed in public. There's no way to tell what's inside their underwear. Penis or not, any fool would call them 'man'. To all appearances, they were a hundred per cent bloke.

Best of all were the before-and-after pics, posted under the #TransformationTuesday hashtag. Often, the contrast was staggering. A blonde prom-queen with fake tan and winged eyeliner would become a bearded gym bro, sixpack covered in tatts. The paired pics could have been brother and sister or a straight couple, rather than the same person transformed by the magic of testosterone and the surgeon's knife. It was wondrous: a girl given a potion and remade into her male shadow, unrecognisable. Born anew.

The 'before' photos fascinated me. So many of these men had once resembled the girliest of girls, all sparkles and curves. Here was hard evidence that not every transmasculine person was a tomboy from birth. I wasn't the only one who'd once boasted a wardrobe of dangly earrings and red lipstick and lacy bras.

When I first announced my transness to friends and family, I'd encountered widespread disbelief.

'But you've always been so feminine,' they exclaimed.

'You wore dresses! You owned makeup!'

The implication was clear: 'real' trans people refused their assigned gender from day one. Perhaps, then, I was an imposter; perhaps it was all a phase.

#TransformationTuesday quashed those doubts. The Insta posts taught me you could be the belle of the ball—a princess with lip gloss and blonde highlights—then one day you could wake up and realise you weren't a woman at all. It was okay. I wasn't the only one. Others had walked this path before.

Elliot Wake was one of those ahead of me, staking out a route for others to follow. Wake was a novelist, living in Chicago, who—like me—didn't transition until his early thirties. Like me, he'd long published under his birth name, and couldn't afford to disavow his former identity. Now, Wake was documenting his transition on

Instagram. Each day he posted a new selfie, often after working out at the gym. The images displayed his muscled arms, his new wardrobe, the growing thicket of facial hair. We had much in common: age, writing, introversion. Scrolling back to his pre-transition photos, I found a version of me. Despite our different colouring—me blonde, Wake dark—our 'female' selves shared a slim-hipped androgyny, a tentative posture, hungry eyes. We both had the raw and dazed look of someone who'd just admitted the depths of their appetite. Our appetite for masculinity. It was so naked on our soft-skinned, hairless faces. We were all want. It was hard to watch, but I couldn't look away.

Wake's early selfies documented his first incursions into menswear. His narrow frame posed in front of the bedroom mirror, modelling brand-new shirts and jackets that draped and billowed, refusing his still-feminine contours. Just like they did for me. We had similar taste in clothes. His wardrobe was all normcore classics—crews, navy knits, leather jackets, pea coats, slim-fit jeans and boots of chocolate leather.

For months, the clothes remained too big. He swam within the fabric. A kid playing dress-ups. But then, almost imperceptibly, things changed. As the testosterone did its work, aided by long gym sessions, Wake's body transformed. Day by day, he filled out his clothes. The tension in his jaw relaxed. He began to take up space. Day by day, he became man. A beautiful man, muscled yet elegant, just a tiny bit cocksure. The clothes now appeared tailor-made. It was magic. Not incidentally, perhaps, he resembled a younger version of my father. They were both just a little bit wolfish.

Each morning, munching muesli, I inspected Wake's latest selfie, then scrolled back over the image history once again. Like a forensic detective, I inspected the minute changes in jawline, chest circumference, posture, fat distribution, facial hair. Trying to find the exact moment of transition. Trying to find a map for my own future. Trying to summon the courage to take the leap.

We never interacted, apart from the likes I gave his photos. Elliot Wake had no knowledge of my existence. But he showed me I wasn't the only one to take thirty years to recognise my transness. He taught me it was acceptable to arrive late to the party.

Then one day, he was gone. Wake had been sparring with Instagram over image censorship, as the platform kept deleting his topless posts. Finally, he had enough. He posted a farewell message and deleted his account, never to return. Like he'd never even been there at all. It was as though Wake had been my fairy godmother, a trans mentor to guide the journey, only to vanish in a puff of smoke when he'd served his purpose.

It was up to me now, ready or not.

↘

In early 2018, still a woman called Anne, I watched the fourth season of *Transparent*. After three seasons set in Los Angeles, this season takes the Pfeffermans to Israel, where they explore their Jewish identity and reconnect with long-lost family. According to *Transparent* creator Joey Soloway, it's a season about 'borders and boundaries'. At the heart of the drama is Ali, the Pfeffermans' youngest child, who follows the family around Israel under a dark cloud. Ali is distressed to be holidaying on stolen land. She can't look away from the plight of Palestinians, herded behind borders and checkpoints. Most of all, she's discomfited by the gender binary. At the Wailing Wall in Jerusalem, men pray on one side, women on the other, a barrier between them. Upon arrival, the Pfeffermans split in two, each with their designated gender. Ali is appalled.

'It's fucking bullshit, this divide.' She scowls, pacing among the subdued women.

Over the barrier, she sees men singing and dancing. There's laughter, music plays. Ali knows where she wants to be. She exits the women's section, dons a kippah, and re-enters among the men. No one stops her. She's crossed an inviolable border and gotten away with it. Her body relaxes, face clears, distress replaced by wonder. If this border can be so easily transgressed, we see her thinking, what else is up for grabs? What other rules can be broken?

In the next episode, Ali continues to rub against her family. Her trans parent, Maura, asks her what's going on.

'I just don't feel good in my body,' Ali mutters.

'Do you think you're trans?' Maura asks, gently.

'I don't know that I feel like a woman, whatever that means,' Ali responds.

With Maura's blessing, Ali leaves the family, taking a taxi to visit queer activist friends living nearby. That evening, yarning around the campfire, she flirts with Lyfe, a handsome genderqueer person. The pair retreat to Ali's tent, and begin to kiss.

Ali goes to remove Lyfe's chest binder.

'No, not this, I don't take this off,' Lyfe cautions, before leaning in for another kiss.

Lyfe then reaches for Ali's crop top, asking: 'Can I take this off?'

'Yeah,' Ali agrees automatically, but then pauses. She's never been asked this before. Maybe, in fact, she doesn't want to include her breasts in their encounter? She's uncertain, confused, apologetic.

'It just never occurred to me I could *not* take this off,' she explains, gesturing at the crop top. 'It's literally never occurred to me.'

It had never occurred to me either. My breasts had never been a source of pleasure, sexual or otherwise. I went rigid when lovers touched my nipples. But I'd never dared consider they could be removed from the equation. Breasts were meant to be the star of the female body, and so, as a putative woman, I'd allowed them to take a leading role. But maybe I didn't have to. Perhaps my breasts could also be tucked away, flattened beneath tight fabric.

On the screen, Ali asked Lyfe how sex worked for them: did they play the male role?

'I'm just a human person,' Lyfe answers. 'And I just want to be a body, so we can do what bodies do.'

A human person, neither female nor male. Just a body, existing in the world, giving and taking pleasure. What an idea. These words were so simple, yet I'd never heard them uttered before. Hearing them was like opening a new doorway in my mind. Here were new possibilities, previously unthinkable, a way forward I hadn't known existed. Here was permission.

On the couch, watching that scene in the tent, my whole body vibrated with recognition. These, I knew, were people like me—or I was like them. Whatever that meant.

⤙

A few months after watching Ali in Israel, and now in the first throes of coming out, I slunk into a cavernous warehouse of a bar tucked behind a Brunswick carpark. It was a chill Wednesday evening and I was alone. The room heaved with an unlikely mix of pale-faced queers and hulking rugby bros out for post-training drinks. Lurking by the bar, I scrolled my phone, feigning a bored wait for a non-existent friend. My fingers typed urgent messages to no one. My eyes covertly surveyed the crowd. Belly laughs, sleeve tattoos, the reek of man sweat. Jugs of beer on every table. Despite the warm fug of bodies, I kept my jacket on. Swaddled in its bulk, my narrow frame padded out by layers of fabric, I hoped to conceal the frightened little girl within.

After a long half-hour, we were allowed into a darkened back-room. Queerstories had begun. It was a queer storytelling night, a regular event hosted by Sydney performer Maeve Marsden. Still terrified of my own transness, I'd forced myself to go along to find other people like me.

First up on the stage was Alison Evans, a non-binary writer with a fey demeanour and shock of green curls. Younger than me, but far advanced in wisdom, Evans talked about the conventions of trans storytelling. Trauma looms large in stories about trans people, Evans noted.

'Stories written about us focus on our transitions, gender dysphoria, how we have learnt to hate our bodies, how we want to change our bodies. We are so often defined by what we're not, we are defined by a lack,' Evans explained. 'That narrative is so dominant in the media, in the books we read, the films we watch.'

As a consequence, transness and trauma become linked in our minds. When we imagine our own trans futures, we see only acres of suffering. We see hate crimes, unemployment, gender dysphoria, botched surgeries, social rejection, early death. There's not much to hope for. It becomes difficult to consider the possibility of trans joy.

'How might we subvert this narrative?' Evans asked. 'What would it look like to "write queer stories without queer trauma"?' That was their creative goal. Up on stage, Evans unveiled their new project: a young adult novel called *Euphoria Kids*, a tale about trans teens that would stress the pleasures of being transgender. The title took its name from 'gender euphoria'—the opposite of gender dysphoria—the state of being 'comfortable in yourself, in your body, in your gender'.

'I want people to know about gender euphoria,' Evans concluded. 'I want them to learn about it before dysphoria. I want the young trans kids that will read the books I write to be proud of who they are and imagine wonderful lives for themselves.'

Gender euphoria. What an idea. I was all too familiar with gender dysphoria, but this was a completely novel proposition. Transness as a source of euphoria? Not just as the absence of trauma, but as an actual source of pleasure? Preposterous, surely. Walking home through dark streets, I pondered how all the stories I'd consumed had taught me to imagine barest survival as the best possible future for myself. Not getting rejected, not getting harassed, not killing myself—these were my limited objectives. A life of dodging bullets, nothing more. Nothing to hope for but a mere lack of trauma. My imagination had been starved of trans flourishing and joy.

Euphoria Kids was published eighteen months later, in early 2020. It was everything Evans promised, and more. The three trans protagonists exist in a cosy world of parental affirmation, lasagne-fuelled movie nights, potent crystals, and never-ending hot chocolate. They're teenagers negotiating high school in contemporary Melbourne but they're also magical creatures born from fire and plants. They cast spells, hobnob with faeries and dryads, travel through time, battle curses and hunt witches. In Evans's story, transness is not monstrous but rather powerful and magical.

The trans characters are wise and magnetic, and far too busy visiting other realms or learning spellwork to hate their bodies. Transness is also commonplace: special, but far from freakish. The moon is trans, the dryads are trans, as are many of the humans. Even (spoiler alert) the dreaded witch turns out to be a beautiful trans woman, queenly in her cottage of plants.

How different might my life have been had I'd grown up with *Euphoria Kids* instead of *Ace Ventura*? How much shame and self-loathing could have been averted if, as a child, I'd learnt that trans people were magical rather than vomit-worthy? *Ace Ventura* and the vomit scene hadn't stopped me being trans. Like all conversion therapies, it had failed to do anything other than breed self-disgust. Maybe, with *Euphoria Kids* as my handbook, I could have skipped the decades burdened by dysphoria and gone straight to the euphoria part.

At least, for children now, things are different. At least *Euphoria Kids* is on the bookshelves of a new generation. This isn't the same as trans liberation, but it's not nothing either. On good days, it's enough to give me hope that the rising generation of trans people will live lives infused with gender euphoria. Perhaps, eventually, we'll even once again be recognised as the magic people we truly are. Until then, I'll keep practising my spells.

EVERYDAY ARMOUR

THE CHEST BINDER WAS THE kind of object that knew its own worth. It didn't set out to charm. Slate grey, boxy lines, nylon and spandex without ornament—it resembled a long-lost artefact from the USSR. A communist corset, bluntly functional and more than a little severe.

It wore its history proud. The sides were stretched by use, the label faded from countless washes, the pilled fabric evidence of long hours rubbing against skin. Its owner had worn it often. Day in, day out. The stiff fabric had bound their breasts, compressing unwanted curves, for months or years even—until one day, the owner had top surgery, obtained a permanent flat chest, and the binder became redundant, ready to be passed on to the next person hungry to conceal a bosom. That person was me.

It sat atop a pile of donated binders, arranged on a trestle table at the monthly meeting of the transmasculine support group. All were up for grabs, free for anyone in need.

'Have a look, help yourself to any that might fit,' the facilitator urged me.

He turned back to the urn where the other attendees clustered with cups of Nescafé.

At the table, I sorted through the binders. A binding virgin, I was on the hunt for a freebie to pop my cherry. Most were too big for my narrow frame, serious objects designed with hefty bosoms in mind. The old grey one was the closest fit. Measuring its girth against my body, I smelt laundry powder and the memory of sweat.

In the bathroom, under fluorescent lights, I squeezed my torso into the binder's embrace. There were no buttons or zips, so the garment had to be forced over my shoulders, down onto my chest. It hugged me tight, dancing on the edge of pain. With each inhale, my lungs strained against the unyielding fabric. Once fully dressed, I looked a different person. In the mirror, my chest was boyish, a smooth expanse of T-shirt, green and white stripes circling flat terrain. At the neckline, there were flashes of grey, the binder peeking out to wave hello. I shrugged on my denim jacket, adjusting its bulk to conceal the corsetry. Collar up, sleeves rolled. Perfect. My reflection beamed. New body, new me.

I took a selfie, eyes wide and mouth agape, and texted it to friends.

Spot the difference? I asked.

When the support group ended, I cycled away into the night, bound for a friend's birthday party. I flew through damp Carlton streets, legs pumping, wind stroking my face, heart thrumming against the grey fabric. I was impatient to show off my new shape. Most of the time, I was no fan of parties, feeling awkward amid crowds of strangers. But today was different. Today, I'd chat and flirt and dance like a pro. I'd strut into that party like I owned the joint. With my flat chest jutted out like a ship's bow, I was invincible.

Chest binders are a kind of armour. In the words of Melbourne comic Scout Boxall, a binder is 'somewhere between a hug and a breast plate'. A binder is 'everyday armour', Boxall writes.

Like armour, a binder is not designed for comfort. At best, it's suffocating—postmodern corsetry that squeezes the lungs and bites into soft flesh, leaving red marks and chafing in its wake. At worst, it moulds the body in its own image, distorting the curve of a rib cage and inviting chronic pain. The tight fabric allows no ventilation. On the mildest of summer days, it becomes stifling, swaddling the torso in clammy heat like an electric blanket. No matter the time of year, binders inhibit deep breathing, making it near impossible to exercise. Manufacturers recommend wearing them for no more than nine hours a day. As with a heavy iron breastplate, weighing down its wearer, a binder never learnt the meaning of gentle.

But, also like armour, binding gives a different kind of comfort— the comfort of feeling safe. It grips the chest so tight to ensure all the softness beneath is contained within a hard exoskeleton, all that unwanted tissue hidden from prying eyes. That grip, while suffocating, is not so very different from a hug. Both enclose, both promise protection. Within the binder's embrace, shirts and blazers fit more easily, falling from neck to waist without obstruction. The lines are right.

And the world begins to treat you differently. With a flat chest, it's harder to be wounded by the words *miss* or *ma'am*; you might even be called *sir*. Above all, a binder gives the comfort of being seen as you see yourself.

↳

Each morning, fresh from the shower, I squeeze into the grey binder, the synthetic fabric sticking to my damp flesh. Once inside, my breasts disappear, a woman's chest remade into something else.

From the waist up, I could be a twelve-year-old boy. It's a magic trick that never gets old.

Before inheriting the binder, I'd worn crop-tops, compression devices designed to secure breasts during sport. These were comfortable, lacking the vice grip of the binder, yet offered only a modicum of flattening. You could still spy the tell-tale lumps of womanhood. It was a step in the right direction, a step that whetted my appetite for more.

Further back in the past, my wardrobe was filled with bras engineered to enhance my B-cup chest. Bras that crafted cleavage out of nothing. Bras with ribbons and bows and lace and underwire, the kind of bras sold to young women from hot-pink boutiques. Bras that made me feel like a sex doll, a generic Lolita trussed up in accordance with straight men's fantasies.

Even then, in my push-up days, my breasts were strange to me. I ignored them as much as possible. We could go days, weeks, without a close encounter. They weren't familiar parts of me like my hands or face; they were alien appendages that defied understanding.

One night, in my early twenties, my hand brushed my right breast and I felt a lump. A tumour? Cancer? Panic set in. A sleepless night followed, haunted by scenes of my imminent death. The next morning, I headed straight to the GP.

She inspected me, and her face clouded.

'It does feel like there's something there. I'd recommended you see a specialist.'

After an anxious month of waiting, I found myself in the surgeon's office. Stripped to the waist, I lay on the bed, ready for her cold hands, fearing the worst. It was over in less than ten seconds.

'That's not a lump,' she said, voice full of disdain. 'That's your rib.'

'My rib?' I asked, confused.

'Yes, the hard thing beneath the breast tissue is just your rib cage. There is no tumour. Only bone.'

The surgeon turned to wash her hands, dismissing me from her presence. I'd wasted her time. I redressed in silence, fingers fumbling, awash with shame.

Turns out, I knew my own breasts so little that I'd mistaken a rib for a cancerous tumour. Turns out, I lacked even the most basic understanding of my own flesh. After the rib incident, I stopped touching my breasts altogether. I averted my eyes in the shower. It seemed safer, somehow.

Now, thanks to the binder, I pushed my breasts down and to the side, out of sight. It was a relief. Binding was a daily medicine, a necessary confinement. In my communist corset, I was ready to face the world.

Who was the previous owner? All I knew was that it was someone who'd once bound their breasts and no longer had breasts to bind. Someone who'd donated their binder to a trans support group.

Perhaps they were a fresh-faced Zoomer, part of the generation below me, the kind of enviably precocious trans youth who boasted the self-knowledge to transition when barely out of high school. I'd seen kids like that on YouTube and Instagram. At only nineteen, twenty, they knew who they were. From their bedrooms, they made viral videos about pronouns and packers. They showed off surgery scars to thousands of followers.

'Remember to like and subscribe!' they chirped at the end of each video.

They wore their transness without apology, ready to take on the world. I liked to imagine some of that confidence had soaked into the binder, ready to be absorbed by me.

Or perhaps the binder's previous owner was older, Gen X or Boomer, someone who'd made the choice to transition after a lifetime as a woman. Perhaps it was someone who'd been a wife, a mother, an aunt—then finally, already wrinkled, hair greying, they'd told the world they were trans. What bravery to upend a life already far down a well-trodden path. What a daring leap into the unknown. So much easier to keep walking in the same old direction, to follow the rules of gender, to ignore the whispers urging insurrection.

Whoever the previous owner, I wondered how they like their new chest. Do they stand with quiet awe before the mirror, fingering the fading scares, turning sideways to marvel at the flat profile? Do they sunbake topless, drunk on kisses of sunshine across their skin? Perhaps they swim in board shorts, caressed by the currents, no longer worried about covering their torso.

Then there are the breasts themselves. Does my binder-donor ever miss them?

E-J Scott, a trans curator, kept his breasts after top surgery. Scott's amputated boobs now sit in twin mason jars of formaldehyde, on display at the Museum of Transology in Brighton, England. Scott calls the exhibit his trans 'show and tell'—a nod to the removed tonsils kids once brought in for 'show and tell' at school.

No longer compressed by a binder, Scott's breasts float full and perky in their liquid home, like exotic jellyfish specimens. You can still see hair around the areola. The skin shows the faded green and purple ink of an old tattoo. The nipples themselves have been removed, to be reattached to Scott's body.

It's uncanny, to see objects so unwanted now carefully preserved, placed on public display. The breasts speak of rejection, jagged tissue evidence of the surgeon's knife, but they also testify to the love of close attention and care. There's a kind of reverence in this mammary display. But perhaps Scott's breast preservation is less about reverence than reasserting control. The unwanted breasts, which sprouted on Scott's body without consent, outside his control, are now ordered and contained, locked safe in their jars. Unable to cause further harm. The genie is back in the bottle.

Scott's breast specimen is unusual, though: it's the only physical record of surgical transition within a British museum. All other breasts are destroyed after surgery, presumably incinerated in some hospital furnace alongside the breast tissue of cancer patients who've undergone mastectomies. I imagine plumes of smoke made of mammary cells, banished by the breeze.

↶

'You should get a binder from this company in the States,' Cam says, from across the table. 'I've bought my binders there forever. They're the best.'

She takes a drag of her cigarette, world-weary at twenty-eight. Cam has been binding for years, she's a veteran of the art, but still calls herself *she*. She likes to fuck with gender like that.

'Really?' I reply. 'What makes them so good?'

'They have, like, insane compression. You can't even feel the breasts at all. Here, touch my chest,' Cam orders, gesturing towards her woollen jumper.

'Are you sure?' It seems too intimate.

'Yeah, just do it.'

I reach out a hand and am met with unyielding hardness. There's no give beneath her jumper. Flat as a tack. You'd never guess there were C-cup breasts hidden under there.

'Wow, that's incredible. Much better than the second-hand one I'm wearing.'

I look down at my chest, a gentle undulation still visible beneath my blazer.

'I know, right?' Cam grins.

She stubs out the cigarette and runs a hand through her short hair.

I want that hardness, that flatness. I need it, like air.

'How can I get my hands on one?'

The new binders arrive from California, taut and factory fresh. I'd ordered two, black and beige. They smell of chemicals and hope. These are not communist artefacts; these are pure essence of America—shiny, streamlined and quick to violence.

It's a struggle to get them on. I wriggle like a fish, arms flailing, forcing the compression fabric over my head and shoulders. Inch by inch, I pull it down my chest. It's a battle between lycra and torso, a contest both are refusing to lose. Finally, the tussle ends with the binder in place over my chest. In its grip, I gasp for breath. One minute is torture; surely a full day will be unbearable. Maybe I should've stuck with the second-hand binder after all.

Then I button up my shirt and joy pulses through me. Flatter than I ever thought possible. I preen before the mirror, a peacock in white cotton. I'm fully armoured; ready to face the day. Downstairs, I mount my bicycle—this knight's loyal steed. Onwards to the battle-fields of the university. Nothing can hurt me today. As I cycle along the creek, my ribcage and the binder grip each other in an uneasy truce. But in ten hours, give or take, they'll finally go their separate ways—for the night, at least.

⌁

Like most aspects of trans health, binding is under-researched. Chest binding dates back centuries, but medical professionals have never shown much interest. The experts on binding are not doctors but ordinary trans folk, who pass down knowledge like a secret handshake, person to person, across the generations.

The first peer-reviewed study of binding's health effects was only published in 2017. That study, conducted by researchers at Johns Hopkins and Boston universities, investigated the experience of binding among 1800 female-assigned adults, most of whom lived in North America. All had some experience of binding. Around half used binders daily. The results showed that 97.2 per cent experienced at least one negative physical side-effect, including back pain, chest pain, overheating, shortness of breath, itching and bad posture.

But binding also had incalculable benefits. Participants reported improved emotional wellbeing and reduced dysphoria. Anxiety, depression and suicidality also decreased. The study concluded that binding is 'associated with significant improvements in mood and mental health'. The 'participants consistently affirmed that advantages of binding outweighed the negative physical effects'. In short, science confirms what we already knew: binding causes pain in the body and eases pain in the soul. For me, for many of us, the latter is well worth the former.

~

Binding exacts a heavy toll, however. Alongside the daily discomfort, it's ruined summer for me. High summer was once my favourite season, a carnival of salt water and mango flesh danced to a soundtrack of cicadas. Summer was blue days that stretch forever, fading into hot nights made for prowling. It was the season of bodily appetites, a pleasure palace that rewarded the hard work of the year.

Now, its approach fills me with dread. I quail as the supermarket shelves fill with sunscreen and Christmas tinsel, shudder at the carols on the loudspeaker. When the mercury rises, my corset-clad body is quick to overheat. Warm days become torture. I'm a basted sausage, tender flesh roasting under the sun within the second skin of my binder. Sweat drips down my back, in vain pursuit of a cooling breeze. But no air can penetrate this sausage skin. The heat has nowhere to go.

Atop my binder, I wear a crew-neck T-shirt or a collared shirt buttoned to the neck—something with enough coverage to keep the corset hidden. No singlets, open to the air. No unbuttoned shirts. I go about dressed for autumn, skin covered, while all around me there are bare arms, exposed chests, naked shoulders. The binder demands bodily disciplines that take no heed of the weather. In January, I no longer wish for time to stand still. Now I count down the days until March. Until the leaves turn, there'll be little chance of relief.

'Sorry I'm late, I've been at the pool,' Clare says, plopping down at the cafe table, hair dripping. 'I had the best swim; it was the perfect day for it.'

Her denim sundress reveals tanned arms, browned during thrice-weekly laps. Outside the cafe, the day is a furnace.

'How great,' I reply. 'I haven't been swimming this summer.'

'Why not? You live so close to the pool.'

'Oh, I've just been really busy. Hey, let's order, I'm starving.'

I hand Clare a menu, closing the subject.

What I don't say is that I yearn for the water, craving to stretch out my limbs in its liquid embrace. I'm a water baby, born under the sign of Pisces. The astrological fish. Like my star sign, I've always been at home in the ocean. The beaches of northern New South Wales were my nursery school. Even a council pool will do. Every summer, my shoulders grow strong from laps of freestyle, my hair bleached by chlorine and sunlight.

Since I've been binding, though, the water has become alien to me. The binder's synthetic fabric is waterproof, but its grip constrains the muscles needed to swim. I'm hobbled in the water. Freestyle and binders just don't mix. Yet without the binder, in a standard swimsuit, I'm naked. Too exposed. My breasts loll about, taunting me with their curves. There's nowhere to hide.

The local pool has no gender-neutral bathrooms, so I'm forced into the female change rooms, where pendulous breasts and dimpled thighs jostle for space on the wooden benches. It's a temple of woman-hood in which I feel myself disappear. The local matriarchs, towelling themselves after a swim, greet my arrival with suspicious eyes.

Who is that person, with the flat chest and short hair? their cold gaze asks. *Are they a man or a woman? Do they belong in here?*

I don't belong; they're right on that score. But there's nowhere else for me to go.

Soon, I stop going altogether.

'I had this great idea during my laps this morning,' Clare says, after we've ordered lunch. 'My brain always works best in the water.'

'Me too. Swimming is the best thinking time,' I agree. I adjust my torso, feel the binder cut into my armpit. 'I need to get back to the pool, one of these days.'

⤙

As I write this, I'm binding. Beneath a navy wool jumper and black T-shirt, I wear a black racer-back binder, faded from use. I've worn it for six hours already today; I'll probably wear it six more. I'll only remove it to shower, sleep and run. For exercise, I swap the binder for an extra-small crop top, a compromise that allows me to breathe.

After two years of binding, the discomfort has largely receded into the background. Unless it's a hot day, I can forget that my torso is squeezed by corsetry that resists my every breath. It's a kind of disassociation, I guess. My mind edits out the compression in my chest. It's become numb to what it cannot change.

But today is different. Today, with binding front of mind, the discomfort has returned to me. I *feel*, in a way I haven't for a long time. My upper back aches, pain radiating from my spine. My ribs long for release. My lungs strain against the fabric. I'm claustrophobic, on the verge of panic. I want out.

You could say that binding is self-harm. Something deranged. Pathological. The crazed actions of a disturbed mind. People do say these things. They want to save us from ourselves. But why are we the ones who need saving? The decision to bind is not so different to fashion choices that women make every day. Mainstream fashion encourages bodily pain in the pursuit of a desired aesthetic. Think of stiletto heels, Brazilian waxes, eyebrow threading. Skinny jeans so tight you need to hold your breath to fasten the zip. Clip-on earrings that pinch the lobes. Sandals that rub at the heel. Tattoos. I've tried all those things; I can vouch they hurt. Pain is to women's fashion what death is to life: hard to avoid. If pouring hot wax on your genitals is 'normal', surely binding can be too.

In the 2017 study of chest binding, two-thirds of participants planned top surgery in the future. For them, binding was an interim measure, a stopgap en route to a permanent solution. Among the remaining third, surgery wasn't on the agenda. It was too expensive, too permanent, just not for them. In their case, binding was an indefinite adventure.

I'd always known which camp I was in. The surgery question was never *if*, but *when*. *When* would I have the necessary ten thousand dollars, *when* would the surgeon be available, *when* could I afford to take weeks off work to recover from major surgery? *When* would I be ready to claim this for myself? It took years to get all the ducks in a row.

Boobs was staged at the Melbourne Arts Centre in January 2020, amid the toxic smoke of a savage summer. It was a one-woman show, part of the annual Midsumma Festival. In the audience, I held my breath as Selina Jenkins, armed only with an acoustic guitar, sang the story of her elective double mastectomy. Jenkins isn't trans. She's a woman, born in a female body, a queer lady who still embraces *she* and *her*. Yet this woman did the unthinkable: she lopped off her boobs. There was no tumour, no disease, no gender dysphoria. Jenkins just wasn't keen on her breasts. They got in the way; they were uncomfortable. So she pursued top surgery, the first cisgender woman in Australia to do so.

The doctors were bemused, forced her to jump through hoops galore. Anyone with sufficient cash can get a breast enhancement, but breast removal requires medical permission. The likes of Jenkins aren't trusted to know their own minds.

She did, though. Jenkins knew exactly what she wanted and refused to be deterred by sceptics. She brushed those medical men aside like so many buzzing mosquitos. Eventually, she located an amenable surgeon in Florida. Over in the United States, she remade herself into a proud breastless woman.

'Take the tit out of identity,' Jenkins croons to the audience.

In my seat, I feel she's speaking directly to me. She's telling me to feed my appetites, no matter how unconventional or inconvenient. She's granting permission—or more precisely, she's teaching that my body belongs to me, is beholden to no one, and can be changed according to my desires. The only permission required is my own.

Outside, afterwards, the sky is red. Kayaks slice along the Yarra like bats. On Princes Bridge, a busker serenades the weeknight crowd with jazz standards. I pause, look up at the sky. My chest is light, despite the binder's grip. It won't be mine for too much longer now. Soon, one day on the near horizon, it'll be time to pass on my armour to the next person in need.

THEY

DURING THE SECOND YEAR OF my transition, I'm interviewed by a
colleague from overseas. She wants to chat about podcasting. This
professor is teaching about history in the public sphere and wants me
to give her students a real-life example. We agree on a pre-recorded
Zoom interview that she'll play in class later that week.

On the appointed morning, we launch the platform, chat for
a few minutes. Then she hits record and begins an introduction.

'Yves is joining us today from La Trobe University in Melbourne,'
the professor tells the audience, reading from prepared notes. 'She
is a lecturer in history and she writes on Australia in the world.'

I blink, startled. This colleague has known for over a year that
I am not *she* but *they*. This colleague can see my pronouns listed
in my Zoom name. 'Yves (they/them)' says the text below my face.
This colleague is a feminist, an ally, and even has her own pronouns
listed in her email signature and Twitter bio. But none of that seems
to have stuck.

'She is the co-host of the history podcast Archive Fever and she
also makes regular appearances on radio,' the professor continues.

There are three *she's*, four, five. Each one lands like a slap I haven't braced for.

I burn with humiliation but force myself to keep smiling. The interview is being recorded, after all. Within seconds, my facial muscles ache from the effort of maintaining an 'engaged professional' expression.

In the Zoom chat, I type out an urgent plea.

'Just a reminder that my pronouns are they/them—not she/her.'

The message sits there, unread, for a good five minutes. We keep recording the interview. We talk about the boom in podcasting. Then all of a sudden, the professor's eyes widen.

'Oh god, did I use the wrong pronouns?' she interjects, halting the conversation.

'Um, yes, you did. A few times.'

'Oh god. We need to stop the interview.' She suspends the recording, face flustered. 'Let's go back to the beginning and start again.'

'Okay, sure. If you want.'

I swallow, more uncomfortable than ever. Here I am causing trouble, making a fuss. I didn't set out to be a troublemaker. I don't want to make things difficult; I just want to be seen.

Second take. Camera rolling. The professor's voice is faster this time because our allotted hour is running down. 'Today I'm speaking to Yves, a historian at La Trobe Uni, and she's the co-host of Archive Fever. Her interests include . . .'

She, her, again. Always, forever *she*. There's no escape. Being called *she* feels like having my limbs shoved, one by one, into a detested costume, and then paraded about before a gawping crowd.

Still, I smile, encouraging, determined to grin and bear it. I just want to get this done. I can't summon the fortitude to correct her a second time. She's my superior, a senior figure in my profession. Someone I can't afford to have offside.

But then, a minute or so later, the professor stops herself.

'Oh dear, did I do it again?'

'Uh, yes. You did.'

'Oh god, oh god. I'm sorry.'

Her face is reddening now, voice shaky. This was meant to be a straightforward conversation, but it's turned into an ordeal for both of us.

'Okay.' She's breathing fast. 'Let's try again.'

The clock is ticking down. Less than thirty minutes remain of the hour she's allocated in her packed schedule. Less than thirty minutes until she has other, more important, meetings to attend.

Third take. The red 'recording' button lights up. I hold my breath.

'Today I'm speaking to . . . ah, Yves . . . a historian . . . um, at La Trobe University.'

She stumbles over the words, now so ruffled that speech eludes her.

'Yves is, ugh, a . . . the co-host . . . of, um, Archive . . . um, um.'

The professor breaks off, stops the recording. Takes a deep breath, closes her eyes, trying to compose herself.

I watch, frozen, willing myself to disappear. This has become a slow-motion catastrophe. The professor is the one making the mistakes yet somehow the fault seems all mine. I'm the one with the 'difficult' identity. I'm the one making things complicated.

The excruciating silence drags out as we each stare into our computer screens. She's ensconced in her home office, a wall of books behind her. I'm crammed into a corner of my living room, the rack of drying underwear pushed out of sight.

'Okay, let's try again,' the professor finally says.

'We could re-schedule for another day,' I suggest. 'We don't have much time left. You have another meeting soon, right?'

'No, no.' She's grim, determined. 'Let's get it done.'

Fourth take. Red light on. I brace myself.

'Today I'm speaking to Yves, a historian at La Trobe University.' Again, the words spill out fast. 'Yves is a historian of Australia who is also a podcaster. So, Yves, how did you first become involved in podcasting?'

I exhale. Finally, we managed it. An introduction without *she*, without being called a woman.

'Thanks for the introduction,' I respond. 'In answer to your question, like many people, I first got the podcasting bug after doing some radio work.'

As I speak into the computer, beginning my spiel, I glimpse movement out of the corner of my eye. There's a whoosh of running water. I glance to the left and discover my rotund tortoiseshell cat, perched precariously on a monstera plant, pissing a stream of golden liquid onto the floorboards. She resembles an acrobat displaying a new trick. Her paws grip the pot as the urine shoots out at a dramatic angle. In over three years, she's never done this before. She's always done her business neatly inside the bathroom litter tray.

Eyes widening in horror, I keep talking about the pleasures of podcasting. The piss puddle turns into a lake, barely a metre from my desk. Ammonia perfumes the air. I soldier on, determined to avoid a fifth take. I just hope the laptop mic won't pick up the noises of feline urination. Who knew a cat's bladder could hold so much liquid?

Finally, with only seconds remaining of our allotted hour, the interview ends, and we log out. I leap from my seat to clean up the piss fast soaking into the floorboards. Up on the couch, Delphi the cat lounges, nonchalant, luxuriating in the scent of her urine as she delicately grooms a front paw.

Below, on hands and knees, I mop up the small ocean of her waste. A mound of used paper towel grows beside me. Above, Delphi surveys my efforts with unblinking eyes.

'Why on earth did you do that?' I demand.

No answer. She returns to her ablutions, angling to lick the fur of her back. I sigh and keep scrubbing the floor. I have no idea what inspired her performance, but one thing is for sure: it's the perfect finale to an absolute pisser of a morning.

↜

When I first adopted *they* pronouns, it seemed a straightforward decision. Being called *she* made my stomach clench and eye twitch, so female pronouns needed to go. But I wasn't a man either, so he/him wouldn't fit. They/them was the perfect alternative. Here was a neat linguistic tool to indicate I was neither male nor female. I was non-binary, genderqueer, trans—part of the great expanse outside or beyond M and F. All it required was one little word swapped out for another. A sentence like '*she* has a cat' would become '*they* have a cat.' '*Her* cat is called Delphi' would become '*their* cat is called Delphi.' No biggie.

There were other non-binary pronouns to choose from, so-called neo-pronouns like *ze/hir* or *ey/eir*. For instance: 'ze has a cat. Hir cat is called Delphi'. Neo-pronouns have a long history; some have been around since the 1800s. At the latest count, there are over two hundred options. For me, however, *they* was the obvious choice because it was already a familiar part of the English language. According to linguist Gretchen McCulloch, singular *they* dates back to Chaucer, appearing in *The Pardoner's Prologue*. 'And whoso fyndeth hym out of swich blame / They wol come up,' Chaucer wrote in 1395. Singular *they* was also used by Shakespeare and Jane Austen. Contrary to what reactionaries like to suggest, it's hardly a new-fangled trend.

They was open, expansive, a blank page that could be filled with anything or nothing. It was an elegant refusal of the gender binary, defiance in a single syllable. *They* could be single or plural, a single person or a crowd, a quirk that made me feel connected to a global community of people like me. We were each an individual *they*, all dancing our own distinct dance. Yet we simultaneously formed a fearsome collective. *They* were an army of gender rebels, seeding revolution around the world. *They* was me; *they* was us all.

All in all, *they* worked for me and should pose no great difficulty for anyone else. From late 2018, I began announcing my new pronouns via emails and tweets. Soon, everyone had been told—my friends, my family, my work colleagues. Simple, problem solved.

In truth, the problems were just beginning. Apart from a handful of friends, no one got my pronouns right. It was an unrelenting chorus of *she, she, she*. Of course, I'd expected mistakes. I'd been *she* for thirty years. I didn't assume anyone would make a seamless shift to *they*, and anticipated months of awkward conversation as we made the transition. I prepared myself for exchanges that would play out something like this:

'Hey, there's Yves,' someone would say. 'Is she coming to the park later—oops, sorry! I meant *they*. Are they coming to the park later?'

In response, I'd smile and stay silent, pleased that my interlocutor was making an effort. The conversation would move on, and the next time—or the time after that—the other person would use *they* with ease. We'd get there together.

None of this actually happened. What happened instead was, well, nothing. I'd announce myself as *they*, my announcement would be acknowledged, and nothing would change. *She* stuck to me like glue.

'She's coming to the park later, once her call finishes.'

'Her cat's called Delphi.'

Almost without exception, the speaker had no idea what they were doing. They didn't accidentally use *she*, then correct themselves, as anticipated. Instead, they were—as far as I could tell—completely oblivious. Entire conversations would pass, a hailstorm of *she* and *her* flung in my direction, while I stood paralysed, wondering how to respond. *Should I say something? Will they get angry?*

It was like being spat at, repeatedly, by someone convinced they were gracing you with a polite smile. The mismatch between their reality and my own made me question my sanity. *Did they really say* she, *or am I hearing things? Do they really have no idea what they're doing?*

It was excruciating and it happened multiple times a day.

In response, I experimented with different strategies. When I was feeling brave, I corrected people on the spot.

'They,' I'd interject mid-sentence, trying to keep the tone light. 'You mean *they*, not *she*, remember?'

This strategy didn't go down well. I'd be met with eye-rolls, exasperated sighs, clicking tongues, unconcealed frustration.

'Yeah, sure, whatever,' my interlocutor would respond, before hastily changing the topic.

Sometimes, the other person would deny using the wrong pronoun.

'I didn't use *she*, of course not! I would never do that. You must have misheard.'

Either way, I was the problem. It became easier to just let it slide.

But the barrage took a toll. Each time *she* was lobbed at my face, the other person told me I was a woman in their eyes. I was getting reminded, dozens of times a day, that my knowledge of myself as not-woman wasn't real or valid. I was being schooled through language, shown my place. *Get back in the woman box, how dare you try to rock the boat.* Each day I'd come home weary, half-crazed from being gaslit by the world. This is what they call being misgendered.

⤻

Rather than correct people on the spot, I started seeking out a quiet moment to reiterate why pronouns mattered.

'One of the best ways to support me is by attempting to use the correct pronouns,' I'd explain. 'I don't care if you make mistakes;

it's the effort that counts. I know it probably doesn't seem a big deal to you. But it means a lot to me. Being called *she* all the time feels terrible.'

'Yes, yes, but *they* is just so hard,' I'd be told in response. 'I mean, it's grammatically incorrect. You can't expect us to get it right. It's a huge adjustment.'

Is it so very huge? I always found this line disingenuous. It felt like an easy excuse. Singular *they* is already embedded in everyday English. We use it constantly, without thinking, without conscious effort.

Imagine you're in a busy cafe, enjoying a latte and croissant. It's Saturday morning, you're perusing the newspaper as jazz mingles with the hiss and grumble of the coffee machine. After you finish the crossword, you look up from the paper and notice a phone left behind on a neighbouring table.

'Someone has forgotten their phone,' you might exclaim, before handing the device to the barista.

Their phone. In this scenario, we don't think the phone is owned by multiple people. We know it belongs to an individual. But we don't know their gender, so we automatically adopt singular *they*.

Another example: imagine you're at home, cooking dinner after a long day at work. You're sipping a glass of red as you brown onions in the pan. The landline rings and your son runs to answer it.

'Dad! It's for you,' he yells down the hallway.

'What do they want?' you respond. *They want.* You know it's one person on the phone, but you don't know their gender, so—again—we use singular *they*.

Admittedly, in these examples, *they* is a stand-in for someone of unknown gender. For non-binary people like me, they/them is not a placeholder but our permanent pronoun. It's a pronoun that signals our gender is irreducible to either male or female. But no matter whether *they* is a placeholder or permanent choice, the sentence constructions are exactly the same.

'What do they want?' you ask of the unknown person on the phone. But imagine your son had called out: 'Dad, Yves is on the phone for you.'

Your response could still be: 'What do they want?'

If we unthinkingly employ *they* in some contexts, why do we pretend it's so hard to use for trans and gender diverse people like me? Perhaps the difficulty is not about the words at all. Perhaps it's about the rebellion behind the words, the provocation embedded in the refusal to use *she* or *he*. Perhaps the difficulty is the discomfort we feel when others break rules long taken for granted. Perhaps this tussle over language is all about keeping people in their place.

Then there's the idea that singular *they* is 'grammatically incorrect'.

'It's so hard for me,' I'm told, time and again. 'It's grammatically incorrect! I learnt proper grammar in school, and I know this is wrong.'

The 'rules' of grammar are thrust in my face, an injunction from on high, as though that settles the matter once and for all. But what are these rules and who makes them? Singular *they* dates back to Middle English. You can hardly get more traditional than that. True, they/them as a non-binary pronoun is a more recent phenomenon, something that's only taken off in the last couple of decades. But that doesn't make it 'incorrect'. Languages are living entities, made and remade by ordinary humans. There is no god of language, spelling out dos and don'ts in a fat tome. Words and usage evolve with each passing year. Most of the time, we take this in our stride. Did you use *google* as a verb in 1997? Of course you didn't. Do you use it today? I'm willing to bet yes.

They/them pronouns are no different. As singular *they* becomes commonplace, language guides have updated their conventions accordingly. The Associated Press has used singular *they* since 2017. The American Dialect Society (ADS), which has been studying North American English since 1889, voted for *they* as its 2010s 'word of the decade'. The gong was given in recognition of 'its growing use to refer to a known person whose gender identity is nonbinary'. Even the venerable Merriam-Webster Dictionary has got on board, choosing *they* as its 2019 'word of the year' in response to a 313 per cent increase in searches.

If leading arbiters of the English language are comfortable with singular *they*, surely individuals can follow suit. We easily accommodate other forms of identity change. If a newly married woman changes her surname, we don't quibble about this choice. We readily undertake the labour involved in reimagining the former Miss Johnson as Mrs Lee. There's no reason pronouns should be any different.

The flipside of pronoun pain is the exquisite pleasure when someone gets it right. Whenever *they* is used with ease, I receive a verbal hug. It's the linguistic equivalent of being told, 'I see you. You matter.' I notice it, every single time. If you wanted to serenade me, you couldn't do better than trill *they, they, they* in my direction. I'd swoon, guaranteed.

For the past few years, I've had a regular history segment on local radio. There's much to love about this gig: the fascinating stories we uncover, the thrill of live performance, the engaged community of listeners. Too often, academic historians only speak to each other, so it's a treat to talk history with the general public. But my very favourite part of the radio gig happens right at the beginning, before I'm even on air. The best bit, the bit that keeps me coming back, is when I hear the announcer introduce me.

'Soon we'll be joined by Yves Rees. They are a historian at La Trobe University. Every couple of weeks they come chat to us about Melbourne's history. They'll be with us right after this song.'

They, they, they. It rolls off the announcer's tongue. In her mouth, *they* is effortless, natural. There's no fuss or struggle. It's delicious. The sound prompts my stomach to unclench. My body knows it's safe. Even though I'm hyped up to do live radio, blood pumping with adrenaline, the deepest part of me is at ease.

There's no reason why this broadcaster should have a special knack for *they* pronouns. She's not queer or trans herself. She's a white, straight, cisgender blonde woman, partnered with kids—on the surface, as 'normal' as they come. She just makes an effort. She cares. Perhaps it's connected to her chronic illness, which means she's also different to the norm. She knows, in her own skin, the slow violence of living on the margins. Perhaps her own lived experience of exclusion motivates her to proactively include others.

Whatever the reason, it's a gift. Each *they* she utters is a tiny jewel, swaddled in velvet and ribbons, handed to me across the airwaves. With each jewel, I am less a freak or burden, more a creature like any other.

'We've been speaking to Yves Rees. They join us each fortnight to talk about parts of Melbourne's history we've forgotten.'

They, they. The jewels glint in my palm. For these few minutes each fortnight, I am real. I exist in the eyes of others—not-woman, not-man, but no less human than anyone else.

These jewels arrive at unexpected moments, small delights that inject colour and sparkle into grey days. One might not appear for weeks, then suddenly the riches rain down. *They*, I hear in a friend's mouth. *They*, I read in an email. I cherish each one, hold it up to the light.

Winter 2019. A frigid day, night by late afternoon. I'm at the Arts Centre with my friend Clancy, about to see a performance of John Cage's 'Lecture on Nothing'. The foyer is crammed with gussied-up punters, scarlet carpet barely visible beneath flocks of theatre-goers in Melbourne black. A hundred conversations clamour to be heard. While Clancy's picking up the tickets, I dart into the toilets. There's a queue, of course. Only minutes until the curtain goes up. I tap my toe as the line inches forward.

Outside, Clancy's trying to locate me amid the crush. He hovers nears the bathrooms, tickets flapping in his hand. *Where has Yves gone?* A young woman notices his searching face.

'Your friend went into the toilets. She's still inside,' she informs Clancy, as she exits the bathroom, heading towards the theatre.

Clancy darts after her.

'Hey, thanks,' he says. 'But just to let you know, my friend isn't a *she*. They're trans.'

'Oh! I didn't realise. Thanks for letting me know. I shouldn't have assumed,' the stranger replies.

'No worries,' Clancy says.

I emerge from bathroom in time to see the woman walking off.

'What was that all about?' I ask.

'Oh, she just misgendered you, so I corrected her. She called you *she*, so I told her you use *they*,' he explains. 'Quick, let's find our seats. It's about to start.'

Clancy marches off towards Door E. Trailing behind, mouth agape, I blink back sudden tears. I've grown used to negotiating the pronoun minefield alone, and it never occurred to me that someone else might act on my behalf. I never imagined that anyone would believe in my not-womanness so completely that they'd insist upon this fact in public. During the play, I barely register the action onstage, too preoccupied by this new evidence that I might, after all, be able to take up space. A real *they*, not an unwilling *she*. In the dark theatre, I sit solid in my limbs, feeling my transness kiss the air.

'Thanks for correcting that woman,' I tell Clancy afterwards, as we ride the escalator back to street level. 'No one's ever done anything like that for me before.'

'Oh, it was nothing,' he answers, forever nonchalant.

But it wasn't nothing, not really. It was someone believing me and then acting on that belief, making themselves vulnerable in the process. It was having my reality validated by another. It wasn't the usual grudging acceptance; it was love. And that's every-thing, in fact.

⤙

It's easy to mock pronoun policing as the solipsistic fixation of over-coddled youths, a distraction from the actual problems of the world. 'Snowflakes', naysayers like to call us when we complain about being misgendered. 'Political correctness gone mad!' they exclaim when we list our pronouns in our Twitter bios or email signature.

But in truth, it's not about the pronouns. It's about the big ideas behind those humble little words. To argue that pronouns are self-evident, and can be assumed from someone's appearance, is tantamount to saying that perceived anatomical sex is equivalent to gender identity. It's tantamount to saying that trans people do not—cannot—exist. It's an erasure of trans experience that's breath-taking in its arrogance.

Moreover, when someone remains wedded to *she* and *him*, and makes no effort at *they*, what they're saying is that only two genders exist. That there's M and F and nothing else. That anyone who says otherwise, anyone who names themselves as neither male nor female, must be lying or crazy or worthless. Or some combination of the three. This position ignores the countless people, across time and place, who have lived outside the gender binary, and this is not only blinkered but quite bonkers—akin to suggesting that the moon landing was faked.

They is also about respect and basic kindness. It's a word that can swell another's heart with glee. A single *they* can make a day. With a pronoun, a single syllable that costs us nothing, we can gift joy and dignity to a fellow human. Why withhold that bounty?

↴

Alongside gendered pronouns, we also have gendered titles. Mr or Mrs or Ms or Miss? Man or woman? Pick a side. Every time we complete a form, we're asked to choose. It's not enough to give our name and date of birth; we must contort ourselves into the gender binary as well. Each time we face this choice, we're reminded that the binary rules supreme.

In July 2016, I was awarded my PhD from the Australian National University in Canberra. The inland capital is always arctic in winter, but that day it was snowing. We shivered in our thin gowns and floppy hats as we gathered outside the university hall. This was the culmination of ten years of tertiary study, including four years of doctoral research. By the time I crossed the stage to receive my degree, while my parents snapped blurry photographs in the audience, I'd been a student for almost twenty-three years straight. Now, aged twenty-eight, I was finally giving up my student concession card.

I was ecstatic, but not for the reasons you might expect. I didn't really care about the status of having a PhD. Nor was I especially fussed to be the first person in my family with this degree. Even the prospect of finally earning a salary didn't spark much joy. To my mind, the real benefit of having a PhD was gaining the right to call myself 'Doctor'—the gender-neutral title of my dreams. Finally, I'd escaped *Miss* and *Ms*. No more feminine titles, locking me into womanhood. Instead, for the rest of my life, no matter what happened, I could call myself 'Dr Rees'. Doctors were not women or men. They were just people who knew stuff. It was identity that denoted education rather than gender. As a doctor, I could be any gender or none.

That day, at the graduation, the vice-chancellor didn't just hand over my testamur. He also gave me a superpower: the ability to linguistically extricate myself from the gender binary.

Doctor is not the only gender-neutral title. Since the late 1970s, Mx has been used as a gender-neutral alternative to Mr or Ms. It's pronounced 'Mux', or thereabouts. The 'x' denotes a wildcard—the user can be male, female or something else. Today, Mx is recognised by the *Oxford English Dictionary* and a growing number of British institutions, including Royal Mail, the Royal Bank of Scotland and the bank HSBC. It's also listed in the *Merriam-Webster Dictionary*. Mx is less common in Australia, however. Outside of queer settings, it's almost never an available option.

The airline Qantas is a typical example. As of early 2021, the carrier's website offers an impressive range of titles—seventeen, in fact. On a Qantas flight, you're not limited to the basic options of Mr or Miss or Mrs or Ms. You can be a Captain, a Reverend or an Honourable. You can even be a Brigadier or Ambassador. Yet you can't simply be Mx. The nation's oldest and biggest airline won't allow its passengers to be gender neutral. Yes to Lord; no to Mx. What century are we living in?

This is repeated across Australia. In practice, most of the time, the Mxs of this world are forced to choose between Mr or Ms.

To its credit, La Trobe University—my workplace—is a rare outlier. Whenever staff or students receive an email from the university library, the automated greeting reads *Dear Mr/Ms/Mx [insert surname]*. A small thing, really. But that tiny institutional acknowledgment gives me a glow every time. I like to imagine it does the same for the university's gender-diverse students. *Dear Mx* the email reads. Only that's just the words. What it really says is: *we see you, you are welcome here.*

Unfortunately, however, La Trobe is the exception that proves the rule. Outside a few progressive institutions, Mx is rarely used.

The benefit of Dr is its ubiquity. Almost always, it's an option listed alongside Mr and Mrs. And unlike with Mx, everyone knows how to pronounce it and what it means. At present, in fact, Dr is the only gender-neutral title that's sufficiently commonplace to be practical. That's unfortunate, because doing a PhD or studying medicine (the other reason to use Dr) are each a privilege. It's a path that comes with a hefty price tag, in both time and money. Not every trans or non-binary person can make themselves a Doctor—and not everyone wants to, either.

I was one of the lucky few. White enough, affluent enough, nerdy enough to obtain a title that matched my gender. The PhD was a slog, but it was more than worth it for this glorious honorific.

In the days following my graduation, I changed my title to 'Dr' across the board. Banks, Medicare, frequent flyer accounts, utility bills. Ms and Miss were abandoned without a qualm. At that point, in 2016, I hadn't yet named myself as trans, but already I knew that feminine titles would never sit right. Ms or Miss had always been a burden, the cost of doing business in the world. Heavy, sticky words that clung to my skin, refusing to be shrugged off. Until now.

Soon after, I arrived home one evening, weary from a long day, to discover a letter in the mailbox. It was a generic official envelope, a slim, white rectangle with a plastic window for the address. The kind of envelope that stamps of impersonal bureaucracy, of bills and fines and obligations. The kind you might be tempted to leave unopened. But this envelope was different. It was addressed to 'Dr Rees'. My new name was now real, a live beast circulating in the world, making its way from computer databases and post offices into my shabby Chippendale terrace. There it was, printed in black and white.

My weariness evaporated. I broke out into an impromptu dance in the dark hallway of the share house, waving the envelope in the air. *Doctor, doctor, doctor!* I chanted to no one. Or, more importantly, not Miss or Ms. The letter could've been a traffic fine but still would've been worth framing. One for the pool room, you could say.

BLOOD WILL TELL

THE NEW WORDS BEGAN TO accumulate: *Yves, doctor, they. Anne* and *Ms* and *she* fell away like dead skin. By infinitesimal degrees, the mess of me re-solidified into a trans shape. But I couldn't renounce my womanness that easily. My biology had other ideas. It wouldn't let Anne go without a fight. Because it was only once I stopped calling myself a woman that I started bleeding like one.

Ever since I'd first started menstruating, aged thirteen, I'd gone years at a time without regular periods. First there was the anorexia-induced amenorrhea that lingered for much of my teens. Eating only a spoonful of muesli for breakfast, an apple for lunch, there was no energy to spare for ovulation. As I starved my body to carve away the newfound curves of womanhood, my monthly bleeding vanished in step. I'd reversed the clock back to childhood before my body betrayed me with blood, fat and hair.

For trans people, puberty and disordered eating often go hand-in-hand. According to a 2018 Australian study, two-thirds of transgender youth restrict food intake. One-fifth have a diagnosed eating disorder. For me, like many others, anorexia handed back some measure of control over a body that was hurtling in the wrong direction.

It wasn't a conscious decision to reject a female physiognomy. In a teenage universe shaped by Britney Spears and the Backstreet Boys, I didn't know it was possible to refuse the gender I was assigned at birth. All I knew was that I was terrified, and that a flat chest and no periods made me feel safe. Their disappearance was a triumph of will over biology.

In my twenties, when I swapped food restriction for compulsive exercise, my low body fat and high cortisol levels again halted my menstrual cycle. A series of half-marathons, a five-year passion for Bikram yoga, a recurring dalliance with HIIT, regular Pilates, occasional barre, the odd weights session, cycling to work, over-night bush walks, and endless laps of the pool kept me slim and contained, no longer heroin-chic skinny but still androgynous, with only the merest hint of hips and breasts. As little 'woman' as I could get away with.

Streamlined, angular, oestrogen under wraps. Just how I liked it.

On holiday in Bali, a massage therapist exclaimed that my torso was like a boy's.

'So thin, all muscle,' she cried, as I lay prone under the slow-moving fan. It wasn't intended as a compliment. But for me, this is what victory looked like. My body was right for a moment.

In photographs from that trip, I have brown stick-insect arms and a mad gleam in my eyes. My head looks too big for my torso.

My body was smart enough to know this was no time for repro-duction, and my periods all but vanished. With my mother, at the GP, I feigned concern. *Was this amenorrhea setting me up for osteo-porosis? What about my fertility?* But these expressions of worry were just another performance. I was, in truth, delighted. None of that messy woman business to worry about. I'd mastered my body again.

For years, I was on the pill. Every twenty-eight days I'd get a reliable 'pill period', but I never mistook it for the real thing. It was a simulacrum of fertility, nothing more. Like wearing make-up or donning heels, this pill-induced bleeding was a form of drag that helped me impersonate a woman in the world. Pop a tablet each morning; excrete some bloody matter each month: bingo, instant female.

Even during the rare months I did manage to bleed without a pharmaceutical nudge, it was never like the periods my friends described—whole days lost to cowering on the couch, armed with hot water bottles and daytime TV. For me, there was no cramping, no PMS, no leakage. Instead, there was a trickle of red liquid that lasted a day or two, a flow so half-hearted I barely required a tampon. I never knew when it was about to come, and it was scant inconvenience while it lasted. Light pads were more than sufficient. Even toilet paper would do.

This was not all that unusual. Female athletes often stop bleeding for the duration of their career. As the rise of HIIT and 'fitspo' led ordinary women to push their bodies to the limit, exercise-induced amenorrhea was becoming an epidemic. I read blog posts by gym-bunnies who hadn't menstruated for years. The photos showed toned, steely-eyed women with muscled arms, broad shoulders and sixpacks. I was content to be in their company. If I had to be female, this was the femininity for me.

Then my mother went through menopause and mourned the loss of her menstrual cycle.

'I miss feeling in sync with the moon,' she told me.

The monthly rhythm had connected her to nature. It had been a little remnant of wildness in her urban professional life. Without it, something was missing.

She spoke like I would understand, like we were two women discussing our common bond with the earth. But her words only revealed some unnameable gulf between us. I'd have gladly sped ahead to menopause tomorrow. Surely most women felt the same.

Or did they? Locked inside my own brain, it'd been easy to assume my horror of menstruation was 'normal', typical. Now, after witnessing Mum's menopausal grief, the doubts began. Maybe I was the outlier here.

I never once got pregnant, and half-suspected—half-hoped—I was infertile. I played along when my partner talked of marriage and children, but in truth could no more imagine bearing a child than travelling to Mars. The idea was fantastical.

Testing fate, I grew reckless with contraception, trusting that my reproductive system was down for the count. There was never once a positive on the pregnancy tests I'd buy in a panic and then unwrap, hands shaking, in the toilets at work. Every time, peeing on the stick would elicit only a single bar—the bar that told you the test was working. I'd exhale, then bury the evidence under layers of used paper towel, deep in the bathroom bin.

Clearly, I had a female reproductive system in name only.

Then, I told the world I was trans. I acquired a masculine name, discarded 'she/her' pronouns, threw out my dresses and heels, cropped my long hair, bound my wee breasts. Anne was history; Yves had landed.

Then, my period arrived with a vengeance. Suddenly, aged thirty-one, I was bleeding every thirty days—once again regular-as-clockwork, but this time *au naturel*. The flow was viscous, scarlet, and it lasted three days, four, five. After seventeen years with a malfunctioning menstrual cycle, I was suddenly a well-oiled bleeding machine. At the very moment I'd renounced my purported womanness, my female physiognomy woke up from its long hibernation.

My entire body went along for the ride. Sore breasts for ten days beforehand, the swollen tissue emitting a fresh sigh of pain with each step on the treadmill. My chest was the biggest it'd been since puberty. I needed new crop-tops to contain the alien mass. At its worst, running was impossible.

Then there was the persistent ache in my abdomen as the bleeding ran its course, pain that had me doubled over and eating Nurofen like lollies. In work meetings and classes, I struggled to concentrate, my body remade into a throbbing pelvis with limbs attached. One month, the pain was so bad I called in sick and spent the day contorted in bed, sweating under the hot water bottle prescribed to ease the cramps.

Then there was the tension, so much tension, that rose like a barometric chart each month until I was desperate for monsoonal relief. I would be antsy, angry, a bunch of raw nerve endings, looking for a fight. They were rarely hard to find. I'd snap at my mother, send irate texts to bewildered friends, glower at strangers on the street.

Here I was: Yves the trans person, who'd also morphed into a bad stereotype of the bleeding woman, of the body given over to womb, with a textbook case of the PMS I'd once believed was a patriarchal construct.

What the hell?

Perhaps it was because I was eating bread for the first time in years, munching thick-cut rye toast with a generous coating of peanut butter. (Or avocado—I am a millennial, after all.) Since coming out as trans, my weight hadn't shifted but I'd certainly relaxed my diet, no longer subsuming all my dysphoria into obsessive rumination about food.

Now that I understood the source of my fears of feminine fat— could name it as part of my transness—the fear itself lessened. I could (almost) eat a meal without analysing its nutritional content and calorific fallout. I was branching out beyond almonds, tofu and kale. After close to a decade in a low-carb semi-Paleo twilight zone of 'healthy' eating, I was recovering from my mortal fear of grains.

I even ate pasta occasionally. (Pizza was still beyond me.) Were these long-denied carbohydrates giving my body the fuel I needed to menstruate?

Or perhaps coming out as trans had triggered some deep psychic release, unlocking the tension that had bottled up the flow all those years. Even though my body remained biologically 'female', and the world still treated me as such, the act of announcing myself as transgender had brought unprecedented peace and ease. Now that Yves was in the world, the furies within were quietening down. The self-hatred and disgust abated.

Perhaps this psychological shift was the essential difference? Had I needed to accept myself as 'not-woman' before my body felt safe enough to perform this 'womanly' cycle?

Over coffee in a Flinders Lane cafe, an older friend confesses she didn't menstruate regularly until her forties, when a breakdown sent her into therapy and loosened her grip on control. Her body unclenched, she tells me, and the periods followed. A decade on, she still bleeds regularly each month.

Yes, I think, yes. The body knows the score. My stained under-pants may be the fruits of my own great unclenching.

But these are sour fruits, by no means welcome.

One small part of me is thrilled at this evidence of health. My body has finally deemed me healthy enough to make another human being, and I can't help read this as an endorsement of my transition. Here is a tick of approval from my biochemistry, a sign I'm on the right track. Even as my brain continues to second-guess itself—*are you really trans? How can you be sure?*—my body is giving me the thumbs up. *The war is over,* I can almost hear it trumpet. *Peace and safety are here. Now is the time to breathe easy, to grow life.*

But I recoil from the physical reality of menstruation. Each bath-room encounter with bloodied toilet paper sends me into a tailspin of dysphoria. At yoga, head down near my crotch in a wide-legged forward fold, I gag at the rich smell. At work, beneath my men's suits, my aching pelvis taunts me with the hard fact of biology.

Normally, during the long hours alone at my desk, I could almost forget about gender, but now each menstrual ache and whiff is a foghorn in my brain: *woman, woman, woman, woman—and don't you dare think otherwise.*

There's no escape from the bleeding and all it represents. Curled up in my apartment, a locked door between me and other humans, I am made into a feminine being.

At home each night, swollen breasts unbound and lolling free, my hands measure the engorged flesh, cupping fatty tissue in horrified fascination. I fantasise about slicing the strange lumps clean from my body, reclaiming the almost-flat chest long taken for granted. Each month I research surgeons who perform top surgery, only to be deterred by the six-month waiting lists. I need these invaders gone now.

Wine and whiskey become essential to help me forget, to escape my biology. Just one generous glass, alone on an empty stomach, to send me floating into the pink evening. Maybe add some nicotine, courtesy of my newly acquired vaping habit. Finish up with an episode of *The Crown*. Oblivion. I try not to notice how quickly the whiskey bottle empties.

Each morning, the truth returns. My body is going in the wrong direction, it has betrayed me.

If asked, I'd insist that womb does not equal woman, that men and non-binary people can menstruate and that women can have penises. I know trans men who've become pregnant, muscled blokes boasting a swollen belly beneath their beards. In the 2019 documentary *Seahorse*, the British journalist Freddy McConnell tracked his decision to bear a child. A trans man, McConnell had been on testosterone for years, and looked like any other bloke. Aged thirty, he took a break from HRT and become pregnant via IVF, remaking himself into 'the dad who gave birth'. His son, Jack, is now a healthy toddler.

McConnell's active womb does not invalidate his masculinity. My politics are built on rejecting simple equations between anatomy and identity. My periods, I know, do not make me any less trans, any less non-woman.

Why, then, are they a problem? I berate myself.

There is no escaping the wrongness that accompanies each cycle. I cannot argue myself into making peace with my female fertility. I yearn for the androgyny of amenorrhea, even as I have no wish to reprise the punitive disciplines that poisoned those years.

And so I bleed each month beneath my male underwear, leaking redness into the gaping crotch made to fit an absent cock.

There are tampons and Nurofen in the pocket of my blazer, a menstrual toolkit tucked snug into that handy interior pocket that's only granted to men.

~

Driving me to the airport after a weekend at his Queensland retirement idyll, Dad asks about being trans.

'What's it like?' he ventures, eyes straight ahead on the road.

I'm touched by the question. From the passenger seat, as we speed through the charred remains of recent bushfires, I tell him about my new-found menstrual cycle and the agonies it inspires. With this concrete example, I seek to bridge the gap between us, help him fathom the unfathomable.

'Well,' he responds, not missing a beat, 'you've probably only got about fourteen years until menopause. That's not long to wait.'

Fourteen years. One hundred and sixty-eight cycles. If the current bushfire season is any indication, we may not even have a habitable planet by then.

'You'll probably live to ninety,' Dad explains, 'so you'd have the second half of your life without periods.'

I stare out the window at the blackened eucalypts, trying to formulate a response.

Fourteen years is nothing in the life of the earth, nor in a ninety-year human life.

But in this moment, fourteen years seems an eternity, an impossible length of time to be spent in monthly dread of my own body. It's taken me thirty years to become Yves; I don't have much patience left. More to the point, the next fourteen years may be the only 'good' years we have left, before the changing climate makes war, disease and famine the norm. These are years to be cherished, too precious to be lost in waiting.

Six days later, I have my worst period yet, a raging storm in the pelvis and the heart. I spend a Saturday evening sobbing on my kitchen floor, before forcing myself onto the treadmill at 9 pm to run the hurt away. Running, always running, from pain.

The next week, I make an appointment with my GP.

'Can you do anything to make the periods go away?' I plead, after explaining my predicament.

'Well, we could try you on the pill,' she says. 'You could just skip the sugar pills to avoid bleeding. You could do that for a couple of months in a row.'

'Really? Would that work?' I ask, not daring to hope.

'It's worth trying.'

It does work, better than I thought possible. One little pill each morning, and the monthly hormonal storm disappears. No bleeding, no emotional seesaws, no swollen breasts. I'm taking a drug for women, pumping myself full of oestrogen, to make my body less woman, more me. It's counterintuitive but it does the job.

Evelyn, the drug is called. Evelyn to make me Yves. She's my little helper, the daily technician who keeps my oestrogen nice and steady.

The contraceptive pill is celebrated as an invention that, since the 1960s, has given women control over their bodies. They could now have sex without fear of pregnancy, enjoy orgasms without being tethered to marriage and motherhood. The pill set women free. The irony is that the same pill is now giving me freedom *from* womanhood. It's given me control over my body, but for entirely different reasons. There are no penises or semen involved in my liberation, only an absence of blood. Evelyn is flexible like that. A woman for all seasons.

Each month, I work through three weeks of white pills, then throw out the foil packet when only seven yellow sugar pills remain. Next, I open a fresh packet and begin again. The tampons sit unused. The whiskey stays in the bottle. I picture Evelyn in shoulder pads and permed hair, fingers expertly manicured with coral nail polish, an old-school girl boss who rolls up her sleeves and gets the job done. Even now, she's buzzing about my bloodstream, flattening out the peaks and troughs of a menstrual cycle until I can forget that I ever menstruated at all. Good old Evelyn; she keeps me on an even keel.

WOMEN'S SPACES

WHEN I WAS SMALL, I FELL asleep to stories of women's liberation. Each night in bed, my blonde head peeking out from the doona, Mum would lull me towards slumber by recounting her glory days in the Movement. In 1975, International Women's Year, she was a law student in the thick of Sydney's feminist activism. There were tales of bohemian Glebe share houses with wild parties, political theatre in the streets, and going down to the prison cells to expose domestic violence. Everyone wore overalls and made their own muesli. They were taking down the patriarchy and proving women could do anything. Mum conjured that world in my bedroom, her voice soft under the lamplight.

'Tell me another one, another story,' I'd plead, even though I'd heard them all before.

Feminism was my lullaby.

In 2020, the world of my bedtime stories was recreated on film. *Brazen Hussies* was a long-awaited documentary about the Women's Liberation Movement compiled from archival footage and present-day interviews by filmmaker Catherine Dwyer. After years of labour, working on a shoestring budget, the feminist doco was finally ready. My inbox was abuzz with the news.

I called Mum.

'We should watch the opening-night screening together,' I said. 'You'll probably know heaps of the women interviewed. All your old mates from the seventies!'

On opening night, we settled in on the couch at Mum's place, cocktails at the ready. Melbourne was still in lockdown, so we had to make do with an online screening and virtual celebrations.

Brazen Hussies begins its story in the mid-sixties when feminist consciousness began to reignite after the conservatism of the Menzies years. The film opens in 1965, when Merle Thornton and Rosalie Bogner chained themselves to the bar in the Regatta Hotel in Brisbane, protesting women's exclusion from public bars. Then there was the fight for equal pay, led by Zelda d'Aprano down in Melbourne, who chained herself to the Commonwealth Building. In January 1970, the first Women's Liberation meeting was held in Sydney, inspired by similar campaigns in Britain and the United States. By the early seventies, the Movement was in full swing nationwide.

At the heart of Women's Lib was consciousness-raising. The movement created dedicated spaces for women to gather and share stories of their oppression. The idea was to build solidarity among the sisterhood and help individual women feel less alone. *Brazen Hussies* featured rare footage of one group from Sydney. Long-haired women were packed into a room on Glebe Point Road, passionately dissecting sex roles between puffs of cigarette.

'Femininity is, I guess, a great pointless martyrdom,' concluded a woman on screen, her T-shirt printed with the raised fist of Women's Lib.

'I remember those!' Mum exclaims from the couch, almost toppling her drink in excitement. 'Consciousness-raising groups! They were incredible. We would talk for hours. It was so eye-opening.'

Back on screen, feminist Anne Summers reflects on the importance of consciousness-raising in women-only spaces.

'It involved learning to trust other women and that was something we'd never done before,' Summers explains.

The film makes it clear: this was a fight for women, by women, who were building a new world apart from male domination.

On the couch, I drink in the idealism of these youthful pioneers. Their refusal to follow the rules—their sheer brazenness—is more than a little exhilarating. My skin tingles at their raised voices, so deliciously unladylike.

But I also can't help wonder, where does the idea of 'women's liberation' leave someone like me—someone trans, someone not-woman, yet raised as a girl and very much a feminist? Would I have been welcomed into women's consciousness-raising spaces? Would I have *wanted* to be in such spaces?

Where does my consciousness belong?

As *Brazen Hussies* draws to a close, the film moves to the present, showing footage of a new generation of women's rights activists carrying on the fight.

Martha Ansara, a veteran libber now in her seventies, cheers them on.

'Women should always band together. Whenever you have the chance, band together!' Ansara urges, ending the film on a rousing note.

Afterwards, Mum is giddy, buzzing about the kitchen, drunk on memories of the sisterhood. She talks a mile a minute. The hair! The clothes! The roneoed newsletters! The excitement of it all.

'I still have a bunch of those old newsletters in the front room,' she says. 'You know I never throw anything out. I remember using the roneo machine to make copies. They had that distinctive purple ink, you know.'

I listen, slumped at the kitchen table. I'm eager to share in her joy, but instead find myself weighted down by something that resembles grief.

Mum, her head in the seventies, doesn't notice my silence. She keeps talking, tongue loosened by whiskey, while my heart knots with sadness.

I'd grown up thinking this was my fight, my lineage. These were meant to be my people: women fighting for women.

Women's Liberation was my inheritance, its principles imbibed with my mother's breastmilk. I've never not identified as a feminist. On rainy childhood afternoons, I'd pour over Mum's photo albums, studying faded photographs of theatrical troupes in costume and uni students cross-legged on campus lawns. On long walks by the beach, our talk circled and re-circled those years.

'What did your parents think?'

'Did you ever try out lesbianism?'

Soon, I knew all the stories, word-perfect.

As a teenager, I perused Mum's library of paperbacks about women and medicine, women and law—fierce tomes from the 1970s and 80s that mapped how female rebellion was punished by male institutions. For centuries, 'difficult' women had been locked up, declared insane. On the same shelves, I found Mum's research on domestic violence. The hand-typed pages told of women pissed on by their husbands, women driven to murder by decades of abuse. Too young, I learnt what men were capable of doing to us. I learnt the importance of fighting back.

In my twenties, I even did a PhD in women's history. For four years, I dedicated almost every waking hour to the Australian women who, a century ago, fought to have careers and travel the world. I hunted out the flotsam of their lives in archives from Canberra to Chicago, digging out long-forgotten letters and squinting over scrawled handwriting.

The story of women battling for emancipation was the story of my life.

But now? I'm not so sure. The idea of being in a 'sisterhood' makes me squirm. I'm sister to no one. I can't be a woman banding together with other women anymore. These days, Women's Liberation feels like a party that didn't invite people like me.

Yet feminism never stopped being my fight. Quite apart from my solidarity with victims of injustice, I've spent my life in a 'female' body. I know what it means to be afraid on deserted midnight streets, or have men speak over me in meetings. I know the taste of wolf-whistles, body shaming, unwanted hands. Aged only eleven, I was groomed on the internet by a man who threatened to rape me. I may be trans, yet I've experienced many common women's struggles, and the world still largely treats me as a woman.

Feminism will never not be relevant to me.

But how can I fit within its walls? Five decades on from Women's Lib, white liberal feminism—the kind of feminism we call 'mainstream'—remains oriented around the figure of 'woman'. Feminism is still imagined as a political project for women, by women, who gather in women-only spaces. At the March4Justice rally in Melbourne in March 2021, organisers urged the crowd to embrace 'sisterhood' and led a rendition of Helen Reddy's anthem 'I Am Woman'.

On the surface, this makes perfect sense. It's women, mostly, who get shat on by patriarchy. Sexual violence, family violence, unpaid or underpaid labour, workplace harassment, depression, eating disorders—these all mainly happen to women. Of course, this oppressed group deserves spaces free from the men who, by and large, perpetrate their oppression.

But this idea of feminism is built on the gender binary: woman vs. man. 'Woman' is imagined as a monolithic entity, oppressed by

an equally monolithic 'man'. This thinking has obvious limits. For
one, it sidelines or even ignores how race, class, religion, ability,
sexuality and age also shape our experience. Given the vast gulf
between, for example, a young poor Black straight woman and a rich
white lesbian, is it even meaningful to speak of 'women's' experience
at all? Both may be women, but their lives are miles apart.

Then there's the question of trans people. Where does all this
talk of man vs. woman leave people who don't fit within the gender
binary? What does it mean for people who are feminists, who've
experienced sexism and gendered violence, who aren't cisgender men,
but who aren't in fact cis women at all? Do we fit in the ecosystem
of women's spaces—and if not, where else?

That night, after watching the launch of *Brazen Hussies*, I can't
help feeling stranded out on the footpath, watching a glorious revolution that has no space for me. Not-women, not-men, we trans
people are outside, wandering the streets, trying to work out where
we belong.

↲

In an article from 2017, trans writer Cameron Awkward-Rich
unpacks the fraught relationship between trans and feminism. The
two have been at loggerheads for decades, with no sign of easy
resolution in sight.

What's the problem here? According to Awkward-Rich, the stumbling block is not trans women. To be sure, there is a loud minority
of so-called 'feminists' who take issue with transfeminine folk.
These 'trans-exclusionary radical feminists' (or TERFs), also known
as 'gender critical' feminists, employ a mix of separatist logic and
biological determinism to dismiss trans women as 'men in skirts'
who seek to infiltrate women's spaces. In their thinking, someone
born with a penis and raised a boy can never claim womanhood.
Anyone who seeks to do so must be a man with sinister intent.

This is a bigoted position that denies the reality of transness. It's discriminatory, unsupported by evidence, and exposes trans women to harm—making it hardly 'feminist' at all. If trans women aren't allowed to use female bathrooms, where are they supposed to go? To male bathrooms, where they risk verbal or physical abuse? Seeking to exclude trans women from women's spaces is both a cruel denial of their gender and a very real threat to their safety, as it reinforces stigma against trans women and exposes them to violence at the hands of cisgender men. Given that one in two trans people experience sexual violence or coercion, this is far from a trivial concern.

Many feminists, however, accept that trans women exist. For them, it's not so difficult to imagine a feminism that includes transfeminine people. All that's required is for the 'women' in Women's Liberation to encompass *all* women—both cis and trans. Sisterhood not cisterhood, so the saying goes.

If trans women can fit within feminism, what's the difficulty? According to Awkward-Rich, the real barrier to marrying trans and feminism is transmasculinity. This is because the transmasculine person, or the female-assigned not-woman, challenges the idea that feminism is for and about women. In other words, if a not-woman like me is part of feminism, if I inherited the torch from women's libbers, then is feminism really a *women's* project after all?

This challenge creates 'bafflement', Awkward-Rich suggests. Can feminism, formerly Women's Liberation, cease to have women at its centre? On face value, this idea seems laughable.

And so, we reach an impasse. A fully trans-inclusive feminism, one that incorporates transmasculinity, threatens to displace '*women* as the imagined subject of feminism'. That can be difficult to stomach. On the other hand, a trans-exclusive feminism, the TERF position, denies the very existence of trans people. It refuses to recognise trans women as women and denies them access to the safety of women's spaces.

Both alternatives face fierce resistance. The trans-inclusive position is accused of erasing women. The trans-exclusive line enacts
transphobia. The battlelines are drawn.

Soon, we're back where we began: how can trans and feminism
flourish together?

⌐

'I worry that I'm betraying feminism,' I confess.

It's 2018 and I've just started to admit my transness. I'm a hot
mess of fear and confusion, a terrified animal running in circles,
eyes glazed. On this Saturday afternoon, I'm at a deserted Carlton
cafe with Sam, the non-binary sibling of a close friend. Sam is
younger than me but older in trans time, having 'come out' several
years before. Now, they're a mentor of sorts. Over green tea, we
discuss the best places to buy gender-inclusive fashion and the
problem of finding non-binary swimwear.

Then I summon the courage to admit my fears. Pouring another
cup, Sam bears witness to my confession.

'I grew up thinking that feminism was about challenging
gender norms. It was about expanding what women can be and
do. If I announce myself as not-woman, haven't I just turned
my back on that project? Maybe this is all about internalised
misogyny. Has living under patriarchy brainwashed me into
wanting to be a man?'

Sam smiles. They've clearly heard all this before.

'That's a common fear,' they reassure me. 'Most female-assigned
people worry about that. But I don't reckon it's true. I mean, what
about all the cis women who live under patriarchy? They also inter-
nalise misogyny, but they still regard themselves as women. If it
was just about brainwashing, wouldn't they be brainwashed too?'

'That makes sense,' I concede.

'Plus,' Sam continues, 'being trans is hard, bloody hard. It's not a free pass to male privilege or a way to dodge the challenges of being a woman. If you think you're trans, you probably are.'

'But what about feminism?' I insist. 'Doesn't this make me a bad feminist?'

Sam snorts.

'No, of course not. What kind of feminism asks people to deny who they are?'

The following year, when I'm now fully out as trans, my friend Clare forwards me a flyer for a women's podcasting conference.

'Check this out! You should go,' she says.

'She Podcasts LIVE' promises 'women audio creators a chance to learn and experience community in an environment created JUST for them.' Over four days in Atlanta, Georgia, women podcasters could learn new skills, experience community and build relationships. Everything was 'women only'.

Clare and I had just launched our own podcast, and all things podcasting was my current obsession. Unlike Clare—who had decades of broadcasting experience—I was new to audio and eager to learn. So, in theory, 'She Podcasts LIVE' was a perfect fit. A tailor-made professional development opportunity. There was just one problem.

'Thanks, Clare,' I email back. 'Looks great! But I'm not sure it's the place for me. I'm not a woman, so I probably don't belong at a "women's conference".'

Clare seems surprised. Bemused, even. She knows I'm trans and embraces that fact. But she still appears to think that women's spaces are my spaces.

Why, then, am I so convinced otherwise?

No doubt, the organisers of 'She Podcasts LIVE' would be happy for me to attend. I haven't medically transitioned; I still live in the 'female' body I'd had from birth. As someone socialised as female, I'd experienced many of the same challenges as women podcasters.

Yet the thought of attending the conference induces nausea. I grow hot and agitated at the mere idea. It's not because I don't want to be around women. (I adore women—both cis and trans.) It's not because I think the event shouldn't exist. (Podcasting is a blokey world; it makes sense to support women creators.)

It's because to attend a 'women's' event as a not-woman would be tantamount to denying my own existence. To turn up at 'She Podcasts LIVE', or something similar, would mean saying to myself: *you're not really trans; you're still really a woman*. It would mean erasing myself. That might not sound like much, but when you've spent thirty years inside an ill-fitting box, the idea of squeezing yourself back into that container begins to feel like self-mutilation. You might just manage to get back inside, only to sacrifice a limb in the process.

I already knew what this erasure feels like because it happens all the time. Every single day, the world told me I was still really a woman. Sometimes, this was as small as being called 'ma'am' on the phone or 'she' in an email. Other times, it felt more pointed, harder to shrug off. The cumulative effect was exhausting. To be told, again and again, that I didn't exist, that my gender wasn't real, was like an unending sequence of paper cuts. Each cut is only a minor irritant, easy to ignore. But with enough cuts, over time, you're reduced into one big open wound, bleeding all over the place.

This was my daily reality, and I wasn't keen to expose myself more than necessary. So no, 'She Podcasts LIVE' wasn't for me. To attend would be an exercise in masochism—a four-day fiesta of gaslighting myself.

And it wasn't just about me. I didn't want to take up space better occupied by an *actual* woman, cis or trans. If we were going to have

women's spaces, it seemed a no-brainer that women themselves
should be given priority access.

Then there was the broader symbolism. If I went along to 'She
Podcasts LIVE' as a not-woman, I wasn't just erasing my own transness, I was also casting doubt on the reality of the whole TGD
community. It was one thing to undermine myself; it was quite
another to deny the existence of non-binary kids struggling to be
recognised as real. I was determined to make things easier for the
people who came after me. That would only happen if we refused
to be erased.

⌐

Trans and *women* and *feminism*—how to make them reconcile?
How to know where I belong? I wrestle with these ideas until I'm
exhausted, chasing thoughts into the corners of my mind, trying
to force my transness and my feminism to embrace each other like
pieces of a jigsaw puzzle.

'What about biological essentialism?' Mum asks, one hot summer
evening after a glass of wine. 'When I was young, feminism was
meant to be about rejecting biological essentialism—rejecting the
idea that women were inherently weaker than men. Feminism was
about showing that women could do anything men could do. But
doesn't being trans, and wanting to change your body, mean you
think there is some innate difference between men and women?'

My mind is clouded by the wine, and I struggle to arrange my
thoughts.

'No, no, they're not the same,' I manage. 'Biological essentialism
is sexist science, an idea used to justify oppression of women. It's
a weapon of patriarchy. But transness is embodied knowledge, it's
something you just know. And it's a matter of individual authenticity
and freedom—unlike biological essentialism, which makes sweeping
claims about entire groups of people.'

Mum is unconvinced. 'But surely your sense of being not-woman implies that there is a fixed thing called "woman". Isn't that biological essentialism?'

Back and forth we go, for hours at the kitchen table, a tennis match of intellects. As the night thickens, the cavoodle naps to the melody of our raised voices. Our thoughts grow muddled by the labyrinth of bodies, sex, gender, society. How do they all fit together? Which is chicken and which is egg? Mum and I are both people who live in our heads. Together, we grow determined to solve the conundrum, once and for all. Analysis, debate, language—these are the tools we trust to make the world known. But the more we push for clarity, the more insight recedes.

'I think we should call it a night,' I concede, eventually. 'We're going round in circles.'

Back home, I collapse on the carpet, defeated in my attempts to wrestle the ideas into submission, no wiser for the hours of talk—but still no less trans, no less not-woman. Is this what it all comes down to? There are just things the body knows, things that defy reason. Things irreducible to language. I can't argue myself out of feeling trans, no more than anyone can pray the gay away.

We, all of us, know things about ourselves difficult or impossible to explain. How do *you* know you're a woman or man or something else? How do you know you're attracted to men or women or both? How do you know you prefer chocolate to vanilla, apples to bananas? Every single human has self-knowledge impossible to prove in a court of law, which no one else is qualified to refute. We are all the experts on our own experience. It's just that those with 'normal' identities—straight people, cis people, white people—aren't required to justify themselves to the world.

There is a danger in ignoring the body. It knows things, deep in the guts. Things we can't quite explain. But why do we always need to explain everything? Perhaps some things can just be as they are.

↗

White liberal feminism has a long history of excluding or even harming other oppressed groups. In Australia, the suffragists who fought for female voting rights also threw Indigenous women (and men) under the bus. *The Commonwealth Franchise Act* (1902) made Australia the first nation to give full political rights to white women, but that same legislation also disenfranchised Indigenous Australians. White women's freedom came at the cost of First Nations subordination.

This foundational dynamic has proved hard to dislodge. Despite efforts to reckon with its exclusionary origins, mainstream feminism continues to be critiqued as a movement for affluent white women that overlooks the interests of Indigenous, migrant, queer, poor and disabled communities.

Viewed against this backdrop, feminism's vexed relationship with transness becomes less surprising. Feminism struggles to reckon with many axes of difference and oppression; why should its relationship with transness be any different? Perhaps the problem was much bigger than trans/feminism dynamics; perhaps the real problem was the limited horizons of the political project that we call 'feminism'. Perhaps it was the 'women's movement' that needed to change.

I was far from the only one grappling with these questions. Feminist organisations, conscious of the growth of trans communities, developed language that aimed to acknowledge and welcome not-women like me. The phrase 'women and non-binary people' began to circulate. Within months, it was everywhere. Poetry nights, prizes, festivals, conferences, support groups, research studies: all former women-only domains now identified their constituency as 'women and non-binary people' or 'women and gender-diverse people'. Even the Stella Prize, Australia's premier award for women's writing, expanded its eligibility requirements to include non-binary people.

Had feminism, once the preserve of women, thrown open its doors to not-women and ushered us into the party? Perhaps we were all one happy family now.

This new language seemed inclusive, a gesture of recognition and welcome. Unlike TERFs, defined by hostility to trans identities, this 'women and non-binary' feminism appeared to embrace trans folks with open arms. *Come one, come all! All ye not-men can shelter here.*

Problem solved. Or so it appeared.

But something felt wrong. I did not want to attend the 'women and non-binary' slam poetry night. And not because of the slam poetry.

It was because 'woman' was still the master category. 'Women and non-binary' or 'women and gender-diverse' collapsed transness into womanness. Instead of recognising non-binary as a distinct gender, this language implies that trans identities are 'woman adjacent'. Almost woman, but not quite. Woman enough, however, to partake in a women's event.

'Effectively, these groups feel like women 2.0 or women* or women+,' noted critic Jinghua Qian in a 2020 essay published by the Feminist Writers Festival. 'Women—which is to say cis women—and people with footnotes. Women plus women-lite. After all these are feminist spaces converted from (cis-centric) women's spaces, and they show their bones.'

Women+ is not meaningful trans inclusion. The 'women and non-binary' slam poetry event still asked me to do trans within the woman umbrella—which, at its core, was just another form of erasure.

There's also the question of *which* non-binary people are welcome. Non-binary identity can encompass both those assigned female at birth (AFAB) and those assigned male at birth (AMAB). They are equally non-binary. AMAB non-binary people may still be perceived as male, just as I'm still perceived as a woman. Both assumptions are incorrect. We're not on opposite sides of the gender binary; in fact, we share a gender: non-binary.

Out in the world, however, AMAB and AFAB non-binary people are treated very differently. As Qian notes, the phrase 'women and non-binary' tends, in practice, to only encompass non-binary folk capable of being perceived as women.

'As a nonbinary person who is not a woman yet easily accepted as one,' Qian explains, 'my presence in feminist and women's spaces is often framed as part of a positive shift towards greater trans inclusion: *oh, trans people, we have those!* But I know the hospitality I receive is frequently also a form of trans erasure—an insistence on seeing us as the genders we were assigned.'

An insistence on seeing us as the genders we were assigned. This, it seems, is the rub. Women's spaces can welcome non-binary people like Qian and me because we were assigned female at birth and are still fundamentally viewed as women. The same welcome is not, by and large, extended to AMAB trans folk—people who may know themselves to be women or non-binary but whose appearance may still lead the world to deem them 'men'.

We're all reduced to the genders we were given, not the genders we are. Everyone is denied their truth. And only some trans people are welcomed. 'The overrepresentation of AFAB non-women in these spaces can reinforce the exclusion and marginalisation of AMAB people,' Qian concludes.

Upon interrogation, then, this new inclusive language hasn't actually changed all that much. Although well-intentioned, the phrase 'women and non-binary' is rhetorical wokeness that subsumes AFAB transness into womanness, and sidesteps AMAB transness altogether. It is a phrase that paints new words onto old assumptions.

What we need instead is to confront hard questions about who and what feminism is actually for. We need to go back to basics and reconsider our fundamental mission.

When we say we want or need a 'women's space', what exactly do we mean? Cis women only? All women—cis and trans? Everyone who was assigned female at birth? Or everyone who is not a cisgender man?

The answer depends on the purpose of the gathering. Perhaps the purpose is to investigate experiences of menstruation—then it may make sense to focus on bodies born with uteruses, women and otherwise. Or perhaps the goal is to create a safe space for people marginalised under patriarchy—then surely everyone apart from cisgender men should be welcome. (Because lord knows that AMAB trans folk face misogyny no less than cisgender women.)

But what if the goal is to gather people opposed to patriarchy? In that case, surely all genders should be welcome, because all genders—including cisgender men—are victims of patriarchy and can be invested in its downfall.

There's no one right way to make feminist spaces. Each space has its own needs and objectives. There can never be a one-size-fits-all approach. This is all a work in progress, evolving at a rapid clip. Everyone is learning and making mistakes. We're all figuring it out together.

But the core point is this: rather than slapping 'non-binary' on an existing framework, we'd do better to ask some basic questions. Questions like: what exactly do we want to achieve in this space? Who needs to be here for that to happen?

The answers to these questions invite new language. After all, 'everyone except cis men' or 'everyone born with a uterus' might be more accurate than 'women', but they don't exactly roll off the tongue. New terminology would be welcome. How could language be used to upend the way we imagine feminist politics and gender categories beyond the stale old binary of women and men?

'Let's invent new languages out of old words,' writes trans poet Alex Gallagher.

Now that is a feminist project I could get behind.

⌣

These days, I don't do much women's history. My PhD on Australian career women was meant to become a book but it languished, unfinished, for years. Instead of revising the manuscript, I invented other work for myself, new projects that didn't have 'women' at their centre. I wrote economic history, migration history—anything, really, that would allow me to avoid thinking about the idea of 'woman' and what it meant for me.

Friends and colleagues were bemused.

'When is your book coming out?'

'Is the book done yet?'

'You have the contract, just finish it!'

Yet somehow, I couldn't. I was a person who prided themselves on seeing things through, not giving up, fighting doggedly to the finish line. But still I spent years circling around my 'women's history' book, that rotting corpse of my old certainties. I didn't know how to write women's history anymore because I no longer understood my own relationship to that concept. Who were women, even? Was their history still my history? Why did 'women's history' have no trans women in its pages?

On bad days, I couldn't even use the term 'women' without wincing at its cruel exclusions and baggage of binary thinking. Language was refusing its old comforts.

Women's history was my inheritance, or so I thought—and that had been central to its appeal. All those sepia-toned women, surviving the forces weighted against them, living lives large and small, waiting to be remembered by another woman in the future. Patriarchy had deprived us of much but hadn't managed to steal this treasure. Now, however, I'd been disinherited—or had disinherited myself.

It was too painful to consider, so I didn't. My book remained in the form of Word drafts and manila folders, collecting dust.

I wrote instead about male economists, stiff in their starched suits. The shame of not finishing the book was preferable to the grief of feeling severed from the lineage of women. I continued to love them, wanted them to love me, but couldn't work out how we fit together.

Nonetheless, I still keep a photo of my great-grandmother on my desk.

Muriel Palmer was an English showgirl, a free spirit who did vaudeville with Charlie Chaplin. She hooked up with my great-grandfather while on tour in Sydney in the roaring twenties. He was a bookie, the black sheep of a respectable family, who dabbled in drugs and petty crime. She got pregnant, they married, but the life of wife and mother held little appeal. Muriel returned to London, where further adventures awaited. There was a Spanish acrobat, two more kids, countless late nights, infinite cigarettes— and always, always her career. Well into her sixties, Muriel remained a working girl, entertaining the punters on a transatlantic cruise ship. (Meanwhile, my grandmother, Muriel's daughter, was raised by an aunt in Melbourne, and never knew her mother.)

Now, Muriel watches me work each day. She's a guardian angel frozen in black and white, eyes quizzical and lips curled in wry amusement. Her whole face is a provocation. Chin tilted, a hint of a dimple. The photo is undated but captures the wonderful insolence of youth. This Muriel is no more than thirty, at the outside. She sports a floppy velvet hat and beaded tunic—one of her theatrical costumes, no doubt. Here is a woman who lives by nobody's rules. Most naysayers, she'd eat them for breakfast.

Muriel died long before I was born, but our shared ancestry leaches from the photograph. Something about the fierce gaze, the wilful chin. If I stare hard enough, I'm convinced we have the same eyes.

For all my discomfort with women's history, Muriel has never discomfited me. She's part of me and the seeds of me are embedded in her. She's someone who also broke the rules of womanhood.

Maybe, if she were alive today, she would have named herself not-woman as well. I might be projecting, but I like to think she has a boyish vibe. In her impish costume, she could be Puck from *A Midsummer Night's Dream*.

Muriel keeps hope alive that I'll return to women's history as a not-woman, some day. Maybe I'll claim back my inheritance, layer fresh bonds over frayed ties, reimagine myself within a lineage of feminists of many different genders. And maybe, as is well overdue, I'll question whether we still need 'women's history' or whether—as with women's spaces—we'd do better to rethink our categories altogether. After all, a trans-inclusive feminism demands a trans-inclusive feminist history. Women's Liberation birthed the idea of 'women's history'; the feminism of the 2020s will doubtless require a new way of looking at the past—one that writes trans women and gender non-conforming people into the story.

⌁

'I've been thinking about our conversation,' Mum announces on the phone. 'The conversation about transness and feminism.'

'Really? And what did you decide?' I ask, holding the phone to my ear as I walk down a tree-lined street.

'I've decided that transness isn't at odds with feminism. It's actually an extension of the Women's Liberation we practiced in the seventies. That feminism was about rejecting social roles based on biological sex, and that's basically the same as what trans people are doing.'

'So you're saying that feminists and trans people share the idea that genitals are not destiny?'

'Yes, but trans people are taking it a step further. Women's Lib was focused on freeing women from social roles based on biological sex, but trans people are doing it for *all* genders. It's a whole new frontier!'

Her voice is triumphant, as though she's solved a thorny maths problem. And in a sense, she has. She's shown me how my feminist origins and trans present can fit together.

A smile stretches over my face, as the two halves of myself lock into place, complementary at last. After we hang up, I feel whole, no longer scattered into conflicting parts. I continue down the street, a new swagger in my gait. Above, honeyed light trickles through the plane trees.

Out in the world, feminism and transness will continue to jostle and snipe, as both are broad churches that attract a great diversity of views. But in my life, in my own personal lineage, the two have recognised each other as parent and child—both part of the great tradition of liberation politics. My mother was a Libber, I am a trans person, but beneath those labels we're fighting the same fight. Mum is engaging in gender resistance within the binary, insisting that women can do and be anything. I'm challenging the binary altogether, asking why we're limited to man and woman in the first place. These aren't antithetical struggles, but different fronts of the same battle.

As non-binary philosopher Robin Dembroff puts it, 'the more sledgehammers we take to gender categories, the better. Some prefer to make these categories gooey on the inside; I prefer to torch them. There's enough room for all at the barbecue.'

In our different ways, we're all drawing weapons against the gender rules that keep us bound and afraid.

WHAT'S SEX GOT TO DO WITH IT?

I WEPT THE DAY ELLIOT PAGE was born. On 1 December 2020, the celebrated Hollywood actor, made famous by teen pregnancy drama *Juno* (2007), posted a statement on social media announcing he was transgender. He introduced his new name, Elliot, and new pronouns, he/they. 'I feel lucky to be writing this. To be here. To have arrived in this place in my life,' Page wrote. 'I can't begin to express how remarkable it feels to finally love who I am enough to pursue my authentic self.'

The internet erupted in congratulations. Late in a dire plague year, here—finally—was something to celebrate. We cheered for Page's self-acceptance and bravery, for the new future he'd chosen for himself. But we also cheered for what this moment might mean for trans people worldwide. With a beloved celebrity now one of us, hopefully, surely, transness would lose some of its stigma. We had a new champion, a new poster boy for the community.

Fellow celebrities from Miley Cyrus to Mia Farrow to Ellen DeGeneres rushed to proclaim their support. Queer websites lost their minds. On Twitter, Page's announcement attracted 1.7 million likes.

At home in Melbourne, I read and re-read Page's statement, skin tingling, blinking back tears each time.

'I love that I am trans,' Page told the world.

To see those words proclaimed by a Hollywood star, at a time when trans people were demonised daily, when my own transness remained tinged by shame, was a much-needed blast of sunshine. I hadn't realised how stiff and cold I'd become until that sudden warmth thawed my limbs. I moved freer, breathed easier, after reading Page's words.

2020 wasn't all bad, after all.

Not everyone saw it that way. In certain (importantly, not all) lesbian circles, an alternative narrative was circulating. For them, Page's coming out was a moment of loss rather than celebration. Page, who was married to a woman and had formerly identified as lesbian, was depicted as having abandoned the lesbian community to become a straight man. His newly acknowledged transness was imagined in deficit terms, as a blow to a dwindling club of gay women. It was as though team trans had poached a star player from team lesbian.

This response was disheartening, yet far from surprising. The idea that transmasculinity and lesbianism are competing identities is rife, both within and without LGBTQIA+ circles.

'Where have all the butch lesbians gone? They've all become trans men,' is a refrain so ubiquitous it's easy to assume it must be true.

Transmasc is just a new word for butch, so the story goes. *Trans men are dykes who've betrayed the sisterhood,* we're told. *Trans is nothing more than a fashion, a way for lesbians to assume the privileges of straight men.*

Transmasc and lesbian: locked in a zero-sum battle, competing for a limited pool of adherents.

Except it's not like that at all.

⤵

Like Page, I too named myself lesbian for a time. It was 2016, I'd just moved to Sydney, fresh from a five-year heterosexual relationship fast barrelling towards marriage. The relationship had met its demise because imagining a future as a wife and mother felt like my own death. In the final months with my partner, I wrote short stories about women fleeing straight coupledom. Out jogging with him, I'd find myself running in the opposite direction from my beloved. Sometimes, I screamed in bathrooms. My subconscious was telling me something.

If I didn't want to be with a man, even a man I loved, I must be gay—or so I reasoned. Obvious, problem solved. And so here I was in Sydney's fast-gentrifying Chippendale, a stone's throw from the queer heartland of Newtown, ready to become an Official Inner-West Lesbian, *par excellence*.

Except I wasn't very good at it. I was terrible, in fact. I tried hard, truly I did. I downloaded dating apps and swiped right on women with Gorman outfits and underpaid jobs in the arts. I joined lesbian support groups and book clubs, sitting for hours on stained couches in queer community spaces. I borrowed *Rubyfruit Jungle* from the library and watched *The L Word* on my laptop. I got my first tattoo. I bought a leather jacket from the Glebe Salvos, then acquired a bobbed haircut my gay housemate described as 'signature nineties lesbian'. Most days, I promenaded up and down King Street, staring at the women couples holding hands or eating vegan Thai, silently willing them to disclose their secrets.

'How does one *be* a lesbian?' I asked a friend, when, after several months, nothing seemed to be working.

'Well, in my experience,' she explained, 'short nails are very important.'

I looked down. I had those already—nails clipped and devoid of polish. What more did I need to do?

More study was clearly in order. I buckled down on reading the back catalogue of *Autostraddle*, the world's premier lesbian website.

What I'd failed to realise was that, unlike running a marathon or doing a PhD, lesbianism was not something you could achieve through hard graft and grim determination. Unfortunately, I couldn't read my way into being a lesbian. It was something you had to do. And therein lay the problem: I didn't, in truth, want to do the doing.

I arranged coffee dates with women, then bailed at the last minute. I fled the lesbian meetings before anyone could say hello. I skipped Mardi Gras. Whenever I suspected a woman might be flirting with me, I immediately changed the topic to Donald Trump or Brexit.

'You like my outfit, hey? That reminds me of the resurgence of xenophobia and white nationalism in the UK. What do you think of Jeremy Corbyn?'

I could consume lesbian culture until the cows came home, but actually dating or kissing or fucking a woman as a woman—now that was a bridge too far.

The problem wasn't homophobia, external or internalised. I was as supported in my lesbianism as you could possibly be. Gay friends, gay colleagues, gay neighbourhood—I had it all. My life was one big rainbow flag. Even my normally reticent father embraced me when I announced my new-found homosexuality during a visit to Queensland.

'I'm so proud of you,' he whispered into my hair, voice thick with emotion.

If anything, it felt like the world was rooting for me to be a lesbian.

Except, I wasn't. Not really. The concept just didn't sit right. It was an outfit I admired on the hanger, but which scratched and itched as soon as I tried it on. I kept adjusting the seams, fiddling with the collar—as though enough fine-tuning would make it fit. I tried for a year, almost two, to no avail.

Women were beautiful, women were smart, women had emotional intelligence and promised to be better partners than most men. Research suggested that lesbian couples had superior sex.

I loved the idea in theory. My mind conjured a lesbian future in technicolour detail: we'd adopt a pet greyhound, go hiking, then discuss our feelings over nips of whiskey by the campfire. We'd read Kate Tempest aloud, cook vegan feasts for our chosen queer family. She'd grow heirloom tomatoes and tend the compost while I pickled vegetables in the kitchen. We'd even make our own kombucha, spiced with ginger. I had it all mapped out.

And yet I just couldn't, somehow, bring myself to do 'lesbian' in the sense that it involved two women together.

Then, in 2018, transmasculinity entered my universe. Everything immediately made more sense. From the first, the idea of transness fit me like a glove, resting snug against my skin where lesbianism had always sat askew. It was the difference between cheap polyester, several sizes too small, and a tailor-made suit of the softest cashmere.

I didn't belong in the world of straight couples, that much was correct. As I'd first intimated back in 2016, I was queer as they come.

But that didn't make me a lesbian. My difference was a matter of gender more than sexuality. The reason that the idea of being a bride filled me with horror wasn't the prospect of wedding a groom; it was the fact of *being* a bride. Straight coupledom was my idea of slow death because of the femininity it imposed upon me, not because of the masculinity of my partner. Swapping out a male partner for a female one wasn't the answer, so long as I remained female. The problem wasn't who I went to bed *with*, it was who I went to bed *as*. Lesbianism didn't work out because it still required me to be a woman. It was womanness I cringed from, not having sex with men.

This, then, is the rub: transmasculinity is not simply a new word for butch lesbian, because the two describe different phenomena. The former is about gender; the latter, sexuality. It's who you are versus who you desire. It's apples and oranges.

That's not to say there's no slippage between the two identities. It's no accident that butch and transmasc are assumed to be synonyms; in practice, the two often get attached to the same individuals. Many people who are transmasculine (their gender) are primarily or exclusively attracted to women (their sexuality). Like Elliot Page, they may have lived as lesbians at some point, prior to coming out as trans. There are also female-attracted people with masculine presentation who continue to identify as women, butch or otherwise—and this 'female masculinity' is just as real and legitimate as transmasculinity.

The erroneous conflation of transmasculinity and lesbianism also has deep roots in history. For much of the twentieth century, same-sex attraction and gender non-conformity were largely conflated, understood as twin symptoms of the same deviance. A male-assigned person in a dress? Must be a homosexual. A female-assigned youth sporting a three-piece suit? A lesbian, obviously. Gender deviance equalled homo. Male effeminacy, female masculinity, same-sex desire—all were lumped together in one big soup called 'gay'.

This thinking stemmed from the sexological concept of inversion. From the late 1800s, sexologists like Havelock Ellis and Richard von Krafft-Ebing theorised that same-sex attraction represented the reversal (or inversion) of gender traits. A homosexual was an invert—a woman or man who'd been 'born in the wrong body' and now had all their desires upside-down. As Krafft-Ebing put it, female inversion was 'the masculine soul, heaving in the female bosom'. This 'masculine soul' inspired the female invert to desire women and adopt a mannish persona. Her gender and sexuality were both that of a heterosexual man. In other words, there were no true homosexuals, just straight people born in the wrong body.

Sexual inversion was soon superseded in medical thinking, but it had a long shadow in mainstream culture—popularised by books such as *The Well of Loneliness* (1928), which fused same-sex desires and gender variance in the popular imagination. As a result, gender-variant people were often funnelled towards homosexual identification. Female masculinity was deemed a sign of lesbianism.

Among masculine female-assigned people who came of age in the 1960s or 70s, concepts like 'butch lesbian' were hence the obvious place to land. By this time, 'transsexuality' was recognised as a category distinct from homosexuality, but it was almost exclusively associated with trans women. Until the 1980s, there was little recognition that female-assigned people could even be trans.

More recently, as concepts like non-binary and transmasculinity entered the mainstream, some baby boomers who started off as lesbians have adopted trans identities. It wasn't that they'd abandoned lesbianism to join manhood; it was that they'd encountered new concepts and words that proved a better fit.

Leslie Feinberg, born in 1949, was raised a girl but preferred short hair and boys' clothes from a young age. 'Is that a boy or a girl?' was the question that dogged their childhood. There was no language in the 1950s to make sense of their difference. Feinberg began their queer life as a working-class butch in the 1960s, dodging police raids of drag bars in upstate New York. Later, they encountered the concept of 'sex-reassignment'. They had a breast reduction, took testosterone, and began living as a man. By the 1990s, Feinberg had evolved again, now locating themselves between genders, neither male nor female.

'I've been called a he-she, butch, bulldagger, cross-dresser, passing woman, female-to-male transvestite, and drag king. The word I prefer to describe myself is *transgender*,' Feinberg explained in 1996. As language evolved, so too did Feinberg's identifications. By 2006, Feinberg termed themselves a 'transgender lesbian'. When they died in 2014, aged sixty-five, Feinberg was known as a pioneer of 'transgender liberation'.

Eileen Myles followed a similar trajectory. Myles, born in Massachusetts in 1949, came to prominence as the great lesbian poet of their generation. They were a woman who wore button-up shirts and loved cunt, so they were a lesbian. A dyke. End of story. For boomers, Myles was the ultimate butch poster girl. Myles's book *Chelsea Girls* (1994), about East Village life in the 1970s and 80s, was *On the Road* for gay women. Then, in the 2010s, aged in their sixties, Myles felt an affinity with the proliferation of trans identities. They began to call themselves trans and adopted they/them pronouns.

'I feel like I am very trans-identified. To some extent, I felt I did, in fact, identify as a man in a women's body,' Myles reflected in 2018.

Yet they hadn't renounced lesbianism. 'I am a gender queer dyke,' Myles tweeted in 2016. Myles told journalists that they contain multitudes. 'I feel male, and I feel female. I feel queer. I feel trans. I feel I'm a dyke, I'm a lesbian. I feel like a fag sometimes,' they explained.

Would I have stuck with lesbian, despite the difficulties, if I hadn't found transmasculinity? Probably. Lesbian sat all askew, it itched at the armpits, but at least it allowed me to articulate my queerness. It gave a framework, however imperfect, to explain that I wasn't like the other girls. It was a step in the right direction.

At the end of the day, these are all just words, imperfect proxies for selves that can never be captured by something so clumsy as language.

'All is heuristic!' Anne Boyer reminds us. 'We make shapes in our mind to understand the world, and even then, we never do.'

Some shapes fit better than others. They all remain shapes, however—abstractions conjured by neurons. These abstractions help us navigate the world yet should never be mistaken for the world itself. 'The map is not the territory,' as Polish philosopher Alfred Korzybski puts it.

We are so much more than the shapes we choose to cluster beneath. We are all irreducible to labels.

⤸

These days, I feel more like a gay man than a butch lesbian. The butch tropes of work boots, craft beer, trucker hats and Bunnings expeditions have never been my thing. I couldn't use a wrench to save my life. What even is a wrench?

If I had a magic wand, I'd remake myself as a twink—a slim-hipped boy-man, with a puckish sparkle and bony wrists. Faggotry as art form.

Whatever the reason, *gay* floods me with a sense of familiarity, of rightness, that I never found in lesbianism. Many of my closest friends are gay men. When we're together, drinking Riesling or cold brew, talking books or politics, I fall into thinking I'm one of them. It feels like home.

Every March, when the Melbourne Queer Film Festival rolls around, the films that draw me are always those about love between men. European dramas about AIDS and nightclubs and activism, the camera lingering on stubbled chins and naked chests. Cigarettes and leather jackets. Monosyllabic conversation. Heartbreak, death. I rock up to the cinema at Fed Square with my gay friend Clancy, a lone vagina among a sea of men holding hands. These are my people.

Does this mean I want to have sex with men, as a masculine person? Maybe. Sometimes. I wouldn't be the only one. There are certainly gay transmasculine people—just as there are straight, bisexual, pansexual, demisexual and asexual trans people. Transgender people can be any sexual orientation.

The pioneer of gay transmasculinity was Lou Sullivan, a trans man from the United States who proudly took male lovers and identified as homosexual. His diaries, published in 2019 as *We Both Laughed in Pleasure*, document his long-term sense of himself as a gay man. As a youth in the 1960s, while still living as a woman in Milwaukee, Sullivan told his diary that 'I want to be a beautiful man making love to another beautiful man'. In 1975, aged twenty-four, he moved to the gay mecca of San Francisco. There, Sullivan went about in men's suits and leather jackets, leading him to be regularly mistaken for a lesbian. But despite his 'butch' appearance, Sullivan had no sexual interest in women. 'I consider myself a male homosexual,' he told acquaintances.

In the late 1970s, Sullivan sought medical transition, but found that doctors were reluctant to prescribe testosterone because his sexuality was at odds with their idea of a trans man (or 'transsexual', as they were then known). Female-to-male 'transsexuals' like Sullivan were meant to be attracted to women—former lesbians who remade themselves as straight men. Sullivan didn't fit this narrow script. If he loved men, why not simply live as a straight woman? Sullivan pushed back, questioning the doctors' logic. Homosexuality was no longer classified as a mental disorder, so why was it 'mental' for him to want to live as a gay man? In 1979, Sullivan finally secured hormone replacement therapy and top surgery, acquiring the male body he'd long craved.

During the 1980s, Sullivan was a fixture of gay San Francisco, renowned as a leading trans activist and enthusiastic lover of men. He died in 1991, aged only thirty-nine, of AIDS. This was the great irony of his life: Sullivan was denied the right to live as a gay man, yet he nonetheless died as one. By the time of his death, Sullivan had redefined what transmasculinity could be. His attraction to men demonstrated that trans men were not butch lesbians by another name; rather, they were masculine people whose sexual orientation could take many forms. Their gender and their sexuality were two separate things.

Sullivan was attracted to men both before and after his gender transition. His sense of himself as a gay man was lifelong. For some trans people, however, their sexual orientation changes alongside their gender. Transmasculine people who'd formerly dated women may become attracted to men for the first time. This phenomenon is featured in the 2019 reboot of *Tales of the City*, the miniseries about queer San Francisco based on the novels of Armistead Maupin. In the opening episodes, Jake Rodriguez, a young Latinx trans man, experiences a sudden attraction towards men after years of dating women.

'I think I might be into guys,' he confesses to his girlfriend Margot.

With Margot's permission, Jake experiments with 'kissing boys'. He joins Grindr, the gay hook-up app, and starts sleeping with Flaco, a cisgender man.

By the season finale, Jake acknowledges that his sexuality has fundamentally shifted.

'I'm gay,' he admits to Margot, now his ex. 'It's so crazy, I feel like I've spent the majority of my life coming out. I'm lesbian, I'm trans, I'm gay.'

Formerly a lesbian woman, Jake is now a gay man.

Quite possibly, I could follow in Jake's footsteps. Lesbian, trans, gay.

It wouldn't be easy, though. Gay male communities are notoriously transphobic. A Canadian research study, published in 2018, found that only one in ten cis gay men would consider dating a trans person. On apps like Grindr, trans users report widespread bigotry. Invasive questions are par for the course.

'Can't you people go ruin another app?'

'Do you have a vagina?'

'What are you doing here?'

'You must be really fucked in the head.'

'You still look like a girl.'

These are all messages received by trans Grindr users. The users recite them in a 2018 video, made as part of the Kindr Grindr campaign—an attempt to purge transphobia and racism from the app. As each individual recites the hateful words directed towards them, their voice reverberates with pain. It's hard to watch.

Tales of the City gestures towards this prejudice, via a scene at a gay bar. Jake is sipping a beer alone when he's approached by a cis man. Flirtation ensues. Several drinks later, Jake's new paramour expresses distaste for trans men—not realising that Jake himself is trans.

'I'm cool with trans guys,' the cis man insists, his face giving lie to this claim. 'I just don't date them. I'm dick gay.'

Dick gay. The message is clear: the phallus maketh the man. Vaginas are feminine; vaginas are gross. No amount of muscle and beard could ever compensate for the lack of penis. Gender is reduced to genitals.

Hearing this dismissal, Jake's face falls. He makes his excuses and flees the scene, sick with the shame of being judged undateable.

This could be my future. A masculine person dating men. Gay. Dodging the dick gays, trying to find my person amid the wild west of dating apps. It might well fit better than lesbian. It would be hard pressed to fit worse.

Mainly, however, I no longer want to date men or women or anyone else. I call myself pansexual, in the sense that I could be attracted to any gender, but most of the time that's a lie. I'm pansexual in name only, theoretically open to the whole buffet but content to keep my plate empty. Most of the time, in truth, I don't want to be sexual with anyone at all.

ᕛ

'Why are all the songs on the radio about love or romance?' I ask my babysitter.

It was 1998, I was ten, and Aerosmith's power ballad 'I Don't Want to Miss a Thing' was the soundtrack to our lives.

Every afternoon, on the drive home from school, Steven Tyler's voice blared from the car radio. Soon, we knew the mawkish lyrics by heart. The song resonated, evidently; it was number one on the Australian charts for thirty weeks.

Why this fixation with love songs?

'You'll understand when you're older,' Barbara the babysitter reassured. She trusted that puberty would have its way with me.

Well, I am older now. I'm old by some measures. Puberty hit a full two decades ago. And I still don't understand the cultural preoccupation with coupledom. Not really. I still find it baffling that nearly every song, novel, movie, advertisement and TV series has romantic and sexual love at its centre. It's almost as if we're supposed to think that romantic coupledom, structured around sex, is the *raison d'etre* of life. It's almost as if anyone who thinks otherwise must be a freak.

Romance is about as attractive to me as chess or kayaking. It's something I've tried, it wasn't terrible, but I'm in no great rush to do it again. (Though I wouldn't rule it out.) I just don't find it very interesting. Romance, sex, coupledom, all that jazz—none of it gets me excited. As US novelist Brandon Taylor puts it in an essay 'on being queer and happily single', sex is an 'insufficiently motivating organizing principle of life.' Like Taylor, I don't find it repulsive, but I'd much rather read a book, or write a book, or have a conversation, or take a bath. Or do most things, in fact. I am sufficiently motivated to brush my teeth; I am insufficiently motivated to pursue romance or sex. *Meh* is my overriding emotion. I can take it or leave it.

As an undergraduate at Melbourne Uni, I wrote an essay, bloated with footnotes and emotion, about the history of the spinster. In my allocated three thousand words, I explained that the stigma surrounding the single woman was an artefact of patriarchy. Spinsterhood wasn't inherently miserable; women were just taught to fear this fate to ensure they remained under male control. A single woman was an autonomous woman, a threat to male hegemony. Patriarchy needed to neutralise this threat. It did so by painting spinsterhood as a fate worse than death.

Back then, I was still a skinny blonde who strutted about in miniskirts and dallied with one-night stands.

'Why are *you* writing about spinsters?' My older classmate leered, eyes on my tanned thighs. We were eating sushi and a few weeks later he'd invite me to eat his dick.

Spinsterhood was an unlikely passion, it was true. As a fuckable young filly who regularly received the kind of sexual harassment that passes for flirtation, I was still on script to settle down with a nice man one day. But I knew, even as a leggy twenty-year-old, that spinster history was my history. One day, not too far in the future, I'd walk away from the dating palaver and settle down with a good book. Another spinster joining the club, ready to spin my own future. Flying solo. No longer a woman, as it happens—but still a spinster, nonetheless.

Over the years, I've consented to sex because I desired what it promises—affection, validation, status, adventure—not because I desired the sex itself. I wanted to feel loveable and alive; I did not particularly want a close encounter with another person's genitals. The latter was simply a route to the former. Once the sex began, there'd always be a point, halfway through, when I became bored. The means would stop justifying the ends, and I'd be impatient for it to be over, my body still on the bed but my mind making a dash for the exit.

These days, I'd rather pursue validation or adventure by almost any other means. Why have sex for adventure when I could just go hiking?

This is not the same as scorning intimacy. I love intimacy, emotional and physical. I crave bear hugs and piggybacks and private jokes and epic D&Ms about the state of our souls. I love dancing in a dim room of sweaty strangers. A full-body massage is my idea of bliss. Still, in my thirties, I love to lie in my mother's lap while her fingers play with my hair.

I just don't have an appetite for what gets called *romance* and *sex*. It's like encountering food when you're not hungry. You might eat the food, you might even enjoy the food, but there's no appetite to fuel the experience. You could easily get distracted by something else. The food may end up abandoned on the plate, cold and forgotten, unable to compete in a universe dense with pleasures.

In 'A Prude's Manifesto', a performance from 2015, trans poet Cameron Awkward-Rich offers 'a list of things I like more than having sex'. His list includes reading, oatmeal, strong coffee, cheap whiskey, wet paint, 'riding my bike away from parties' and 'peeling back the skin of the grapefruit'.

This is my (incomplete) list: baby spinach, wilted with oil, salt and garlic. Getting tipsy alone. Cycling through hot nights. Crisp apples, preferably Granny Smiths. Iced coffee with Bonsoy on a 30-degree day. Scratching the silken fur beneath my cat's chin until her eyes roll back in bliss. Running, drunk on endorphins, to a soundtrack of early 2000s pop music. Gossiping over a G&T

on a balmy evening. Cracking my spine. Headstands. Browsing bookshops. Moleskine notebooks. Sleeping.

These lists are examples of what Ela Przybylo calls 'asexual erotics', the myriad sensuous pleasures of life that are not tethered to sex. In her book on the subject, Przybylo explains that the erotic need not be sexual. Rather, the erotic can be imagined as 'an inner resource of power that fuels action and intimacy in the world'—a definition indebted to Black feminist Audre Lorde. Asexual erotics remind us that a life without sex is not the same as a life starved of joy. Pleasure, elation, sensuality—these all come in many forms. They can come in the form of cunnilingus or in the form of balancing on your head. Whatever floats your boat.

Compulsory sexuality is the idea that sex is normal, healthy, a matchless joy fundamental to individual liberation and human flourishing. *Amatonormativity* (a word coined by philosopher Elizabeth Brake) is the belief that amorous partnerships like marriage are essential to the good life, the ultimate way to love and be loved. Both ideas are fed to us from earliest childhood. They're at the heart of our culture. They're the reason relatives enquire 'are you dating anyone?' at every gathering, then shoot us a pitying smile if we say no. They're the reason low libido, or hypoactive sexual desire disorder (HSDD), is listed as a disease in the current *Diagnostic and Statistical Manual of Mental Disorders* (*DSM*). Compulsory sexuality and amatonormativity are the reason well-meaning friends set us up on blind dates. They're the reason friendship always comes off second-best to sexual relationships. Together, compulsory sexuality and amatonormativity teach us that the single celibate person must be miserable, deviant, unfeeling. Lacking something essential. Broken.

'Don't worry, you'll find someone someday,' we're told.

No one ever considers we might be content as we are. No one considers that love and meaning and happiness might not be dependent on romance and sex. Nor do they consider that our single lives might be fat with intimacies: old friends, new friends, beloved parents, favourite aunts, chosen family, activist comrades, loyal pets, wise-cracking colleagues, patient mentors, chatty neighbours, running buddies, precocious godchildren, keen students with Gen-Z ideals.

No one ever considers that we might luxuriate in our solitude, curling our toes around the shape of each spacious moment.

'What I want is mostly to be alone,' Brandon Taylor explains. 'And to not have to contextualize my loneliness in a way that makes other people comfortable with it. So what if I'm alone. So what if I sit in my apartment and read one book after another or watch period pieces. It's not a wasted life.'

So what, indeed.

Remember: homosexuality was once also deemed pathological. Until 1973, it too was listed as a disorder in the *DSM*. Yesterday's deviance is today's natural variation. I'm prepared to bet that today's deviance will follow a similar fate. Asexuality— eyebrow-raising today—promises to become tomorrow's standard buffet option. Heterosexual, homosexual, bisexual, pansexual, asexual, demisexual, etcetera—take your pick. There's something for everyone at the sexual buffet. A dish to satisfy every appetite. All just different ways to be human.

～

I'm far from the only trans person who'd rather read a book than have sex. The available data points to a distinct correlation between TGD and asexual identities. In 2016, the annual Asexual Community Census found that twenty-six per cent of respondents identified as something outside or beyond the gender binary—far exceeding the reported incidence of non-binary gender in the general population (figures vary, and good research is rare, but one 2011 British study found that only 0.4 per cent identified as non-binary). In a 2018 sociological study of transgender people in the United States, twelve per cent of respondents identified as asexual—again, far exceeding the one per cent incidence of asexuality estimated in the general population.

Why this correlation? Why are so many trans people like me averse to sex and romance? No one knows for sure. There's scant research on either trans or asexual experience; there's next-to-no research on the intersection of the two. But it's not hard to think of credible reasons why they might travel together.

On bad days, the days when I fantasise about taking a carving knife to my breasts and hips, I suspect it's unease with my body that turns me off sex. When your body feels like a mistake, an error best rubbed out, why expose your flesh to another? Fully dressed, I can bind my breasts and wear blazers that accentuate my shoulders. I can craft my own character, fashion an architecture of the self from denim and leather and wool. No one can see my genitals. In bed, amid the sweaty tangle of limbs and sheets, I'm reduced to a little girl, betrayed and ashamed by her girlness. Not wanting to be seen or touched anywhere that'll remind her of the ways she is wrong. This body is no playground; more like an exam made to be failed. Why choose to hang out there? Better to pursue one's pleasures fully clothed, up between the ears.

Gender dysphoria, the doctors would say. *Gender dysphoria inhibiting sexual desire* would be the diagnosis. That's certainly one story to tell.

Another possible story: I discovered the language of asexuality through my immersion in trans and queer subcultures. It was through calling myself trans, and going down that rabbit hole, that I found the words to name my sexual self.

In one view, it's unsurprising that trans and asexual identities travel together because they're both part of a language of sexual and gender difference. As you gain fluency in this language, you discover terms to describe parts of yourself hitherto unnamed. The trans person, devouring queer culture, discovers the concept of asexuality and recognises asexual (or 'ace') tendencies in themselves. Or the asexual person, searching for community online, might come across the idea of gender diversity and find that the shoe fits.

Perhaps trans and ace correlate in the same way as, for example, pearls and golf clubs; not because one causes the other, but because they're twin symptoms of a particular demographic. Owning golf clubs doesn't make you desire pearls, of course. However, you might regularly see pearls on the golf course and come to admire their sheen. Pearls are now part of your world; pearl-ownership becomes normal. *Would pearls suit me?* you wonder in idle moments. If the answer proves yes, the bank balance that funded your golf clubs may also allow you to become a pearl owner. Before you know it, you too sport pearls on the golf course. Your 5-iron didn't cause your pro-pearl position, but it did facilitate the entry of pearls into your life.

In a similar way, joining the LGBTQIA+ brigade as an L or G or T exposes you to other forms of queer culture. The other letters in the acronym become familiar, thinkable. You learn another letter in the alphabet soup and think: *huh, interesting, could this be for me?* And just as the money needed for golf could also fund pearls, the sense of difference that first brought you to LGBTQIA+ might facilitate new forms of queer identification. Like me, you might arrive as T and then acquire A. T didn't cause A, necessarily; but it did enable exposure to A.

I suspect that the people who currently call themselves trans and asexual are just the tip of the iceberg. How many others, out in the world, live with trans and/or ace tendencies nascent, as yet unnamed? How many would clutch at one or both identities if they became available? Perhaps, if asexuality was a habitual talking point at the golf club, golfers may begin to see it in themselves. 'Of course!' they'd exclaim over frothy schooners in the clubhouse. 'This explains why I prefer a round of golf to a tumble with Dorothy. I'm asexual! I never knew there was a word for how I felt. Everything makes sense now.' The other drinkers would nod sagely and sip their beers.

Maybe trans people are no more inherently asexual than anyone else; maybe they're just more likely to be exposed to the idea of asexuality.

Or maybe not.

Whenever I ponder trans asexuality, I'm haunted by the figure of the child. Trans people often remember puberty as a betrayal, the moment when sprouting breasts or facial hair chained them to their assigned gender. Puberty becomes the death of an androgynous childhood self. Puberty is biological chickens coming home to roost. The dawning of sexual maturity is the twilight of gender freedom.

At eleven, I could still be mistaken for a boy. By twelve, I was a lumpen lass, breasts straining against the blue-and-white checks of my school uniform. 'Female' was now a label pinned to my pimpled forehead. Ever since, part of me has hankered to turn back the clock to my eleventh year—the last time womanhood didn't define me. The last time I didn't want to climb out of my own skin.

This begs the question: is my trans body averse to sex and romance because I experienced sexual maturity as a sort of death? Does asexuality appeal because it has resonances of childhood?

We imagine children to be asexual. As Freud and others insist, we imagine wrong. Children can be—are—sexual creatures. They masturbate, they desire. But still, the idea persists. We picture the child pure, innocent, unsullied by sex. The sexless life, then, mimics our fantasy of childhood. From this perspective, my asexual existence may be less an aversion to sex than a craving for pre-pubescence. Twenty years later, perhaps I'm still trying to reverse-engineer that eleven-year-old self. Perhaps part of my brain got stuck there, forever a child without the lumps and bumps and appetites of sexual maturity. You could say I'm a pre-pubescent boy in a thirty-some-thing woman's body, trying to make sense of it all.

On good days, I glimpse that boy in the mirror, flickering into view.

⤙

Childhood promises refuge, a space of possibility before the strait-jacket of puberty. Actual children, however? Terrifying. The irony is that, despite imagining myself as a boy, I tense up around real chil-dren. In the popular imagination, queerness has long been imagined as deviant, diseased, even paedophilic. Queers are seen as a danger to children. They're not to be trusted around young innocents. They threaten to corrupt the youth. *Think of the children!* Keep the perverts far from the playground. Mummies and daddies, beware.

This is the logic behind conservative efforts to keep LGBT education programs like Safe Schools out of our classrooms. This is the thinking embedded in fear-mongering commentary about so-called 'rapid onset gender dysphoria'—the poisonous lie that kids are being brainwashed into becoming trans. Behind it all is the idea that queerness is an infectious pathology transmitted from diseased adults to healthy children.

The queer sex worker Gala Vanting knows this stigma all too well. At a 2019 Queerstories event in Sydney, Vanting spoke about building a relationship with her partner's kids within a culture that deems queers and sex workers unsafe for children. At the zoo one day, one of the girls leant against Vanting's body. In response, Vanting tensed up, not knowing how to respond.

'What do I do with my hands?' she asked herself, anxious to avoid anything that could be misconstrued as inappropriate.

'Because I am a sex worker, and she is a child, and because no matter how hard I work on my own internalised whorephobia,

I can never fully purge my subconscious of the message that these things don't go together. They can't go together,' Vanting reflected.

A similar stigma is buried deep in my cells. No matter how much I know that queers aren't deviant or perverse, despite trusting I'd never harm a child, I continue to feel dirty around children. In their company, I hold myself tight, as though a stray word or gesture might trigger contamination. My transness, that supposed perversity, could leak out like a virus. Like the researcher Ela Przybylo, herself a queer aunt, I fear being accused of 'inflicting deviancy, perversion, or sexualisation' upon my nieces and nephews and cousins.

If I hug a child, piggyback a child, dance with a child, will other adults look askance? In my former life as a cisgender woman, these casual intimacies flowed naturally. I trusted that other adults trusted me. I could tickle and hug without censure. I was a loving aunt, a wholesome influence. Nothing to see here. Now as a trans person, I fear that every interaction is open to misinterpretation. A high five, a pat on the back, even a conversation. Friendly adult or sinister pedo? What monstrosity might lurk here? I'm the same person I always was, only now I'm an imagined threat to children.

Early in my transition, I visited a queer bookshop in Fitzroy and bought a picture book that introduced gender diversity to children. *Who Are You? The Kid's Guide to Gender Identity* explained that 'gender is so much more than the body you were born with'. It had big font, positive messaging and colourful illustrations of kids frolicking around the gender spectrum.

'You are who you say you are, because YOU know you best,' the book explains. 'Be who you are!'

What it doesn't say is: being who you are can frighten the horses. It can frighten people you love. You might start to half-believe in your own monstrosity.

During the COVID lockdown, I joined the bubble of a new friend who lived a few streets away. Kristine was a freelance journalist stress-cooking her way through the pandemic. Her family were overstuffed, and she needed new people to feed. She brought me oven-warm challah wrapped in brown paper and Tupperware containers stuffed with Ottolenghi leftovers. We took masked walks around the neighbourhood park with Harry the cavoodle. Later, when restrictions eased, Kristine invited me around for negronis and vegetarian Thanksgiving and sushi.

At first, I was wary around her children. The two girls, aged nine and eleven, played on iPads or fixed themselves snacks while their mother and I catastrophised about Trump. The kids and I kept out of each other's way.

Soon, however, the girls grew used to my visits. They edged towards the margins of our adult conversation.

'What does "disproportionate" mean?' the elder girl asked, after I used the term offhand. A long conversation about power and justice ensued.

Later that evening, her younger sister read me her latest poem.

Before long, the girls awaited my arrival on the front porch, as enthusiastic in their welcome as the cavoodle.

'Yves!' they would yell. 'Yves's here!'

They knew I was trans and were curious without guile. At the dinner table, their questions rained down, one after another.

'Do you call yourself Mr or Miss?'

'Why did you choose the name "Yves"?'

'Do you want some custard?'

'What are your cats called?'

'How did you know you were trans?'

Their trust in me was healing. Their warmth purged the imagined dirt. I felt more a person, less a monster, in their presence.

I remained careful to avoid physical contact. Never did I let myself hug the girls hello or goodbye. I was still, at some level, worried my touch might corrupt.

One evening, though, the younger girl flung herself at me. We played puzzles, and she batted me playfully when I made a mistake. She draped me with costumes and prodded my nose. Later, as I went to leave, her whole body wrapped around my right leg, refusing to let the evening end. I was pinned to the hallway floorboards, unable to move, locked in place by a bantamweight third grader. Her mother laughed at our antics.

'She normally only does this with her uncle,' Kristine observed.

It was an honour, to be so detained. The girl's wise animal body trusted mine, completely. She knew I was no threat. I'd been vetted and had passed the test. With her, I could be both trans and beloved, a combination I hadn't yet thought possible.

Cackling, hysterical, clutching my ankle with all her might, this tiny creature with wild curls brought me back to my own humanity.

She kept me at her house; she brought me home.

CALLING PURPLE GREEN

AT 5.56 AM MY EYES spring open, ready for action. Over an hour earlier than normal. As though my body has intuited there's a fight ahead this morning.

At 7.20 am the first text arrives from the radio producer. It's June 2019. Victoria's Labor state government is tabling legislation that will make it easier for trans people to change the sex on their birth certificate. At present, trans people must have surgery on their reproductive organs before they can alter this foundational legal document. The new bill would remove the surgery requirement. This is an overdue acknowledgement that many trans people don't want or can't afford surgery, yet still require identification that matches their gender. Under the current framework, trans people often live with a mismatch between their gender presentation and legal ID. For instance, a trans woman might have a birth certificate that labels her M. If she uses this ID to apply for a job or seek housing, she's forced into disclosing her transgender status—a situation that could lead to discrimination, harassment or worse. To stay safe and fully participate in the community, trans people need ID that reflects who they are.

Tasmania's law had been recently changed to remove the surgery requirement. Now Victoria is catching up. The story is all over the news this morning and the radio station wants a trans person to comment. Am I available? the producer asks via text.

I give the matter maybe ten seconds thought. As an academic who until recently had been precariously employed, my default answer is yes. Yes to everyone. Of course I'm available. Always ready to please. You want me to jump? How high?

I call the producer.

'Great! We're thrilled you can comment! It's so important to have the trans community represented!'

They'll slot me in at 8.45 or maybe 9.30. They're waiting to hear back from the minister. Probably 8.45.

I check my watch. I'm unshowered, crouched in front of my laptop on the couch. I'll have to skedaddle to make it to work in time.

Fifty minutes later, I arrive at my office, legs burning from cycling at top speed. I check my phone. It's 8.38. Fuck. On air in seven minutes. But there's also a text from the producer. Can they move me back to 9.35?

I exhale. Turn on my computer, make coffee, jot down some notes, re-read the news coverage on the legislation. Already the comments section is full of hateful words. I scroll down the page, queasy from the poison. The new law is deemed ridiculous, unnecessary, a joke. Political correctness gone mad. It will lead to men impersonating women to perv in female bathrooms. It'll allow attention-seeking millennials to flip genders on a whim. It's the work of a trans cult hijacking the political agenda. (If only trans people were powerful enough to form a cult.)

At 8.52 my phone rings, an unknown number. It's a different producer from the same radio program. Can I go on air now, instead of 9.35? The minister is talking, and they want my response.

Heart starts beating faster. A sudden urge to defecate.

I'm put on hold while the minister is inundated with talkback from listeners opposed to the reform. Angry words pour out of the phone, straight into my amygdala.

'Welcome to the social engineering show.'

'What a joke!'

'Can we have some actual news this morning?'

The voices are loud and scornful. Male. They summon the lurking wrongness, the shame, always hovering just below the skin.

Freak, my brains snarls at me. *Against nature. Perverted, wrong, dirty.* When it comes to 'fight, flight or freeze' my amygdala invariably opts for the fight response, directed towards myself. *All these normal people think you're a joke.*

On air, the minister responds to the talkback with calm authority, explaining the rationale behind the bill.

'Transgender Victorians need legal ID that reflects their gender identity,' he says. 'The current surgery requirement is outdated and pathologising.'

Reasonable arguments delivered in a voice stripped of emotion, distant from the issues at hand. This is another day on the job for him, not a debate about his humanity. He's never had his existence called into question.

8.57 am I'm still on hold. Only three minutes 'til news time. If I go on air now, what will I say? So little time, so much responsibility. My brain scrambles for soundbites that will convince sceptics to change their tune.

The producer comes on the line.

'Sorry, we've run out of time. The news is about to start.'

Back to 9.35 after all. It was a false alarm.

I dart to the bathroom, empty my bowels, then sit slumped in front of the computer. I watch the minutes tick by. Re-read the news article. Check the comments. Already there's more hate, more scorn.

The call comes at 9.34. I'm on hold again as the announcer reads traffic updates, weather reports, news headlines. Finally, it's my turn.

'What do you think about the proposed legislation?' he asks.

I launch into my rehearsed spiel, disgorging facts about trans health, discrimination, suicide. I parade the community's trauma, open a vein live on air. It's the old refrain: *look, we are suffering, we are victims, please feel sorry for us*. Trauma porn offered up in exchange for nuggets of compassion. *We will titillate you with our pain if only you give us accurate ID. Please sir, have mercy*. Somehow, we've been hoodwinked into thinking we need to prove our pain to deserve basic rights—rights that other humans take for granted.

When I pause for breath, the announcer jumps in, a boxer with a surprise left jab.

'But what would you say to the sceptics who call this social engineering?'

He reads out text messages from listeners.

'Say I want to be called a carrot, are you obliged to address me as such?' one reads.

'Changing gender on a birth certificate. What's next? Calling purple green? It's madness!' says another.

Freak, my brain whispers again, louder this time. *Deformed, unlovable*.

On air, I emit a light chuckle, playing the good sport. Internally, I beat my fists in pain and frustration. Why must we always justify our right to live unmolested? Why do journalists always feel the need to platform both sides, when one 'side' is mere uninformed prejudice?

In response to the texts, I offer some words about trans rights, about safety, about the dangers of being outed by incorrect documentation.

'If you have to show ID that reveals you were assigned a different gender at birth, you don't know how people are going to react. You're being forced to disclose your trans status and that's potentially quite unsafe,' I say in rush.

I talk again about the transphobia that steals our peace of mind, steals our lives.

Then, suddenly, it's over.

The announcer thanks me, the producer thanks me, they hang up.

It's finished. A second ago I was performing to an audience of thousands, pleading for their empathy. Now I'm alone in a hushed office, frozen at my desk. Gentle rain patterns the window behind the computer. My screensaver kicks into gear.

It's 9.46 and I'm spent. The news cycle has had its way with me and moved on, marching into the future. I'm left behind, a rotting corpse of sweat and adrenaline, collateral damage in the service of 'robust discussion'.

What now? I'm stupefied, jaw slack. Unbidden, my mind contemplates the sweet relief of blades slicing flesh, of roaring trucks. Of jumping. Anything for release.

Outside in the corridor, colleagues chitchat about the onset of winter. Someone has just got back from Japan. Everyone is overloaded with essay marking. There are muffins for morning tea. It's an ordinary Tuesday morning.

Inside, at my desk, the listeners' texts replay on a loop in my mind.

What's next? Calling purple green? It's madness. The scorn reverberates between my ears. *Madness, madness.*

I sit, statue-still, in the dark office. I'd forgotten to turn on the light. Now I've forgotten how to move.

After the radio debacle, things only got worse. The mooted birth certificate reforms brought all sorts of transphobes out of the woodwork. The media fed on it, vulture-like, platforming bigotry in the interest of 'showing both sides'. One 'side'—those in favour of the reforms—was the trans community, medical professionals, human rights organisations and the state government. An authoritative coalition, so you'd think. The other 'side' was a ragbag of religious figures, shock jocks and TERFs. Somehow, this unlikely alliance managed to make their opposition newsworthy—despite a lack of relevant expertise, experience or credentials. They were not transgender, nor were they experts on law or medicine. There was no compelling reason why their voice should be heard. But that didn't matter in the court of public opinion. Every morning, I awoke to news features and op-eds querying whether trans people deserved accurate ID. It was debasing, to see our rights and our humanity batted about for sport like it was all some high school debate.

First speaker for the affirmative proposes that transgender people are at high risk of violence and require ID that will allow them to safely navigate daily life.

Second speaker for the negative insists that sexual offenders will use the proposed reform to molest women.

I could see them, hectoring from the podium in their school ties, white shirts damp with perspiration, the opposition furiously scrawling rebuttals on index cards.

It was all reduced to words thrown between overgrown schoolboys desperate to win at any cost. At the end of the day, no matter the outcome, they'd all go home safe and sound. Back to their warm houses and hot dinners. Meanwhile, trans people still lacked access to that most basic thing: accurate ID. It wasn't a game to us; it was our lives.

Soon, there were other trans issues in the headlines. Prime Minister Scott Morrison, having already criticised 'gender whisperers' in schools, now attacked Cricket Australia's new transgender inclusion policy. On radio station 2GB, Morrison said it was 'beyond him' why Cricket Australia had moved to welcome trans players. *The Australian* newspaper agreed, expressing concerns that the policy could be used to prosecute 'mums and dads' who resisted trans inclusion. Lyle Shelton also got on board, twisting an effort to make cricket 'a sport for everyone' into a story of cisgender victimhood.

That same winter of discontent, *The Australian* newspaper launched a gender section that soon housed a deluge of scaremongering articles on trans youth. 'They're castrating children' screamed one headline. (Fact check: they're not.) Within only six months, the paper had published sixty-eight articles—or around 56,000 words—on transgender issues, with ninety-two per cent of the coverage negative. During October 2019, there was an average of one article per day. Analysis of the coverage found that 'most of the stories approach transitioning and trans people as threats' and depict 'trans women as bullies who abuse and harass cis women'.

This was the tidal wave of transphobia predicted to emerge in the wake of 2017's marriage equality debate. With the postal survey done and dusted, and marriage equality now the law of the land, conservatives needed a new *bête noire*. The trans community was an easy target, in part because 2017's Yes campaign left that flank exposed. To the chagrin of many queers, the Yes campaign neglected to defend gender diversity and condemn transphobia. Now, as anticipated, the bogeyman of the month had become trans people, especially trans youth. The same old arguments once lobbed at gays and lesbians were recycled to target the trans community. *A dangerous trend. Corrupting the youth. They're all predators. Think of the children!* It was all nonsense, easily refuted by basic facts, but that didn't make it any less dangerous.

The discourse grew ever more toxic, spiralling away from facts into a war of words. Whenever faced with pushback, anti-trans voices liked to paint themselves as victims.

'I've been deplatformed!' they'd cry. 'It's political correctness gone mad. Cancel culture is threatening freedom of speech!'

Somehow, these 'silenced' cultural warriors always found impressive platforms to bewail their deplatforming, their voice amplified to millions. To all appearances, their speech remained free. If only the same could be said for transgender people. Aside from a few exceptions, trans people almost never command a large audience. They can't be deplatformed because they don't have platforms to begin with.

My patience with this circus was soon exhausted. I was sickened by the wilful misinformation, by the airtime given to bigots, by the use of trans lives for political sport. Most of all, I was frustrated by having to be always on the defensive. Enabled by the media, anti-trans voices were setting the terms of the debate.

Indeed, even framing it as a 'debate' was part of the problem. The language of 'debate' implied that there are two legitimate perspectives that could fight it out in the public sphere. But, in truth, this was not a debate at all but a political struggle for trans rights, and those rights are not up for debate. The great ruse of contemporary transphobia is the way it reimagines trans rights—a question of justice and equality—as a matter of competing ideologies. Falsely framed as a 'debate', the conversation descends into a fight about the reality of transness. *Is gender a matter of genitals? Can a person with a penis be a woman? Are trans people valid?*

This 'debate' is eerily reminiscent of earlier debates about the validity of homosexual desire or the intellect of Black people. In each case, bigots sanitised the violence of their position by drawing upon the language of concern and the authority of science. In each case, what is at stake is not competing ideas but the humanity of an oppressed minority.

Today's 'trans debate' works to delegitimise trans identities, nourish ideas of cisgender victimhood, and distract from the real issue: the harassment and discrimination faced by trans people. Unfortunately, large swathes of the media have been seduced by this debate framing, and repeatedly platform anti-trans sentiment in the interests of 'showing both sides'. But both-sideism isn't journalism; it's the abrogation of journalistic duty. As the writer Laila Lalami puts it, 'Handing a bullhorn to "both sides" isn't objective; it's merely relinquishing the responsibility to inform the public.'

This 'both sides' reporting has real-world consequences. Research conducted by the UK organisation Trans Media Watch (TMW) in 2009–10 found that one in five trans respondents had experienced verbal abuse they believed was associated with representations of transgender people in the media. One in five had also experienced negative reactions at work in relation to items in the media. Eight per cent had received physical abuse connected to media portrayals. TMW concluded that 'transgender people are deeply dissatisfied with the way they are portrayed by the media', as negative representation 'leads to considerable real-life suffering on the part of transgender people'. While this research examined the UK, and is over a decade old, it nonetheless points to a disturbing relationship between anti-trans sentiment in the media and transphobia experienced in daily life. As TMW reiterated in 2012, 'the press has shown a distasteful rush to objectify and sensationalise these [trans] stories in a way that places real people in real danger'.

In an effort to mitigate such danger, trans advocates are drawn into a never-ending cycle of words thrown across the fence. Again and again, anti-trans voices make a spurious claim or transphobic dog-whistle under the guise of reasonable debate, leaving trans people compelled to explain why it was wrong. The stakes are too high to risk allowing lies to go unchallenged. Again and again, we are cornered into engaging with this fallacious debate, forced to repeat the same basic facts.

No, trans children are not receiving irreversible medical treatment. Pre-pubescent children only ever undergo social transition, which involves things like wearing new clothes, changing their name and haircut—all of which can easily be reversed, if necessary. Older trans kids might receive puberty blockers to stop the development of unwanted secondary sex characteristics, but only after undergoing thorough medical evaluation and parental consent. Puberty blockers are fully reversible and extremely safe, having been used on cis children who experience early puberty since the 1980s.

No, trans women are not male predators in skirts; they're people who just want to safely use public toilets. There are almost no documented instances of trans women harming cis women in women-only spaces but there are documented examples of trans women being harmed. Overall, trans women experience significantly higher rates of violence than cis women. Anyway, why would an actual male predator go to the effort of pretending to be a trans woman, when they can just assault women in their own homes or workplaces (or even federal parliament), as happens on the regular? Given one in five Australian women experience sexual violence, it seems dubious that men require an elaborate disguise to harm women.

No, trans women don't have an unfair advantage in sport. There are no documented cases of men impersonating trans women to dominate the field in women's sport, nor are there any cases of trans athletes competing at Olympic level. Trans people just want to participate like everyone else, not cheat their way to the top.

It was exhausting, a Groundhog Day of lies and hysteria. The facts never seemed to stick. Would the conversation ever move on?

'The function, the very serious function of racism is distraction,' observed the Black novelist Toni Morrison. 'It keeps you from doing your work. It keeps you explaining, over and over again, your reason for being.'

Transphobia works in a similar way. It keeps trans people locked in the same old sparring match and prevents us from getting shit done. Above all, it's a monumental thief of time.

As the winter days crawled by, anger festered beneath my skin. Each afternoon at dusk, I marched through leaden streets with unseeing eyes, propelled onwards by a fury so hot it threatened to burn me up. Anger dug a gulf between me and the cisgender people in my life. They were baffled by its intensity, wary of getting burnt.

'How can you still be friends with that TERF?' I berated my friend Henry. 'She's caused so much harm.'

'Don't you know that trans people avoid going out because they're afraid of using public bathrooms?' I hectored my WhatsApp chats.

There was a silent plea behind my words: *stand beside me, hold my hand in this storm.* But my need came out as wild-eyed accusation, rage leaking all over the place.

I could sense everyone backing away, anxious I might bite. It was lonely, to be angry alone.

ᐟ

Things turned ugly again in late 2020. That December, I wrote an op-ed for *The Age* about the need to prioritise actual trans voices over the ignorant opinion of cisgender celebrities like J.K. Rowling. Now labelled a 'trans activist', I found myself swept up in a media storm that raged for weeks. The same week as my op-ed, *The Age* was in the firing line for dubious reporting on transgender questions. It had platformed a noted TERF; it had published an anonymous op-ed full of transphobic dog whistles. Online, the newspaper began to face pushback. I joined the critique. In response, libertarians and conservatives claimed free speech was under attack. Soon, the whole thing was a firestorm.

By awful coincidence, that same week saw the disappearance of Bridget Erin Flack, a twenty-eight-year-old Melbourne trans woman who went for a walk near the Yarra and never returned. There were fears for her safety, prompting search parties and pleas for help in the media. All too conscious that trans people—especially trans women—experience elevated rates of violence, the queer community was on edge.

On Friday night, Bridget's body was found. Police reported there were no suspicious circumstances. The implication was that she'd taken her own life. Bridget was a stranger to me; I can't comment on her life or death. But I can testify to its impact. The queer community across Australia was bereft. Even those who'd never met Bridget took the news hard. Her death was heartbreaking evidence that, even after decades of campaigning and advocacy, trans people continue to live brutal lives that too often end violently. We all had the awful statistics etched on our hearts: trans Australians are eleven times more likely to attempt suicide. Nearly fifty per cent of trans youth have done so. Think about that: half of trans kids have tried to kill themselves. Half. Not just thought about it—actually attempted. At an age when the biggest worry should be homework and exams, these kids are seeking their own obliteration. That's how tough their lives are.

So many of us have been there. *That could've been me*, we thought upon hearing news of Flack's death. It could have been almost any one of us. Given the stigma faced by TGD Australians, it's the rare trans person who hasn't experienced depression or suicidality. I know I have—many times. And my life has been far easier than most. Even now, there are still days when, waiting to cross a busy road, I fantasise about stepping out into the path of a speeding truck.

That weekend, after the news broke, I went about in a daze, stupefied by grief. Our heartbreak called for rain and howling gales, but instead the sky had dressed itself in festive cerulean blue, drawing winter-pale bodies out into the parks. On Saturday, I forced my way through a series of Christmas picnics, an automaton making chitchat among friends and colleagues oblivious to the tragedy. Everyone sipped wine, nibbled cherries, finally carefree after our long COVID winter. Cross-legged on the picnic rug, I painted on a rictus smile.

Back home, I wept for Bridget, I wept for myself, and I wept for every trans person who's ever felt freakish, ashamed and alone. Tear-soaked and snotty, I raged that we're still dying too young. I raged that this keeps happening, over and over. I despaired that most people don't know or care.

Against this backdrop, *The Age* firestorm continued. Thanks to my bit part in the saga, I found myself in the centre of the flames. My words and tweets were picked up by reactionary publications. For my sins, I was called a 'heckler' and 'hysterical rainbow bully'. The Catholics accused me of propagating 'neo-Marxist gender ideology'.

On Twitter, I fronted an army of trolls. They took me to task for 'censorship', 'insanity' and 'cry-bully tactics'. I was a 'groomer' who supported 'state-sanctioned child abuse'. I was a 'moron', a 'fascist', a 'stupid twat'. I was 'retarded', 'deranged', 'hysterical'. A 'despicable human being'. Even a 'satanist', according to one unhappy chap. So extreme was the vitriol, it would've been laughable if it wasn't so alarming. Private messages placed curses on my family. 'What an utterly soft, illiberal person you are.' Book burning was mentioned. I was sent a GIF of a burning effigy. 'Fuck off.' 'Piss off, zealot.' 'Grow a spine snowflake.' On the advice of a veteran activist, I ramped up privacy settings on my account.

'Take a break from Twitter! Just ignore all the trolls,' well-meaning friends advised.

'Switch off for a bit, enjoy the sunshine.'

If only it were so simple. The problem was the threat of escalation. With every notification, my heart was in my throat. Would I need to block someone? Would this be the time to call the police? I couldn't walk away, because a school of sharks was out for my blood. For almost a week, I sat frozen at my desk, monitoring emails and Twitter and Reddit around the clock. I ate in front of the screen, slept in snatches. If I turned my back, if I allowed the vigilance to drop, who knew what might happen?

This sequence of events again left me angry. Furious, even. Prior to coming out as trans, I'd enjoyed the unmolested existence of a white, tertiary-educated citizen of an affluent nation. Sexism coloured my reality, and I was embroiled in an ongoing war against my own body, but for the most part I had it pretty damn good. I expected to have my humanity respected. I'd experienced little else. Now, as the same person, only trans, I found myself and my community treated with callous disregard. Our basic existence was debated in public. We were clickbait. Media gatekeepers had washed their hands of the situation. How dare they?

When it came to being shat on by the world, I was as green as they come. I was an innocent, a wide-eyed babe at thirty-two, long swaddled in the cottonwool of privilege. But that innocence gave me fresh capacity for outrage. Never schooled to anticipate injustice, I burned with indignation, the acrid taste of fury on my tongue.

'I'm worried about my anger,' I told my therapist. 'Isn't anger meant to be toxic? What if it poisons me, reduces me as a person?'

'I'm not sure I believe that narrative,' they responded. 'In my experience, anger is healthy and natural. Something would be wrong if you *weren't* angry in this situation. It's just that certain groups— women, trans people, people of colour—aren't allowed to feel anger. Anger is deemed okay for some people but not others.'

'But won't it just fester and make me bitter?' I counter, unconvinced.

'It depends what you do with it,' my therapist answered, implacable as ever. 'Anger is motivating, energising. It can be a useful tool.'

Anger as a tool. That resonates.

There are limits, though, to what certain tools can do. The optimal tool for one situation may prove disastrous in another. Anger fuels action but also has other effects. In general, only the anger of white men wins respect. When men are angry, it is justified. Elsewhere, anger is read as hysteria, irrationality, childishness. Anger is dismissed as excessive emotion, a sign the bearer can be ignored.

The anger of a trans person, no matter how justified, threatens to alienate the cisgender majority. Women and people of colour have long concealed their anger to win a fair hearing. Should I be working to repress mine?

My public platform, such as it is, rests on my being palatable. I am an out-and-proud trans person, to be sure, but I'm also white, cis-passing, affluent and able-bodied. I have a PhD, I'm employed by a university. I conform to the norms of civility expected by white elites. I smile, I make pleasantries. My appearance doesn't rock the boat. By and large, I follow the rules. All this makes it easy to include me as the token trans person in the room. I don't induce discomfort in the way that other, more visibly 'different' trans people might.

My anger threatens to change that. The angrier I am, the less palatable I become. As an angry trans person, I may be judged uncivil. Difficult. An irate so-and-so who makes 'ordinary' people uncomfortable. The invitations may dry up.

Yet, perhaps this is not such a bad thing. There are limits to what can be achieved within the system that causes injustice in the first place. As Black feminist Audre Lorde reminds us, 'The master's tools will never dismantle the master's house'.

Right now, I'm done swallowing my anger. My stomach is bloated with it, unable to house any more. There's only so much bile it can handle. These days, I'm at capacity; one lump more and the whole gutful might come rushing back up, staining the nice rug. We can't have that, can we?

So instead, I say this: we are all entitled to welcome, respect, care. We should all be able to have accurate ID and somewhere safe to empty our bladder. Every human deserves that much. It is indeed outrageous that trans people are so often denied these most basic rights. It's appalling that we're deemed less valuable, that we die prematurely, struggle to find work, and battle stigma and hatred every day. It's outrageous that one in two trans and gender diverse people experience sexual coercion or violence, compared to thirteen per cent of the general population. The dire health outcomes of trans youth—three-quarters have diagnosed depression, half have attempted suicide—are a national tragedy. We should be angry at this state of affairs. Not just because anger is warranted, but because anger is fuel for political action. We cannot afford to be numbed to this situation or accept it as normal.

What we need now, I suggest, is not swallowed anger but angry allies. We need cisgender allies who'll listen to our stories, rage against the injustice, and join us in dismantling the old master's house to make space for something new.

We know those allies are out there. Research conducted by Equality Australia in July 2020 found overwhelming support for trans equality. Of a representative sample of 1026 adult Australians, seventy-eight per cent agreed that trans people deserve the same rights and protections as other Australians—with fifty-seven per cent in strong agreement. Two-thirds agreed that young people should be able to access healthcare that supports them to live as their true selves. And two-thirds believed that religious schools should not be able to fire someone or expel a student for being transgender.

These statistics tell us that the hostile voices in the media and online represent only a vocal minority. Most people are trans allies—or allies-in-the-making. We already have the numbers. All we need now is for those allies to listen to trans people, get angry, and insist that the rights and humanity of trans people are not up for debate. We need allies—especially within the media—to recognise what is truly at stake and refuse to let fringe voices win.

IN THE TIME OF CORONA

'I'VE DECIDED,' I ANNOUNCE. 'IT'S HAPPENING this year.'

We're nestled in the green embrace of Carlton Gardens, lolling on a tartan picnic rug with plastic cups of gin and soda. Warm air carries the rumble of distant trams.

As I speak, Sandro digs a cracker into the tub of hummus.

'You mean transition?' he asks, leaning back on one elbow.

'Yep. I'm gonna medically transition. I've decided, it's time. 2020 is the year.'

'So does that mean hormones? Surgery?' Sandro asks.

'Both, I think. Definitely surgery. Probably hormones, maybe a low dose.'

I stretch out my hand for an olive.

'I've been thinking about it for so long. Years. I'm relieved I've finally made the decision. I still don't want to be perceived as a man, 'cause I'm not one, but I can't bear to be seen as a woman anymore. I need to change my body.'

I pop the olive into my mouth, chew down hard on the tart green flesh.

It was the first day of the new year. Late afternoon. Under the green boughs of high summer, 2020 stretched out before us, glistening and full of promise. As yet untarnished. Bushfires were already raging up and down the east coast, but the true horror had not yet reached Melbourne. It would be another week before the city was blanketed by toxic smoke, a grey shroud that snuffed out colour and hope. Now, on 1 January, the sky was still vivid in spotless blue, a fresh canvas on which to paint our hopes.

2020 could be anything we wanted it to be.

For me, it was to be the year of 'medical transition'. After two years of equivocation, I was ready. Time for that magic testosterone to have its way with me. Time for the surgeon's knife. I'd come out the other end of 2020 a different person. Unrecognisable, even. Not a man, but no longer a woman.

I have it all mapped out.

⤷

Two months later, I meet my mother in Flinders Lane for a hurried birthday lunch. I'm 32 today, but there's little time to celebrate. I've just come from the ABC studios at Southbank, where I was on air for my regular radio history segment. This afternoon, there are university classes to prepare. All busy, busy, busy. Perched on high stools, jammed between besuited office workers, Mum and I gobble down overpriced salads. My birthday cake is a berry smoothie, inhaled through a compostable straw. Once our plates are empty, I jump on the train back to work. There'll be time in a few days for a proper celebration.

It is Wednesday, 11 March, the anniversary of my birth, and I still believe that 2020 was my oyster.

That afternoon, the World Health Organization declares COVID-19 a pandemic.

The next morning, everything has changed. On the 86 tram to campus, my inbox heaves with panicked emails about the threat of workplace coronavirus transmission. I'd taken sick leave earlier that week for what I assumed to be a mild cold. Now my boss is advising me to cancel today's classes. He doesn't want to risk me transmitting COVID-19 to my students. In our new pandemic reality, even the merest cough and sniffle could be a deadly menace.

I get off the 86 at the next stop, opposite a cemetery. Crouched on a nature strip, I tap out a hurried email on my phone, cancelling my classes. Then I catch the next tram back home.

Once home, I never really leave. Apart from a daily walk, I'll be alone inside my apartment for the next eight months.

It is Thursday 12 March, and lockdown has begun.

⌣

In the first weeks, each morning is the same. Waking in bed, my brain still in that murky place between sleep and consciousness, I enjoy a few moments of calm. Normality. Safe in the cocoon of my doona, nothing to dread or fear.

Then I remember. The truth rushes back in: pandemic, infection, death. Skyrocketing unemployment, supply chain disruptions, overwhelmed hospitals. Mass graves. Each morning my brain startles anew at those terrible facts. Shock, anger, denial, sorrow: I cycle through the same emotions every time, all within the first moments of waking. It's a morning grief ritual, a daily count of what has been lost.

It's also strangely familiar. The previous year, in the wake of coming out as trans, I'd spent months in the same mental loop. Awake, remember, startle, grieve.

Back then, it went as follows.

Awake: *Situation normal.*

Remember: *Actually, I'm trans, and everyone knows. I'm officially a freak now.*

Shock: *Holy shit, is this really true?*

Denial: *Surely this is all a bad dream.*

Grief: *This is too hard. Can we return to normal? Things were easier then.*

By this time the adrenaline would be pumping, my stomach twisted with dread.

All through 2019, my awakening brain cycled through that pattern. I was struggling to process the loss of the life I thought I'd have. The life of a 'normal' cisgender person, quietly going about my business. That was gone, forever. Only after months of that morning-mourning ritual did the fact of my transness cease to startle me. Those months taught me about the time it takes a body to metabolise change and loss.

To be clear: I wasn't mourning being trans. Being trans was a homecoming. It was finally seeing myself. It was exhilarating. Magic.

No, being trans wasn't the problem. The problem was the loss of my cisgender privilege. That's what I was mourning—my lost freedom to go about life accepted and unmolested and 'normal'.

Now, a year later, the wake-up 'shock and awe' routine has been reactivated. Only this time for a pandemic. This time, the whole world is grieving as our hopes for the year evaporate. This time, at least, my grief puts me in sync with fellow humans, rather than marking me out as a freak. We're all struggling to process that 'success' in 2020 will look like staying alive.

Again? I think, each morning in bed, moored in familiar grief. *Again, already?* I ask, reaching for my phone to see if the world ended overnight. *I'm not ready for this. I'm still recovering from the last upheaval.*

But the familiarity of morning-mourning has its comforts. I've been here before. My body and mind have already weathered disruption and loss. I know how it works. I know it does get easier. Well, perhaps not easier, but easier to fathom. Less shocking. Eventually. With enough time, the body can absorb almost anything. The trick is to just keep walking.

Is this what they call 'resilience'?

⤙

Within days, elective surgeries are cancelled. Medical services get scaled back. Only 'essential' treatment keeps going. I realise: coronavirus has thrown my medical transition plans out the window. Indefinitely. No one is getting top surgery right now. Even starting hormones may well be impossible. Melbourne's few gender clinics are suspending services.

Everyone is concerned that supply chain disruptions will cause shortages of testosterone and oestrogen. I have phone calls with friends who recount frantic efforts to fill a script for T before everything shuts down. Forget toilet paper; trans people are panic-buying hormones.

The medical world is in crisis mode, unable to accommodate a baby trans person looking to craft a masculine frame. My dreams will have to wait: 2020 will not be the year of medical transition, after all.

This fact sinks in on daily walks along Merri Creek. On still autumn afternoons, I march up and down the banks, glowering at the brown depths framed by eucalypts. In my mind's eye, my masculinised self drifts away on the current. Out of reach. The future that briefly became thinkable is lost to me again.

Every afternoon, male runners overtake me on the path, all pumping legs and fast breathing. Gazelles in Nike on the move. The elegant geometry of lean legs and flat torso disappearing around a bend in the creek.

In my mind I am one of them. In reality, my body retains its stubborn curves.

It hurts, more than I'm willing to admit.

↳

Trans healthcare worldwide is disrupted by coronavirus.

Most significant is the suspension of elective surgery. In May–June 2020, Transform, a University of Melbourne-based study of trans health, surveyed 778 trans and gender-diverse Australians about their experience of the pandemic. This research found that, of those who had scheduled gender-affirming surgery, seventeen per cent had their surgery cancelled due to the pandemic. A further fifty-five per cent had their surgery postponed.

For many, this was a devastating blow. Trans people often spend months or years saving up for gender-affirming surgery, which is not fully covered by Medicare or private health insurance. Costs vary, but the gap can easily be at least ten thousand dollars. Often much more. Then there's the cost of taking time off work to recover. Few, if any, workplaces offer gender transition leave.

Once they've saved enough money, trans people then need to negotiate medical gatekeeping. Unlike cosmetic plastic surgery, which is available to anyone with sufficient cash, gender-affirming surgeries can only proceed if the medical profession has given permission. Anyone can walk in off the street and buy bigger breasts. But trans people can only have gender-affirming surgery if they convince doctors that they're 'trans enough' to warrant surgical intervention. It's infantilising and invasive—not to mention a double standard.

Finally, once you've got the money and permissions, there are long waiting lists for the surgery itself. Few surgeons specialise in these procedures and those who do can barely keep up with rising demand. In Melbourne, there are only two surgeons who perform 'top surgery'—the colloquial term for elective double mastectomy and chest masculinisation. Waiting lists can be up to a year.

All in all, it's a long and arduous road between the decision to have surgery and actually going under the knife. To be on the eve of long-awaited surgery and then have it postponed or cancelled would be a knock-out blow.

'My top surgery was cancelled just a few weeks before it was supposed to happen,' one survey respondent reported. 'I had been looking forward to it for months, and suddenly not knowing when or if it would happen caused a big spike in my depression. I found it really hard to look after myself for weeks afterward as I couldn't find anything to look forward to.'

Other trans folk had access to hormones disrupted. Although the feared shortages did not eventuate, pandemic restrictions did inhibit access to doctors who prescribed HRT. Restrictions on movement, fears of public transport, and scaled-back medical services all made it hard for trans people to get the hormones they needed. Many also struggled with the loss of face-to-face psychological services and the abrupt shutdown of specialist trans clinics like the Monash Gender Service in Melbourne's east.

Transfeminine people, meanwhile, mourned the loss of electrolysis. With beauty salons shut down, they were unable to keep their skin smooth and hair-free. It's easy to dismiss hair removal as 'trivial' or 'cosmetic', but for transfeminine people it can be essential to affirming their identity. It's vital to health and wellbeing. Without it, they struggle to feel like the women they know themselves to be.

'Due to the current pandemic I am unable to continue my laser hair removal and electrolysis sessions,' one person explained. 'I have had to go back to shaving and watching the hair creep back in, which is causing my dysphoria to spike.'

My dysphoria does not spike. In fact, the opposite occurs.

When not pacing along the creek, I'm alone inside my one-bedroom apartment. There, with no eyes on my body, my curves are easier to ignore. My female shape is concealed by a new uniform of trackies, old T-shirts and oversized jumpers. I throw on whatever is comfortable and clean. The bigger the better. No more morning agonies before the bedroom mirror, trying on and discarding piles of clothes, hunting for the elusive outfit that will remake me into the right shape. Now I float through the days swaddled in elasticated androgyny, my body a formless prop for my brain.

My binders sit unworn. Those corsets that flatten unwanted breasts languish in the back of the closet. In lockdown, there's no longer anyone to assess the shape of my chest. Crop tops will suffice. Less flattening, but who's to know? The binders were a necessary evil, armour I'm happy to set aside while away from the eyes of the world. No more wrestling my shower-damp body into the suffocating compression vest. No more days of straining to breathe, lungs restricted by the tight fabric. Goodbye to underarm chafing, back pain, sweat.

The pandemic has its upsides, it turns out.

But it's not just the clothes that make gender easier in lockdown. It's the lack of other people. Gender is relational: it's something that comes alive in relation between humans. Other people make assessments about our gender and treat us accordingly. We perform our gender—through clothes, hair, make-up, body language, speech—to this audience of fellow humans. This performance is shaped by the perceived gender of those around us. We enact 'woman' or 'man' differently depending on whether we're with men or women or both.

You could say gender is a dance between people. It's performative, as Judith Butler put it. It's something we do rather than something we are. When we do gender, we're forever tweaking our performance to fit the audience.

When there's no one to dance with, when the performance loses its audience, gender changes. It becomes less important. Or, at least, it did for me. In lockdown, there is no one to assess my gender. There is no one perceiving me as male or female. There is no one calling me 'she' or 'her' or 'miss' or 'ma'am'. Instead, I'm just a human, sprawled on my old couch with a view of the sky, an oversized mug of English breakfast in one hand and a book in the other.

Instead of humans, I now pass my days with cats. On impulse, I adopt a kitten in the first week of lockdown. While the rest of Melbourne is panic-buying tinned tomatoes or making futile attempts to secure one of the few remaining rescue dogs or pedigree pups, I bring home a tiny fluffball whose luxuriant tail gives her the look of a brushtail possum. Arabella joins Delphi, my existing cat, as a stalwart companion. She has tiger stripes and silken fur and amber eyes quick to close in bliss. She is a natural alpha, a creature without fear, who overnight becomes the head of our household. Delphi, timid in tortoiseshell, is happy to serve as loyal retainer, tongue ever ready to groom her younger mistress.

We three become inseparable. They follow me from bed to desk to couch and back again. They groom themselves, they groom me, they doze in a tight embrace next to my legs. In the evening witching hour, they chase each other, nails scraping at the wooden floorboards, a mad glint in their eyes. Through sheer force of numbers, the pair remake our household into a feline kingdom, with humans welcome on sufferance.

Delphi has never been a lap cat, but bold Arabella is quick to colonise my chest as a favoured perch. Her purrs, vibrating from her heart to mine, keep anxiety at bay.

We are kin, we are family, we communicate through our language of touch and meows and glances. We gaze into each other's eyes and sleep in the same bed.

Gender could not be less relevant to our interactions. This is an interspecies communion miles away from those crude human concepts of 'man' and 'woman'. There is solace in connecting to another creature without the weight of pronouns. No *she* or *he* or *they*. Just purrs. Scratches on the belly. The kiss of a sandpaper tongue. Lockdown with animals opens my eyes to the possibility of love without the weight of gender performance. If I believed in souls, I'd say these companions see mine.

I'm clearly not alone here. Each time I Zoom with a fellow trans person, a cat invariably stalks across the screen. Do gender-nonconforming types, being set apart from the majority of fellow humans, gravitate towards the companionship of animals? I suspect our messiness, our refusal to fit into gender boxes labelled 'man' or 'woman', might incline us towards messing with that other neat division: 'animal' and 'human'.

Eileen Myles hints at these possibilities. In *Afterglow*, a tribute to their deceased dog Rosie, the non-binary poet suggests an alliance between gender deviance and interspecies camaraderie. 'I felt the tugging from the male side, and another from the female,' Myles writes of their childhood. 'Yet this inbetweeness, this aloneness, hear it now, is holy. I begged my parents fervently for an animal to be an army with me. My story would have moved so much faster if that dog friend had come aboard so early on.'

You can see it: a holy army, genderqueers and their animal-kin, alongside other creatures of the borderlands, all marching across sunbaked plains towards liberation. Picture us there: Arabella leading the troops, brushtail erect with purpose, with Delphi trotting in her shadow and me two steps behind, lugging kibble and catnip on my back, emboldened by my dauntless feline comrades.

Together, all us inbetween things, we gain courage to stride forward.

⌣

My dysphoria eases in the absence of other humans, but this same isolation sets me adrift from Melbourne's queer and trans communities. The loss of affirming queer spaces is hard to bear.

Only weeks before lockdown, I'd attended Midsumma Carnival, the picnic-cum-dance extravaganza that's the highlight of Melbourne's annual queer festival. On a sweltering day in late January, thousands upon thousands of sweaty bodies poured into Alexandra Gardens, on the southern bank of the Yarra, to preen, gossip, drink and dance the day away. There were twinks in crop tops, party gays fresh from the gym, drag queens sashaying on platform heels. Pimpled teens draped with trans flags. Rainbow families with prams. Tattooed hipsters sporting undercuts. Grey-haired lesbians with sensible shoes. Leather daddies holding hands. All arranged onto a thousand picnic blankets crammed onto the lush grass.

Food trucks sold vegan burgers and berry slushies. Community stalls handed out pamphlets. Everyone had an Esky packed with booze. There was a hundred-metre line for the portaloos; the desperate relieved themselves in the surrounding bushes. It was a queer Noah's Ark, an annual gathering of every possible species of LGBTQIA+, all jammed into a few hundred square metres of riverside lawn.

It was impossible to find anyone in the crush.

'Where are you guys?' new arrivals yelled into their phones, trying to hear over the music from the stage.

'On the rug next to the tree,' came the reply.

'Which rug? Which tree?'

I surveyed it all from my perch at the Transgender Victoria stall, where we sold badges, stickers and lanyards in the pink, blue and white of the trans flag. Before me, a constant stream of humanity rolled past. Every second person sported rainbows or glitter. Everyone shone with bonhomie. As the afternoon wore on, the humidity approached a hundred per cent and dark clouds threatened to drench the scene.

Every few minutes, a friend dropped by. There was Alexis and Iby, decked out in matching pink tees, en route to the dance floor. Then there was Clancy, on break from his own stall, pale face glistening beneath a panama hat.

'Looks like rain,' I said, pointing at the dark clouds.

'Either the rain will get us or the coronavirus will,' he replied, with a wry smile.

Coronavirus? That word had barely registered with my brain. Wasn't it something happening over in China?

'Coronavirus?' I scoffed. 'Yeah, whatever.'

I took a swig from my water bottle. 'Seeya later.'

Clancy receded into the crowd and I turned my attention to the next customer. We did a brisk trade in pronoun badges.

Midsumma Carnival was chaotic and sweaty and overwhelming. It was exhausting. It was paradise. A place where every queer—no matter how strange—could feel safe and normal, just for a few hours. A temporary reprieve from the heteronormative world. A place where we could gather and be ourselves.

Now, in lockdown, all that was gone. Now we queers were alone in houses, separated from our chosen family. On television, the besuited politicians talked about lockdown as if everyone lived in a suburban quarter acre block, complete with a lawn, three kids, two parents and a family dog. They spoke as if we could all spend the long homebound days baking with the kids, then crack out a jigsaw puzzle or Monopoly, while hubby did some DIY in the garden. Later, everyone could huddle on the couch for a family movie night.

In this official vision of lockdown, anyone who didn't conform to the heteronormative fantasy became invisible. All the queers and assorted others who lived in alternative family structures were written out of the story. No one was talking about our experience of the pandemic—not the politicians at the daily press conferences, not the public health messaging, not the media. We ceased to exist.

News outlets reported on disruptions to IVF, profiling childless couples bereft by the pause in treatment, but there was a deafening silence about the trans people who'd lost their chance at surgery. Was our pain not also worthy of reportage?

This confirmed what we'd always suspected: we didn't matter. We lived on the sufferance of the straight majority, who were quick to cast us to the winds. Sure, they liked queer creativity and were keen to secure the pink dollar. But in tough times, they would always close ranks. Straight couples who wanted babies were important; trans people suffering from dysphoria were not. Faced with this resolutely vanilla messaging, it was hard not to feel terribly alone.

Of course, lockdown loneliness was not restricted to trans folk. Everyone—cis or trans, no matter their circumstances—suffered under the isolation. But the pain was especially acute for trans people, who rely upon gathering together to offset a lifetime of stigma and prejudice.

When you're cisgender, the whole world is made for you. Our cities are structured around the idea that there are two sorts of people: penis-people who are men and vagina-people who are women. Every workplace, school, pub, gym, boutique, hairdresser and public toilet operates under the assumption that its occupants are the (binary) gender they were assigned at birth.

In this model, there is no allowance for penis-people who are women or vagina-people who are non-binary. Nor is there room for people with intersex variations that make their genitals and/or gender ambiguous. When you're 'other', spaces designed with you in mind barely exist.

There are only a few exceptions. A queer party or bookshop, a trans meet-up. A queer-friendly cafe. In those spaces, you could be surrounded by other people like you. Other trans men and women, non-binary folk, drag kings and queens, butches and femmes. Other people who break the gender rules. You could stop feeling like a freak, for a brief while.

So rare are these spaces, they become impossibly precious.

In lockdown, those spaces disappeared. Unable to congregate, trans and gender diverse people retreated into the shadows, each in their own separate houses. Each surrounded by a cisgender ocean that threatened to drown them altogether.

As Benjamin Riley argued, the pandemic hit LGBTQIA+ communities hard because queers rely upon physical encounters to affirm their identity and belonging. In Riley's words, 'queerness exists in [embodied] moments—not as an abstraction of identity but as something enacted and shared between people in queer spaces'. Without those spaces, he continues, 'I forgot how to be queer'.

So did I. Even in my otherwise queer inner-north suburb, the people like me all seemed to vanish. On daily walks, I was faced with mums powerwalking in activewear, dads steering strollers, retirees walking poodles. Where had all the tattooed weirdos gone?

In the absence of fellow travellers, I grow acutely conscious of my own difference, my own freakishness. On the street, I hunch my shoulders, stare at the pavement, avoiding eye-contact. Afraid to see disdain in a stranger's eyes. Back in my apartment building, going downstairs to the mailboxes, I take the stairs to avoid encounters in the lift. It isn't the virus I fear so much as cisgender humans, whose very normality will remind me of my strangeness. I grow skittish and surly, unable to acknowledge the perky blonde forever wrangling her golden-haired toddlers in the lobby. We cross paths almost daily, but never exchange a word. She is everything I was meant to be. Everything I failed to be. And now she's the only person I see. It hurts to look, so I don't.

With each passing week, it becomes harder and harder to breathe.

↜

In some ways, the trans community was well equipped to deal with the pandemic. As Sydney trans advocate Teddy Cook reflected in a May 2020 forum on 'Trans and COVID-19', trans people have long been familiar with isolation, loneliness and uncertainty. Having discovered ourselves to be part of a stigmatised minority, we know how to survive our world collapsing. We are used to our imagined future being upended. Like the disability community, we already know what it's like to spend weeks at home, afraid or unable to go out into a dangerous world.

We are seasoned at hardship.

The fact that we are still here, despite all the forces railed against us, is testament to our resilience and adaptability. We trans people entered the pandemic as tested survivors. If we had made it to this point, we could surely survive lockdown.

But still, the pandemic took its toll. Nationwide, trans wellbeing went downhill. Some trans people were trapped in actively hostile situations. Almost one in five were living with someone who made them feel unsafe or afraid. Trans youth, in particular, reported being locked down with transphobic family, unable to escape. Stuck with hostile parents or other relatives, they were deadnamed, misgendered and even exposed to physical violence.

Trans people were also vulnerable to the economic stresses of the pandemic, as they tend to cluster in the most affected industries: the arts, hospitality and retail, sex work, and higher education. According to the Transform research, sixty per cent were experiencing financial strain related to buying food. Almost half were struggling to pay the rent or meet mortgage repayments.

Faced with these circumstances, trans mental health went down the toilet. The TGD community already had elevated rates of depression, anxiety and suicidality, but now the numbers were off the charts. The same survey found that eighty-four per cent had felt down, depressed or hopeless in the past fortnight. Three-quarters had felt like a failure. Over half had thoughts of self-harm or suicide.

In my voluntary work with Transgender Victoria, we met the faces behind those statistics. As a facilitator for online peer support groups, we encountered trans people in crisis, barely hanging on by a thread, stuck on endless waiting lists for overloaded free counselling services. In the absence of actual care, they were relying on repeated calls to emergency hotlines. They were unemployed, lonely, estranged from family, fearful of going outside. There was nothing we could do except offer a sympathetic ear. I was barely hanging on myself.

It's all very well to 'ask for help', as the government campaigns instruct us, but what if there's no appropriate help available? Even for those able to afford psychology sessions, there are few psychologists with expertise in trans or queer mental health. Those who do work in this area are rarely trans themselves. Over the past two years, I'd cycled through a parade of cisgender psychologists, only to find that each time I felt like a strange specimen under their gaze. Each session, I'd have to explain basic concepts and terminology; I was paying for the privilege of educating them. Always, their ignorance and the chasm between us, made me feel unsafe, like a crustacean in need of a shell.

Soon, I stopped going. It was easier just to fumble along alone. Faced with the prospect of being scrutinised by a cisgender shrink, isolation seemed the lesser of two evils.

No one was talking about any of this. Our lockdown experience got no airtime.

Instead, the media and politicians told stories of white picket fences and nuclear families. Homeschooling, sourdough starter, quarantinis, Bunnings projects, family Tiktoks. A run on rescue dogs and jigsaws. Hunker down, get cosy with the family. Grow a veggie patch. Watch the footy with a beer or two. This will be a winter like no other, but we'll get through it together. Hold your family close.

But what if you don't live with family? What if your family has rejected you for being trans? What if your only family are the fellow queers who are now banned from gathering? What if you can feel yourself disappearing after weeks and months starved of anyone like you?

What then?

⌁

In spring, after more than six months of lockdown, I'm invited to the Zoom launch of the latest issue of *Archer*, a Melbourne-based queer magazine. I've contributed an article, and they want me to read from my piece.

I agree, but out of duty. It's another task, yet another Zoom to add to the hundreds upon hundreds attended this year. There have been so many soul-crushing hours staring at a montage of faces. At this point, just the sight of the blue-and-white Zoom logo triggers nausea.

The week before the launch, an Australia Post package arrives: decorations. The *Archer* team have sent me rainbow banners, magazine posters and confetti to liven up my backdrop. Vivid reds and blues and purples and greens. It's unnecessary and I love it. With life now reduced to bare essentials, all endless shades of grey, there's something defiant about spending time and money on mere colourful paper. It reminds me of the joys of frivolity.

On the night, rainbow decorations duly strung up behind me, the launch begins with an aerobics routine led by drag performer Betty Grumble. Adorned in high-cut leotard and eighties sweatbands, Grumble gets us to shimmy and shake.

'Thank your bodies, thank your bodies!' she instructs, wrapping her arms around herself.

Next, contributors read from our pieces. Besides me, there's a gay man talking about the ravages of HIV; a lesbian confessing her Catholic guilt; an Indigenous community leader. All different, all cherished here. In this space, we're the VIPs, not the freaks. At the centre, not the margins. As we read, the chat fills with love and affirmation from the audience of fellow queers. We can't be in the same physical place, but we reach each other with words. I haven't touched my G&T but can nonetheless discern a glow in my veins.

Already, this is a Zoom like no other. No longer a chore.

Then, the dancing begins. DJ Gay Dad, a non-binary performer, leads us through a set of queer anthems, early 2000s pop classics, and classic disco. The 'crowd' goes wild. We writhe and bop and shake in our loungerooms, kicking legs and swaying hips, apart but together, shaking off the tension of many months.

Somehow, I find the nerve to leave my video on. I'm dancing like nobody is watching—but the truth is that many people are. The difference is that they're my people. The people who never got the sympathy vote on TV, who were never acknowledged by ScoMo or Gladys or Daniel Andrews in his North Face. The people who know what being invisible feels like. Those who don't have any fucks left to give. This is our own alternative universe, where we make the rules.

The faces on the screen cheer my enthusiastic dancing, which is high on energy if light on finesse. High kicks, waving arms, bouncing feet. Never stop moving. Sweat soaks my T-shirt; the cats have taken refuge under the bed.

The DJ's set is meant to run for an hour but ends up going for more than two. We have last song after last song, only for us to plead for another.

We are all making stars of ourselves tonight. A constellation of pulsing aliveness. Tonight, we insist on our existence. Together, we are real.

Dazzling, even.

BLONDIE

THE CLIPPERS SAT UNUSED FOR weeks before I summoned the courage
to switch them on. It was a cordless contraption, bought online, that
resembled a dildo with teeth. Heavy for its size, gleaming silver, the
clippers sat snug in my palm, waiting to be awoken.

Once oiled and electrified, the blades came alive, gnashing
together with a ravenous whine. I considered the possibility they'd
slice open my skull. This seemed feasible, but not so likely as to
warrant calling off the whole endeavour. After all, we were in hard
lockdown: there was no one to shave my head but me.

All that morning I'd been propped up in bed with a pot of
tea, trying and failing to read. My brain was preoccupied with the
problem it'd been chewing over for months: should I, dare I, shave?

Over the five months since the pandemic hit, I'd managed only
a single visit to the hairdresser—something I normally did every
five weeks. Deep into Melbourne's second wave, and with no end of
lockdown in sight, my hairdresser would not reopen anytime soon.
On my head, things were getting out of control. My queer haircut,
one of those asymmetrical creations perched atop an undercut,

had entropized into a mop that ran down my neck and fell into my eyes. No amount of gel or hairspray would hold these locks in place.

But hair over my eyes wasn't the real problem. I didn't particularly mind not being able to see. After all, stuck at home all day, what was there to see, apart from my cats?

No, the problem was the return of my femininity.

⤳

It had been four years since my first major adult haircut.

On the day Trump was elected in 2016, I directed a bearded Chippendale barber to remove the mane that had hung down my back for the previous fifteen years. He pulled the locks into a ponytail, then amputated with one neat snip. As a red stain seeped across the United States, a mountain of blonde accumulated on the tiles beneath my chair.

That day, I couldn't tell you why I was asking for this clip. My natural blonde hair was, everyone told me, my greatest asset. There was no logic to discarding this fortune, this source of status. I felt only an inchoate urge to do something drastic.

In hindsight, that first cut was a step towards coming out as transgender. Two more years would pass before I could name myself as trans, but that day in 2016 was a beginning of sorts. It was the moment I first chose to be myself rather than be pretty. It was the moment I first dared to thumb my nose at the demand that 'women' highlight their femininity. *Fuck femininity* was the real meaning behind the gold hillock on the hairdresser's floor.

Over the four years that followed, my hair grew shorter and shorter, ever more androgynous, as I remade myself from a woman called Anne into a transmasculine person called Yves. My short hair was what made this transition feel real. Apart from a new wardrobe of menswear, only my cropped hair marked out my transgender self.

Because my hair carried the weight of my transition, I stomached the exorbitant cost of salon haircuts. I penny-pinched over groceries, could be racked with guilt over a four-dollar flat white, but would happily hand over ninety bucks every five weeks to keep my hairstyle fresh. On the walk home up High Street, I'd stroke the fresh undercut and search for my reflection in shop windows. The sharp cut carving a path through the coffee-scented air. All was right, again.

⌁

Now, thanks to the constraints of a pandemic, my hair was growing back fast. Yves was disappearing before my eyes.

Each day, my hairstyle lost definition. Sculptural forms collapsed into soft waves around my cheeks. Each day, the fresh growth shoved me back into womanhood. Each day, the urge to climb out of my skin got stronger.

This was what doctors called gender dysphoria.

This was what I called being terrorised by my own body.

Hence, the clippers. If I couldn't get a haircut, the only alternative seemed to be to shave it all off. Start afresh. A clean slate, so to speak. Why not? Surely there was no better time than a pandemic, with its social distancing and enforced working from home, to take the plunge into egg-head territory. If necessary, I could hide out inside, away from people and cameras, until my hair grew back.

But still, I prevaricated, like a swimmer frozen on the edge of a frigid pool. Even without a girlish mane, I still relied on my golden hair to win praise and attention. Being a 'natural blonde' was a safety blanket and a form of currency long taken for granted. I'd never experienced the world without its comforts and privileges.

Who would I be without any hair at all?

⌁

From childhood, blonde hair defined me. It was my signature, my calling card, the thing that made me recognisable in a crowd.

'You're so easy to spot,' friends would say. 'Your hair's like a beacon.'

My hair was the thing that made me special. The source of my worth.

I learnt this fact early.

'Don't you dare cut your hair!' exclaimed my grandmother, when, aged six, I voiced a passing desire for a haircut. 'It's so long and beautiful, you can't cut it off.'

This is one of our only exchanges I remember.

Hair was what bound me to my mother. In face and body, I have few traces of her side of the family. I'm tall and lean whereas she's short and curvy; she's got neat, symmetrical features, while I boast the bulbous nose and strong jaw recorded in photographs of my paternal ancestors.

But I did inherit Mum's straight blonde hair. Somehow this was enough to mark us out as mother and daughter. Our identical hair would overshadow the fact that, in every other way, we are carved from different moulds. We were the blonde girls, mother and mini-me, walking hand-in-hand down the street. Our common inheritance, our treasure.

For decades, every hairdresser visit followed the same script.

'Oh my god, is your hair natural?' the stylist would ask.

'Yep. Yep, it is.'

'Wow, that's incredible! People spend, like, hundreds of dollars to get hair like that. You're, like, so lucky.'

Lucky. That was always the word that was used. It never failed to rankle, to induce a queasy sensation in my guts.

Why, exactly, did being a natural blonde make me 'lucky'?

I didn't live in a bubble. I knew that blonde hair was high status, something that aspirational women spent good money and long hours to obtain. In the early 2000s, during my teenage years, magazines and billboards featured a relentless parade of blondes in spaghetti straps, straightened hair cascading from a central part towards a tanned midriff.

My hometown crawled with surfers, and surf culture loves a blonde. At school, the hot girls, the popular ones, always looked like they'd stepped straight from a Billabong ad: tan, thin, salt-crusted and, most importantly, armed with long, bleached hair.

Marilyn Monroe, Princess Diana, Grace Kelly, Cate Blanchett, Britney Spears—all those pin-ups and movie stars, elevated by their fair hair. Gentlemen prefer blondes, after all.

I was 'lucky' because I'd been handed that trophy for free. My hair just grew like this. Instant blonde bombshell, straight from the womb. No effort required.

But why was blonde hair so desirable to begin with? Because it was rare—and hence precious? After all, blonde hair is a recessive trait. Only an estimated two per cent of the global population are natural blondes. I was part of a tiny global minority.

But then, red hair is even less common and women don't dye their hair crimson en masse. We speak of 'bottle blondes' but not 'bottle redheads'. Instead we mock 'rangas' for their ginger locks—a hangover from the anti-Irish prejudice widespread during the nineteenth and early twentieth centuries. Red hair was a symbol of 'Irish otherness', explain researchers Amanda Third and Diane Negra. It signalled their 'off-whiteness' or 'not-quite-whiteness'. Today, the Irish are no longer questionably white, but the ambivalence around red hair remains. This history was invoked in the 2020 season of *The Bachelor*, when contestant Zoe-Clare went viral after she accused fellow contestants of anti-ranga prejudice.

Apart from red hair, there are many other human attributes just as rare as blondism yet without the same cachet—being intersex, being transgender, being albino. These are all estimated to feature in around one per cent of the population. Rare and 'special', indeed.

But no one is pretending they're intersex to get a promotion or a Tinder date.

So no, the rareness argument didn't hold up to scrutiny. The real basis to blonde cachet was white supremacy. Blonde hair is, after all, a symbol of whiteness, the hallmark of the so-called 'Nordic race' from northern Europe. From Hitler to Trump, there's a long history of blondes being fetishised in the name of racism and eugenics. Within this schema, the blonde (and ideally, blue-eyed) person is acclaimed as the apotheosis of whiteness—and hence, of desirability. As whiteness scholar Richard Dyer observes, 'blondeness and beauty are synonymous in Western myth and fairytale'. By extension, dark hair is coded as inferior. The hierarchies of beauty are mapped onto the hierarchies of race: the fairer the better.

The same logic shaped modern Australia. In the wake of World War II, when the country opened its doors to migrants from war-torn Europe, 'Beautiful Balts' were given priority because Australian officials admired their fair hair and blue eyes. Unlike 'darker' Europeans, these blondes were no threat to White Australia. '[Prime Minister] Chifley liked them blond,' was the word on the street.

Viewed in these terms, the hype over natural blondes felt like white supremacy by another name.

Then there was the association with youth. Blonde hair is more common in children than adults. Many people born blonde will go darker over time. The cherubic infant, crowned with golden curls, becomes the adult with unremarkable dun-coloured locks. (This was the fate of my brother, whose white mop went brown before puberty.) Blondeness is hence evocative of childhood and its imagined innocence and purity.

This would be fine, if blondes weren't also hypersexualised. So, a trait associated with peak female status and desirability is a trait concentrated among pre-pubescent children. What does this say about our culture? That we sexualise little girls or that we want adult women to be infantile—or both? Either way, it's perverse.

All in all, the hype over blondes felt a little too much like the mutterings of a Ku Klux Klan stalwart with paedophilic tendencies.

And so I would squirm under the hairdresser's hands as they marvelled at my tresses.

'You're so lucky, this colour is amazing.'

Every time it was the same. I'd grimace at their exclamations and wait for it to be over.

And yet: I was not immune to the blonde mythology. I was human, after all. I squirmed at the compliments but also fed off them, ravenous for the honeyed warmth of a stranger's praise.

Best of all, the hair praise soothed my gender anxieties. I was a woman, or so I'd been told, and therefore I was meant to be attractive. But my face was no one's definition of pretty. Big nose, deep-set eyes, strong jaw. As the mother of a boyfriend once told me, I had 'strong features'.

Handsome, maybe. Striking, perhaps. Pretty? No way.

There were ways, I knew, to cultivate prettiness. Potions and lotions, products and rituals. Yet I was baffled by the rituals of female beautification. It was a world as alien and impenetrable as outer space.

But was I really female, then? Blondeness was my saving grace here. Otherwise unfeminine, I relied on high-status hair to secure my place as a legit woman. Shining in the sun, my mane compensated for the parts of me that were wrong.

I saw how it worked: men chose me because they wanted a blonde on their arm. They weren't interested in me; they were in the market for a Barbie doll brought to life. With my hair, a short skirt and a smear of lip-gloss, I could be that Barbie for a night.

Once, at a Southbank restaurant, my date took my photo to text to his brother.

'I want to show him this blonde girl,' he said.

Later that night, he bought me Jaeger bombs at Crown, then fucked me in his car. I was just a mix of hair and holes.

At a gallery opening in Collingwood, an older man crossed the room to spin me round the dance floor.

Next morning, in bed, he explained: 'I saw this little blonde girl and couldn't resist.'

Years later, on a Sydney summer eve, a man on Crown Street picked me up, took me out for beers, then insisted on buying me dinner.

'I was walking behind you and saw your amazing hair and thought "I have to meet this blonde girl",' he told me, before sticking his tongue down my throat.

Then there was the predictable pick-up line.

'Are you Swedish? You must be, with hair like that,' the men leered again and again. Everyday hunters, looking for a tasty morsel, in cafes, on buses, in grocery stores.

The evidence was clear: the hair drew the men, like honey to a pot.

When men chose me, I felt secure in my impersonation of a woman. Their mauling hands and wet kisses were evidence that I'd tricked them, that I could perform 'woman' like a natural. Perhaps, if enough men made me their blonde, their generic fuckable girl, I could trick myself into forgetting that it was all an act. I could forget, for a night, that I was no woman at all.

The men were, as individuals, irrelevant. They were as generic to me as I was to them. I couldn't tell you their names. They're just a blur of hungry mouths and swollen crotches and lustful eyes— an assemblage of male desire that existed to validate my tenuous femininity.

Blonde hair was my secret weapon in all of this. And so I kept it long, washed it daily, and carried a brush at all times, so it would always gleam in the sun and, through gleaming, distract the eye from everything else. All you'd see was a Barbie doll, brought to life.

ᒧ

This kind of overcompensating is common among trans folk. Like actors cast in the wrong role, we may exaggerate and overact our assigned gender, desperate to keep the illusion alive.

Transfeminine people, also known as MTF (male-to-female), might have a hyper-masculine phase prior to transition. The writer Vivek Shraya was a keen bodybuilder before coming out as trans. Then living as a gay man, Shraya gorged on protein shakes and haunted the gym in an attempt to cultivate the masculinity she'd been shamed for lacking. 'I lift weights despite incurring injuries,' Shraya wrote, 'hoping to be both wanted and left alone, all the while reprimanding my body for not conforming.'

The same impulse sends future trans women into the military. In this most masculine of spaces, MTFs are found in disproportionate numbers. As the authors of *Serving in Silence* explain, incipient MTFs are 'motivated to enlist to conform to social pressures to align to hegemonic masculinity.' Not yet living as women, and struggling to be men, gyms and army barracks envelop trans women-to-be in the masculinity that adheres to these spaces.

For me, while still Anne, hair served much the same function. Not yet able to name my transness, and ill at ease in the role of woman, my blonde tresses cloaked me in compensatory femininity. It was my permanent Barbie costume.

To get maximum effect, I wore my hair out. No ponytails or buns for me. Just a river of blonde, cascading down my cheeks. With a full mane and big sunglasses, you could barely see my face. I could remain hidden in plain sight.

ᒧ

That first cut, in 2016, then all the ones since, had ushered Yves, my trans self, into the world. No longer was I trying to be woman. But even so, my hair remained a crutch. Its blondeness, and the white privilege that conveyed, helped offset the tattoos, the hairy legs, the men's shirts, the undercut—all my parts that were deviant and strange. Even short, my hair protected me.

Non-binary writer Roz Bellamy feared shaving their head because 'I knew it would make it a lot harder to pass as straight, which was a safety mechanism I still relied on at times.'

The same fear churned in my guts. After the clippers, there would be nowhere left to hide. There would just be my raw face, and my queerness, plain for all to see. A shaved head would mark me out as a gender traitor. A shaved head would invite the discomfort and scorn of others. I would become a walking provocation. As Bellamy notes, short and especially shaved hair on seeming 'women' constitutes 'an act of defiance'.

The world doesn't take kindly to those who defy gender rules. Hair, in particular, is often a site of contention. In the 1920s, the fashion for bobbed hair in women provoked hysteria precisely because it appeared 'unfeminine'. By cutting their locks, women made themselves androgynous. Shorn of their crowning glory, they muddied the division between women and men. It was an insurrection, and it was met with fierce backlash. Barbers refused to crop women's hair; husbands and fathers denied permission for the cut; some workplaces and churches even banned the bob. In the United States, the Bobbed Hair Bandit—a woman who held up a Bronx restaurant in 1924—fused androgyny and criminality in the public imagination.

Then, in the 1960s, the opposite occurred: men grew out their hair, becoming disturbingly 'effeminate'. After the long reign of the short-back-and-sides, Long Haired Hippies were suddenly everywhere. The gender binary was under threat once more. Men resembled women, throwing conventional ideas of masculinity and femininity into disarray. *What next?* pundits asked. *Was this a slippery slope towards the collapse of civilisation?* Again, these hair rebels were shamed and censured. 'Longhairs' were linked to drug addiction, promiscuity, degeneracy, even criminality. Parents dragged their children to the barbers, and many workplaces and schools enforced restrictions on hair length. Anything to restore order. To turn men back into men.

Today, the moral panic over androgynous hair has subsided. Cropped women or ponytailed men no longer raise eyebrows—most of the time. But the fear and hatred towards gender rebels remain. Trans and gender diverse people, especially those who don't 'pass' as cisgender, are routinely harassed or attacked just for existing. Hate crimes are on the rise. During 2019, twenty-six trans people were murdered in the United States; at least twenty-seven were murdered in the first seven months of 2020. Worldwide, over three thousand trans people have been murdered in the past decade. This violence is disproportionately directed towards transfeminine people, especially trans women of colour. But transmasculine types are also abused, beaten and killed for failing to perform 'woman'.

Shaving my head was unlikely to get me killed, but it might well make me a target for hatred. After all, Australian research from 2012 found that forty-seven per cent of trans men and thirty-seven per cent of trans women had experienced verbal abuse that year. The odds didn't look great.

There was another fear. Would my hair, post-shaving, change colour? Shaved leg hair regrew a darker shade; perhaps head hair would do the same. What if I lost my blonde cachet, not just temporarily, but forever? I'd never used hair dye due to anxiety that the original colour would fail to return. The clippers seemed no less fraught with danger. As much as I recoiled from the racism attached to blonde status, I wasn't ready to forego that status for good.

There was still a small, infantile part of me that needed to be special.

This hair vanity was a big part of what kept me from hormone replacement therapy. One of the irreversible side-effects of testosterone is male pattern balding. Once you start injecting T, you're liable to develop a receding hairline, thinning crown, or even go completely bald. Even if you stop the testosterone, the balding will remain. It's genetic, on the maternal side, so your mother's father and brothers are the best guide for what will happen.

In my case, the evidence was inclusive. My maternal grandfather was near bald by the end of his life. He died, aged eighty-five, with just a few white ruffles around a shiny crown. My maternal uncle, however, still boasts a ginger mop, only lightly thinned, in his mid-sixties. There were rumours of other relatives—some bald, some not—but they were little more than sepia memories from my mother's youth.

Even with a clear family trend, there's no guarantees what HRT will do. It's a lottery.

'Like unlocking the DNA of a male twin,' the gender psychologist explained.

On T, I might develop the musculature I craved, but at the cost of my hair. Muscles for follicles, so to speak. Or not. No one knew. Though the odds were against me. According to the American Hair Loss Association, two-thirds of cis men experience appreciable hair loss by age thirty-five. Over eighty-five per cent have significantly thinned hair by age fifty.

At this stage, it wasn't a risk I was ready to take.

⌐

Like most of my decisions, this one comes in a rush. Standing in the kitchen, in front of the mirrored splashback, I take the clippers to my skull. No towel, no preparation. Just steel assaulting follicles.

It's easier than expected. The clippers purr around my head, great hunks of hair falling to the floor. I start with the 2-cm blades, and then progress onto the 3 mm, the shortest setting. Within minutes, it's done. I haven't even nicked myself.

I sweep the floorboards, making a neat pile of hair. There's a shocking amount, a mix of sun-bleached gold and darker sections that never saw the light. No longer part of me, but still of me. A liminal object, halfway between human and trash.

I recall that hair was central to Victorian-era mourning rituals. Locks were kept in lockets, rings and brooches; cuttings were braided into bracelets. Hair as a metonym for an absent loved one.

I take a photo, then stuff the hair into the rubbish, where it embraces kitty litter, orange peel and teabags.

'You should keep the hair,' Mum instructs, over the phone. 'I wish I'd kept hair from when I was young.'

Again: blonde hair as currency, treasure. Something to hoard.

'Too late,' I tell Mum. 'I've binned it.'

But my hair won't leave me that easily. I'm left with the detritus on my body. Rogue hairs itch at my face, neck and down my back. It takes a long shower to scrub myself free of the shards. My clothes are harder to clean. Flecked with stray hairs, they scratch at my skin. Even after washing, my jumper remains unwearable. It's my own literal hairshirt, torment embedded in cotton weave.

The post-shaving rush is better than any drug. (Not that I've tried many.) The violence of the act, its hint of taboo, are felt in the body as pure adrenaline. Like plunging into icy water, only to emerge elated, hyper-alive. Reborn.

The hair that remains is a pelt, velvet made for stroking. In bed, I run my hand over the surface, learning the new texture, stroking myself into reverie as you would a cat. Smooth one way, crunchy the other. It's somehow feline, more animal than human. Tigers

come to mind, stalking through the long grass. There are worse
animals to resemble.

Within days, the pelt grows uneven. Tufts stick out, here and
there. In certain angles, the tufts catch the light, sparkling gold.
Ginger, in places. Almost white in others. Under the sun, I wear a
crown of sparkles. A queer baby, baptised in glitter.

I look like my brother, in his angry teenage years. I look like
my twenty-one-year-old cousin. I look like Yves. Boyish, unadorned,
a little fierce. No longer am I quite so eager to escape my own skin.

Outside, I don a beanie. Pulled low around the ears, black wool
swaddles my skull, hides it from staring eyes. But the exercise warms
my blood and the wool becomes cloying. Within days, I leave the
beanie at home. Down along Merri Creek, crowded with locals
walking their way through lockdown, I stride the paths, eyes down,
weathering a barrage of curious eyes. At least my state-mandated
mask keeps me anonymous. With cloth over my face, and Ray Bans
perched on my nose, I could be anyone. On the street, friends and
neighbours stride past, oblivious. There are still places to hide.

For the next fortnight, I keep my camera off in Zoom meetings.

'My internet connection has been shaky,' I dissemble. 'We'll get
a better connection if I keep the video off.'

With my egg head hidden, colleagues speak to my Zoom avatar,
a professional headshot taken a year ago. I'm not ready to let that
person go.

While running, I'm newly streamlined, aerodynamic. There's no
hair to collect sweat or hang in my eyes. The breeze whisks over
my pelt. I'm an animal, powering through space.

A fortnight after the Great Shaving, stage 4 lockdown is extended.
Hairdressers won't reopen for another six weeks, at least. A collective howl reverberates across Melbourne at the news. Everyone is
shaggy and unkempt. Roots are growing out. Fringes encroach upon
eyes. On Twitter, the desperate weigh up the pros and cons of a

self-administered trim. Stylists take to Zoom to advise on home haircuts.

I sit back and watch, reassured I'd made the right decision. Using the clippers a fortnight ago had saved me two months of hair-induced dysphoria. Two months of being terrorised by my own body. The stares of strangers are a small price to pay for dodging that fate.

⌁

My shaved head is not the only reason strangers stare. Eyes also widen at my legs, covered by golden tendrils. I'd stopped shaving eighteen months earlier. Ever since, my leg hair had grown with abandon, free and untamed after two decades of depilation. It was another way to refuse womanhood, to embrace masculinity without testosterone.

This bodily hair growth is no less transgressive than head hair removal. In contemporary Western cultures, body hair is deemed 'uncouth, even downright repulsive', notes historian Rebecca Herzig. Recent research found that ninety-nine per cent of American women voluntarily remove body hair. Around eighty-five per cent do so regularly—even daily. It's a taken-for-granted part of feminine grooming, as expected as wearing deodorant or brushing your teeth. Increasingly, men remove body hair also. As of 2005, sixty per cent removed or reduced hair below the neck.

In this context, visible body hair becomes an insurrection—especially for someone, like me, perceived as 'female'. My verdant calves, tanned beneath running shorts, broadcast deviance to the world. They prompt strangers to double-take and furrow their brow. But here again, my blondeness protects me. Low melanin makes my leg hair less conspicuous, less 'disgusting'. In the right light, the pale follicles are near invisible. It's another opportunity to hide.

There's nothing 'natural' about this aversion to body hair. We're not born feeling disgusted by hairy legs. In fact, the practice of regular shaving and waxing is barely a century old. It wasn't until the 1920s that depilation became mainstream. The 'problem' of body hair is a recent invention, fuelled by racism. According to the scientific racism developed in the late-nineteenth century, hairiness was a sign of the primitive, the simian. Body hair became associated with 'less-developed' races, and so white people began to view their own hair with disgust. Smooth skin emerged as a marker of civilisation.

In the twentieth century, the growing requirement to shave was also a new form of gendered control. Just as women won the vote and other political rights, their freedoms were restricted anew by the 'third shift' of beautification (a term coined by Naomi Wolf). Women had their time and wallets colonised by an ever-growing list of 'essential' grooming rituals—a win for patriarchy *and* capitalism!

Back in my leg-shaving days, I'd fume at the bother of this Sisyphean ritual. I don't miss that labour. I don't miss replacing blunt blades, lathering up in the shower, balancing on one leg, the tedious strokes up the calf and around the fiddly knee and ankle regions. I don't miss the nicks and cuts, the scratchy regrowth, the endless disposable plastic. Nor do I mourn the mental labour of planning ahead to ensure a smooth-legged appearance in public.

Sometimes, though, I hanker for the glow of impeccable hygiene conveyed by a fresh shave. I want to feel clean and streamlined in the way that only hairless skin can provide. There's nothing intrinsically dirty about body hair, I know. And yet, I am still unlearning my own disgust. Even as strangers' stares cease to bother me, I'm still teaching myself not to recoil at the brush of leg hair against bedsheets.

Maybe it's the sense of renewal I miss. Smooth legs are a clean slate, a fresh beginning, full of promise.

Now my head serves this function. It's been pruned back like a tree in winter, stripped of excess growth, in readiness for something new.

As the weeks pass, my post-shaving pelt offers lessons in impermanence. My head is only 'shaved' for a day or so before fresh growth asserts itself. Each day, the texture changes, from velvet to carpet to the crunch of dry lawn. Each day, I measure the new length in my palms. The cowlick at my forehead returns. Changing, always, without any effort on my part. Each day, idly stroking, my hands find new evidence that nothing ever stays the same. Here is a new tuft, a new silkiness at the neck. A new wave at the temple. Here is me growing and dying each second.

A month in, the pelt now a forest of bristles, I discuss the politics of hair on late-night radio. The call-back is dominated by women who lost their hair during chemo. They speak about the grief of going bald, the joy of hair sprouting once more. The post-chemo growth is a rebirth, they explain. The new hair, often different in colour and texture, ushers in a new phase of life. Post-cancer, born again.

My own regrowth is also a rebirth of sorts. The shaving was a necessary violence, a shedding of old skin. It enabled me to leave the chrysalis of gender transition and re-emerge as something new. Something that manifests, millimetre by millimetre, with each passing minute.

This regeneration coincides with the first weeks of spring. Jasmine perfumes the night air and angry winds whip my apartment. Like the branches beginning to blossom, I too am bursting with new life. Buds open, shoots rise, gold spills from my scalp. Waiting at the traffic lights, warm air ruffles the hair on my legs.

Despite the long months of winter, despite the carnage of plague and fire, we keep blooming, all of us alive things. The trees and I are not so different. We're all just collections of cells, pulsing with life, reaching towards the sun. In spite of everything.

BPM

ON THE DAY THEY STORMED the Capitol, I panic-bought an Apple Watch. I'd spent the morning transfixed by live footage of red-faced men in combat gear, trampling the vestiges of American democracy with their fists and flags, and I was sick with fear. We knew something like this was coming but foresight didn't stop the bile in my throat. News sites showed gas masks and drawn guns inside the Senate chamber. Live blogs reported that the curfew was being ignored. Further down the webpages, hidden below the Senate story, small print reported that over 255,000 COVID cases had been recorded in the US that day—a new record.

The world was burning, 2021 was proving even worse than 2020, and I could do nothing to quench the flames. So I went shopping. Browsing the internet, I succumbed to a sudden urgent desire for a watch that would track my every step, every heartbeat, a miniature computer that would take up residence on my skin. It was a prosthetic, sleek in black aluminium, that promised mastery over my own body. It would collect data, it would make graphs, it would assert order via measurement. There would be numbers to monitor, targets to meet. My unruly flesh and blood would be made knowable.

As I entered my credit card details, hit the purchase button, I felt the panic subside. Order would soon be restored. I leant back in the chair and took my first deep breath of the day. The fires out in the world continued to rage, but at least there'd be some things I could control.

The watch arrived seven days later, delivered by courier to my front door. It was tiny, barely bigger than a fifty-cent coin. The square watch-face fastened around my wrist with a black leather band that closed with a magnetic snap. The watch wasted no time settling into its new home. Once attached to my body, it began monitoring my stats. Resting heart rate, active heart rate, steps taken, stairs climbed, exercise minutes, standing minutes, kilometres walked, kilojoules burned, VO2 max. Whenever I washed my hands, the watch counted down twenty seconds and vibrated joyously upon reaching zero. Every hour, it sent reminders to breathe. If I'd been sitting too long, I'd receive a stern injunction to stand.

It was my own live-in personal trainer, ever vigilant, with a perky veneer and tendencies towards passive aggression. The watch was removed at night, but it was champing at the bit to track my sleep. I was being remade into data, different metrics for every hour of the day. I used to jeer at the 'quantified self' movement—that army of narcissistic biohackers, spawn of Silicon Valley, who applied the neoliberal logics of growth and optimisation to their own flesh and blood. I'd been repelled by the incursion of surveillance into our most intimate spaces. I still was, in truth. But now I was one of them. Despite my misgivings, I'd joined the ranks of the quantified.

I'd always been a bit too eager to monitor and control my body. In my teens and twenties, compulsive exercise and birdlike eating helped keep the demons at bay. My body was wrong—too fleshy, too feminine—but it could be disciplined into something almost benign. Disgusted by the swell of hip, the softness of belly? Go for a run, mortify the flesh, eat broccoli, scorn sugar. A temporary safety will greet you there.

The Apple Watch, always demanding more, threatened a return to those days of living under the whip. I could feel the old urges pulsing beneath my skin, the siren song of addiction, promising to fix it all with a single step. *Just do this, and everything will be fine.*

The tyranny of numbers was delicious. Move body, meet target, get reward. It was all so simple. The anxious whine of news receded as I applied myself to the watch's demands. If I did what it said, if I followed the rules, I would get fitter, faster, leaner, stronger. Better. Less wrong. That was the promise of living by the numbers. My messy transness, my soft flesh with the wrong bumps and holes, my shame at failing gender, would all be erased by the unassailable virtue of good stats. You couldn't argue with a graph going in the right direction.

There were three core daily targets: standing time, exercise time, kilojoules burned. Each was symbolised by a coloured ring on the watch-face. Red, green and blue, arranged in concentric circles. In the morning, the rings were opaque, empty of colour. Over the day, as you stood and walked and puffed, the rings filled to indicate your progress towards the target. If you met all three targets, you had 'closed your rings'. This was the holy grail.

'Keep moving and close your rings!' chirped the instructors at the end of each Apple Fitness+ video.

The kilojoules target, or the move ring, was the hardest to reach. No matter how much I exercised, the numbers refused to climb to a hundred per cent. Day after day, I closed the standing and exercise ring, but the move ring plateaued at eighty or ninety per cent. The failure nagged at me, an itch I couldn't scratch.

Finally, after a week, I hit ninety-five per cent on the move ring just before bed. Victory was within reach. Instead of brushing my teeth, I grabbed the broom and began sweeping the floorboards, exaggerating my movements for maximal energy output. Like an entrant for the sweeping Olympics, I hunted down dirt in stray corners of the kitchen and beneath my desk. When the floor was clean, the move ring was on ninety-seven per cent. So close. But yet so far. What next?

For the next twenty minutes, I emptied the litter tray, took out the rubbish, wiped the benches, watered the plants, scrubbed the toilet, folded laundry—anything to reach the target. It was well past my bedtime, but I couldn't give up. Eventually, with my apartment now spotless, I resorted to star jumps in the bedroom. In out, in out, in out. The cats watched from under the bed, where they'd retreated to shelter from this unaccustomed late-night frenzy. In the mirror, I caught glimpses of my face, all red cheeks and wild eyes. In out, in out. I checked my watch: ninety-nine per cent. What next? Squats. Up down, up down, up down. My legs burned. A cat yowled in protest. *Go to bed!* I heard her cry.

Then finally it happened: the move target hit a hundred per cent. My rings closed. I'd done it. It was strangely anticlimactic. I'd expected more fanfare from the watch, something more than a simple notification. There was no vibration, no congratulatory messages. What a letdown. I crawled into bed, sweaty and disheartened. *That wasn't worth the effort,* was my last thought before sleep.

If only that was the end of it. But I was in thrall to forces stronger than reason.

The next night, I checked my watch after dinner. The move target again hovered at ninety-five per cent. My pulse quickened, thrilling at the prospect of a goal. I could almost taste the dopamine. Addict that I was, I embarked on late-night calisthenics once more. In out, in out. Up down, up down. Squats, star jumps, running on the spot. Keep moving, always moving. The minutes ticked by, as the numbers on my wrist crept towards the target. Outside the night was black. What on earth did the neighbours think?

It was mad, I knew. Obsession bordering on mania. But sometimes mania is the lesser of two evils, preferable to the leaden weight of grief. As long as I remained fixed on the targets, I didn't have to think about COVID, climate, Trump, the whole world in flames. But most especially, I didn't have to think about the wrongness of my body and its insistence on telling the lie that I was woman. As long as I filled my mind with numbers and metrics, I could ignore the unwanted lumps on my chest, the insistent curve of my thighs, the high pitch of my voice. I didn't have to taste the poison of being a prisoner in my own flesh.

⤳

The watch had an insatiable appetite for data, forever feeding on the facts of my existence. It wasn't content to track my movement; it needed to know the very pulse of my blood. It shone a light on the hidden mechanisms of the body, converting bloody matter into clean numbers. It would leave no mystery uncovered.

I submitted, utterly. I would allow myself to be known.

At every hour of the day, the watch monitored my heart rate. A sensor on its backside measured the pulse at my wrist. Apple likes to boast that this ECG has medical-grade accuracy.

The current heart rate was updated every few seconds, the beats per minute ever refreshing like my own personal stock exchange. The day's data was mapped on a live graph whose serpentine curve showed the shape of each hour. A spike in the late afternoon when I went running. A long valley for the daytime hours at the desk. Rolling hills that marked housework or a trip to the shops. Here was my life, reduced to an undulating line.

My resting rate was low. The average resting heart rate of a healthy adult is between sixty and a hundred beats per minute. I was well below that. Fifty beats per minute, most days. Sometimes, it would drop into the mid-forties. The doctors call this bradycardia: a sub-sixty heart rate, common in young adults and athletes, but also associated with congenital heart defects, heart tissue damage, hypothyroidism and autoimmune disease. Several years earlier, I'd spent twenty-four hours wearing a heart monitor to ensure my brady-cardia wasn't pathological. After reviewing the data, the cardiologist told me everything looked fine but he couldn't give any guarantees. I could live to ninety or I could drop dead tomorrow. Science didn't have a crystal ball.

Five years later, my heart was still pumping, still slower than the norm. Fifty-one, fifty, forty-nine. When sitting for long periods, the number crept down. Forty-eight, forty-seven. It was volatile, though. Even the few paces between desk and kettle would send the rate shooting into the eighties. I imagined the heart muscle, dozing with one eye open, suddenly spurred into action to propel my feet across the floorboards. *Quick, all hands on deck, fellas, we've gotta get this blood pumped.* A frenzy of muscle contraction, the organ test-driving its rapid acceleration, then back to standby, awaiting the next big job.

When I ran, the rate climbed into three digits, sitting at around 140. On the exercise bike, legs whirring, I could push it as high as 165—a number that left me breathless and drenched with sweat, fingers tingling. What a plucky little pump, to have such range.

My heart rate went down as quickly as it climbed. Only a minute or two after stumbling off the treadmill, the beats per minute plum-meted back into the eighties. This heart muscle was a well-oiled machine, ever adjusting to meet demand. Shifting gears in a second, never overextending itself. Around the clock it worked, without a moment's pause, always ready to give my body what it needed.

Like an addict, I checked my heartbeat at every opportunity. The thrill of closing my rings paled in comparison to this constant

news feed, ever refreshing with the latest data. It was the new
Twitter. Instead of checking the bird app, I looked for updates
on the state of my heart. Every time, the number was different.
Standing in line? Eighty-three. Sitting on the toilet? Sixty. Reading
in bed? Forty-nine. Running up a hill, struggling for breath? One
hundred and fifty-five. No matter the time of day, my heart would
be beating away, doing its job without fuss. I half-suspected that
one day I'd catch it unawares, find it had mooched off for a smoke
when I wasn't looking. Surely it would get bored at some point.
But it never missed a single beat. Sometimes fast, often slow, but
always there. The most constant of friends.

In idle moments, I stared at the numbers for long minutes,
watching my heart rate rise and fall. The slower my breathing, the
lower the numbers. I forced long breaths and saw my heart rate drop
to forty-seven, forty-six. How low could it go? The lowest recorded
heart rate is twenty-six BPM, found on an athletic octogenarian in
Surrey, England, in 2014. Mindful activities like meditation and
yoga often generate heart rates in the thirties. At forty-six, I certainly
felt calm. In steering my heart rate down, was I soothing the beasts
of my mind?

I could also make the number rise. If I turned my thoughts
to something stressful, a public humiliation or looming deadline,
the figure would jump to sixty-nine within a second. My heart
was picking up pace to meet a threat I'd conjured in my mind.
Nothing had changed except my thoughts. From forty-six to sixty-
nine without moving a muscle, the number on my wrist pushed
up and down via mere thought and breath. It was like magic. I'd
finally acquired the ability to move things with my mind. Body and
mind, dancing in sync. Descartes was wrong, after all.

It was strange, how a piece of cutting-edge technology, a pros-
thesis worthy of science fiction, was reacquainting me with the
wondrous animality of my flesh. Heart pumping, lungs breathing,

limbs moving, brain running the show—all synchronised, working in concert to keep me alive. It was a marvel. My ordinary human body was the most intricate of machines. I'd never really noticed before. I'd been too busy punishing my ill-shapen flesh to wonder at the infrastructure behind the scenes, the organs that kept me going with nary a word of thanks. No matter my neglect, my heart kept pumping away.

'Here, try my watch, check your heart rate,' I demanded of anyone who got too close. 'Isn't it amazing how the number is always changing? Aren't our bodies incredible?'

In bed, drifting towards sleep, I hugged my chest tight, feeling the heart muscle prepare itself for the night shift. I imagined it labouring through the wee hours, and felt a sudden wave of gratitude.

It was as though I'd discovered a loyal dog living beneath my skin, gazing up with adoring eyes, tail wagging, waiting to be loved. It had been here all this time, and I'd never given it the time of day. How blind I'd been, to ignore such devoted care. Day in, day out. So long as I remained alive, it would never leave me. I'd never be loved better than this.

Maybe, now I'd seen it properly, I could begin to love it back.

I still recoil from my feminine shape in the mirror. Most days, I still want to climb out of my skin. My body remains a prison, punishment for a long-forgotten crime. But within the prison, trapped alongside me, is a dog who exists only to love me. That dog is my heart. It beats out the minutes of my life, its steady work recorded on my wrist. Together, we make it through the days.

DESTINATION TRANS

THESE DAYS, I'VE HITCHED MY wagon to a prefix. *Trans* is what I call myself. Not non-binary or transgender or transsexual or a trans man or even transmasculine. Just trans, from the Latin for *across* or *beyond*.

Used as a prefix, trans conjures movement from one point to another. We take *trans*atlantic flights between London and New York. A *trans*continental train carries us from Paris to Prague. We *trans*late words from English to Japanese; we *trans*fer money from one bank account to another. *Trans*port, *trans*mit, *trans*cend, *trans*verse, *trans*act. Such an active little prefix, forever bustling about, busy-busy, doing the work of the world. *Trans*ition, *trans*form.

These words imply a beginning, middle and end. Something begins at point A, is transported or transformed or transmitted into something or somewhere else, before settling at point B. The trans- word refers to the middle phase, the time of movement and flux between two points of stasis. The trans-ing is the journey, the change that must come to an end.

'When are you going to finish being trans?' I'm often asked. 'When will you be done?'

The implication is that, like a transformation or transition, trans-ness is a time-limited process. I will be trans for a while, I'll journey across and beyond, before reaching a destination where I'll kick off my boots, unpack my bag, scrub off the dirt of the journey and settle down to rest.

'Trans-ing complete,' I'd radio back to home base. 'Mission accomplished.'

For many years, the words *transgender* and *transsexual* did carry this sense of movement towards a known destination. These terms, in their original medical usage, implied transition from one side of the gender binary to the other. A female-assigned person would remake themselves into man, or a male-assigned person would become woman. There was a point A and point B, with a transition in the middle.

In this medical paradigm, the ideal was assimilation back into the gender binary. The transition would be 'complete' when no one could tell you were transgender anymore. Point A was presenting as a cisgender man or woman, and point B was passing as cisgender once more. You might still be transgender, but no one would ever know. You were 'done' or 'finished' when the transness had been tidied away, no longer visible to the world.

Of course, real people have never been that orderly, but this was the medical script of how transgender or transsexual was meant to look.

Trans, though, not transgender or transsexual, just trans—that's something different. There's no terrain of gender or sex to trans-verse. It's just the prefix, standing alone, detached from anything concrete, spinning out into space. Recall that trans means across but also *beyond*—beyond the binary, beyond the categories, beyond the rules and prescriptions. Always becoming, forever unresolved.

'No one had ever told me I could just be trans, that trans could be my destination,' writes Juno Roche in their 2019 book *Trans Power*. A British trans person, assigned male at birth, Roche used to think they were a trans woman. But after gender-affirmation surgery, in which they acquired a vagina, Roche realised they were no more 'woman' than 'man'. Nor were they non-binary. Roche objected to the idea of existing in opposition to something, especially to something—the gender binary—that 'I don't even believe in'. Instead, Roche was something else altogether: trans.

'Trans was always my destination,' writes Roche, now in their fifties and living in Spain. 'The word "trans" is the one that fits me now like a glove. Like a beautiful soft, old leather glove. It feels like I have only ever been this word "trans", even though for many years I didn't know. Born trans, born this way.'

Like Roche, I'm leaning into my transness, refusing to tidy it away. Trans fits me in a way that woman and man and even non-binary never have. It's a destination that's open, unscripted, full of possibility. It allows me the freedom to evolve and change, to do gender differently each day, to be forever becoming. Even though trans is still deemed a dirty word, a place to shy away from, I'm reclaiming it as my chosen destination.

'When are you going to finish being trans?' I'm asked.

To which I say: never. I'm not passing through. This is it, for me. I'm home now.

I've 'transitioned', yes, but not from woman to man; rather from cis to trans. I transitioned from within the binary to beyond it. My destination, my point B, was no fixed point at all, but a vast open plain where I wander, marvelling anew each day at the possibilities.

'I see transness as a synonym for freedom. I see transness as a synonym for escape,' says Travis Alabanza, an English trans performance artist.

Alabanza is right: there's so much space out here. Space enough to run wild across the sand, dance in circles, cartwheel until we're dizzy and collapse on our backs to feast on the endless sky. We're the free ones, the lucky ones, and I only wish more people had the opportunity to savour all this space.

And maybe, soon, they will. If transness is the state of being ill-at-ease with the binary genders assigned to us at birth, you could say almost everyone is trans. Because almost everyone, at some point, suffers from the obligation to be 'man' or 'woman'. Women resent the beauty and caring obligations of femininity. Men feel trapped by the pressure to be strong. Gender trouble is near universal. Trans people are those who name this trouble, but they're not the only ones to experience it.

Today, ever more people are willing and able to name their gender trouble. Trans identification is growing, especially among youth. In Melbourne, the Royal Children's Hospital Gender Clinic has seen a significant growth in referrals, rising from three in 2007 to 250 in 2017 alone. At the Monash Gender Clinic, which caters to adults, referrals increased from 88 in 2011 to 247 in 2017.

Similar trends are evident worldwide. A Gallup poll of fifteen thousand Americans, released in early 2021, found that Generation Z (born between 1997 and 2012) is the queerest generation yet. One in six identified as LGBTQIA+, with 1.8 per cent of Gen Z specifically identifying as trans. This is a big jump from millennials (born between 1981 and 1997), of whom one in ten are LGBTQIA+, and 1.2 per cent are trans. Among baby boomers, only one in fifty are LGBTQIA+ and 0.2 per cent are trans.

The trend is clear: each generation is fucking with norms of gender and sexuality more than the one before. The kids are doing alright. At a time when we're staring down the barrel of a climate crisis, this is a rare trend that gives me hope for the future.

TERFs and other transphobes like to blame the increased incidence of transness on 'social contagion' or 'peer pressure'. But the
truth is much more banal. It's simply that, thanks to increased
trans visibility and the ubiquity of the internet, more people now
have opportunity to put words to the gender trouble that's haunted
us for so long. Transness isn't infection or trend; it's a new name
for an old feeling—a feeling that's deeply human and remarkably
common. In the 2020s, there are not necessarily more trans people,
just more people calling themselves trans.

Today, these people are claiming a space of freedom outside the
stale old notion that penis-babies are men and vagina-babies are
women and no other genders can exist. They're all refusing to be
placed in the predetermined boxes that form the building blocks
of patriarchy.

'Transness really is a new space,' Roche concludes. 'Trans is
uncontrolled and uncontrollable by patriarchy.'

At this point, I no longer worry that transness is at odds with
feminism. In fact, I'm now convinced of the opposite: that trans
identities and perspectives are essential to the feminist project of
smashing the patriarchy. This is because patriarchy is itself rooted
in the gender binary. *Men > women* only works if a) M and F are
the only available options; and b) M and F are fixed categories.
If we add other genders to the mix, and celebrate creative gender
expression for all bodies, then the fallacy of masculine dominance
and feminine subservience becomes difficult to sustain. In other
words, the trans challenge to prescriptive binary gender is simultaneously a challenge to patriarchy.

Take gendered violence, for instance. As Australian and international research has shown, 'rigid gender stereotypes' are a
consistent predictor of violence against women. *Change the Story*,
a 2015 research study conducted by the Australian organisation
Our Watch, found that 'a strong belief in . . . what it means to be

"masculine" or "feminine" are also key drivers of violence against women'. The study also noted that those 'who see men and women as having specific and distinct characteristics are more likely to condone, tolerate or excuse such violence'. As a result, Our Watch is now focusing its preventative efforts on challenging such thinking at an early age. A 2018 report noted that parents have a 'unique opportunity' to prevent gendered violence by 'challenging rigid and harmful gender stereotypes and promoting diverse interests, opportunities and experiences for all children'.

In short, to end the national tragedy of one woman murdered each week by a current or former partner, we need to allow kids to play with gender. Children who run free in the gender playground are children who grow up to build a more equitable and less violent world.

This doesn't mean all children (or indeed adults) are or should be trans. To enforce trans identities would be as oppressive and futile as enforcing binary gender. The point is that narrow ideas of masculinity and femininity are the problem, and everyone is a winner when we learn from trans people pioneering new ways of imagining and doing gender. The point is that feminism, a political project opposed to patriarchy, stands to benefit from the trans critique of binary gender. In fact, to my mind, there's only so much feminism can achieve within a binary paradigm; to truly eliminate gendered violence and inequity, we must unravel the binary altogether. *Smash the cis-tem*, as the slogan goes.

As Roche puts it, 'The word "trans", as a destination, has the capacity to truly shake the patriarchal structures to the ground'.

It's hard, though, to imagine my trans future. All things going well (and depending on climate breakdown), I could have fifty years ahead of me. What would it mean to be trans at fifty, at seventy, in the twenty-first century? When I look ahead, try to picture the possibilities, all I see is a void.

Back when I still believed myself to be a cisgender woman, my imagined future was laid out for me like a buffet. There was an endless array of women, a decade or two older, modelling all the different ways to walk through life. I could be a hard-nosed career woman, a MILF in athleisure, a harried supermum trying to do it all, or a dozen other things besides. To be sure, none of these futures appealed. But at least they provided orientation and direction. I had a map, a GPS and a range of destinations.

Now, I'm walking blind, groping my way through unchartered space, fighting fear of the unknown with every step. It's hard to trust that my feet will meet solid ground.

Juno Roche, in their fifties, is a rare trans matriarch. Although an army of trans people have gone before me, so many died too young, or lived 'stealth', or have been erased from history, or never had opportunity to come out as trans at all. I feel their absence keenly. With relatively few trans trailblazers in my midst, I cling to trans peers only three or five years older, poring over the details of their lives for clues as to what awaits me.

'How was it after top surgery? How is it now with your family?' I demand.

What I'm really asking is: 'Tell me what comes next. Tell me what it means to be trans, ageing and alive. Help me believe I have a future.'

Transness is an uncontrolled space of freedom, rich with possibility, but often I'm lonely and lost out here. Sometimes, you just want to know where you're going. Sometimes, you'd give your right arm for footsteps to follow and a half-decent map.

⤳

After walking away from the gender psychologist, I put my name on the waiting list for Equinox, a peer-led gender diverse health centre in Melbourne's inner north. Equinox opened in 2016, the first clinic of its kind in Australia. It follows a 'trans-affirmative' model that resists the idea that transness is a sickness or a problem. Unlike other gender clinics, Equinox administers hormone replacement therapy (HRT) to trans people via informed consent. Under this framework, there's no need for a diagnosis. No need to prove transness, no need to submit to the medical gaze, nor be infantilised by medical gatekeeping. Instead trans people are given the dignity of being treated like autonomous adults with full sovereignty over their bodies. Equinox views treatment as a 'collaborative effort' between patient and clinician, doing away with the traditional submission of the patient to medical authority. At Equinox, I could be in the drivers' seat, supported by doctors there to educate me and administer whatever treatments I chose.

I sat on Equinox's waiting list for almost a year. Grey winter, windy spring, bushfire summer, and then back into short days and forever nights. Several times during that rotation around the sun, I called the centre, panicked that they'd lost my details or forgotten about me.

'No, no,' I was reassured by a soothing voice. 'No need to worry. You're still on the list. There's just still many people ahead of you. It'll be another few months, at least.'

Finally, after eleven months, the call came. I'd reached the top of the list.

In retrospect, I was one of the lucky ones. As of March 2021, Equinox's waitlist is closed to new patients, with over 175 individuals awaiting their first appointment. Clearly, there is widespread need for a trans-affirmative model, and this one tiny clinic cannot possibly keep up with demand. Similar clinics have recently opened in Preston and Ballarat, but these too are fast filling up.

The day of my first Equinox appointment, I trudged down Hoddle Street through the roar of Friday afternoon traffic, before turning into a nondescript building crouched amid the bitumen. In the hushed lobby sat racks of donated free clothes.

The receptionists were expecting me.

'Welcome!' They beamed. 'You're Yves, right? Did I pronounce your name correctly?'

I was ushered into the waiting area like a VIP at a day spa.

Ten minutes later, I was sitting across from the doctor, chatting about my options. She was a similar age and could've been a friend-of-a-friend. The atmosphere was relaxed, with none of the solemnity I'd come to associate with Transgender Medicine.

'If you decide on testosterone, you have a few options. There's a cream, a gel and injections.'

It was all so matter-of-fact, untainted by shame. We might have been discussing the pros and cons of a new hairstyle or tattoo.

After thirty minutes, the doctor ejected me back into the bright afternoon with a pathology script and a fat dossier about the effects of testosterone.

On the walk home, I called Mum.

'How'd it go?' she asked.

'It was good. Different. Weird, almost.'

'What was weird about it?'

I paused, searching for the right words.

'It was weird because I didn't feel like a freak.'

The day of my second appointment, several weeks later, my brain is a cockroach on coke. All morning, I tab between email and news and socials, eyes twitchy, counting down the hours until the scheduled telehealth call. *This is it. Today could be the day.*

I've done my blood test, read my homework. I've decided upon a low-dose testosterone cream, popular among non-binary folk reluctant to jump from one side of the binary to the other. All going well, my body would masculinise but stop short of full-blown 'man'. I'd apply the cream daily and could stop or increase the dose at any point. My flesh would be remade, turning my female shape into something androgynous, but I'd still retain some semblance of control.

All I needed now was for the doctor to issue the script.

This is it. Today is T-day.

As 2.40 pm approaches, I arrange my phone beside me and pretend to read.

2.41 pm. No call. Is the phone on silent? I double-check the volume. The doctor is probably running a few minutes late, I tell myself. Be patient.

At 2.57 pm I panic that I'd got the time wrong. I scramble for the confirmation email. *Your appointment is scheduled for 2.40 pm,* it says.

At 3.02 pm I ring reception.

'The doctor is just a little delayed,' I'm told. 'She should call within five to ten minutes.'

Forty minutes later, I ring reception again.

'The doctor hasn't called you yet? For your 2.40 pm appointment? Hang on, we'll find out what's going on.'

There's been a minor emergency, it turns out. The call would still come, at some point this afternoon, but it could be hours or minutes. I just need to hold tight, wait by the phone. I stress-eat a wedge of leftover cake, make a cup of tea, scroll the internet. The work I'd planned for the afternoon sits abandoned, a victim of my frazzled nerves.

At 4.43 pm, my phone startles me alert from a post-sugar slump.

This could still be the day. T-day. Day zero. It's happening, it's really happening.

I answer with shaking hands.

On the other end, the doctor reviews my file.

'Did you get the blood test? I can't see the results.'

'Really?' I respond, confused. 'Yes, I did the blood test. Last week.'

'We're having some issues with the pathology lab. Sorry, we'll have to re-schedule this appointment. I need your results before we can proceed.'

'Oh, I see.'

After we hang up, I stare up at the ceiling fan, my cockroach mind now flat on its back, legs flailing and belly exposed. Not today, after all. It was all a false alarm. Now there's more waiting. The endless, endless waiting. The waiting that takes my vain illusions of control, crunches them into a ball and lobs the whole mess into the wind.

The day of my third appointment, I keep expectations low. All morning, I bury myself in work to avoid thinking about that calendar entry and what it could mean. Ostrich-like, I stay inside my to-do list.

Just after lunch, halfway through an email, I'm startled by the church bells of my ringtone. It's the Equinox doctor, calling early, before I even have time to be nervous.

She speaks in a rush.

'So, I've received your bloods and everything's in order,' the doctor says. 'I'll make out the Androforte script now. Shall I fax it to your local chemist? You should be able to pick up the cream later this afternoon.'

And just like that, it's done. The whole thing had taken four minutes and thirty-nine seconds, and I'd never even moved from my seat. It was so frictionless, it barely felt real. If it wasn't for the call-log on my phone, the whole thing might have been a waking dream.

Then the fatigue hits. My nerves had been coiled by wanting, bound tight by a hunger sharpened by the fear that my appetites would go denied. Three years of wanting, waiting, waiting and wanting, three years of contorting myself into a shape that might allow my needs to be believed. Now the locked door had opened, revealing the verboten substances within, and the taut nerves went slack, deflating my flesh like a popped balloon.

Only now that it was over could I taste what an effort it had been.

At the chemist, I'm issued with a slim tube of cream, packaged in nondescript cardboard. Androforte 5. *Apply in a thin layer once daily onto torso.* If you didn't know any better, it could be treatment for a skin rash or fungal infection. An info pamphlet, shoved into my hand by the perplexed chemist, explains that Androforte replaces 'the body's natural hormone testosterone', which is 'essential for the development and maintenance of the male reproductive organs as well as other male characteristics'. Not once in the five-page pamphlet are trans people mentioned. The cream is presented only as a treatment for cisgender men. Even here, at the coalface of medical transition, transness is erased.

Back home, the proud owner of a tube of T, euphoria blossoms in my chest. It's a giddy feeling, similar to the rush of getting a tattoo, a bubbling delight that follows in the wake of self-determination. I have the hormones, no more doctors, I'm in charge now, and my body vibrates in the knowledge of that power. Tonight, crowned full sovereign of my being, I'm as beautiful as I'll ever be.

This is gender euphoria, the neglected twin of gender dysphoria.

I don't know, yet, if I will actually take the testosterone. All my old ambivalences about medical transition remain. But, in a sense, it doesn't really matter. Testosterone won't make me any more or less trans; it won't fix or cure me. All it will do is change my body, something that already takes place every minute of the day. Hair growth, hair loss, cellulite, wrinkles, nail growth, expanding waistlines, new muscle, freckles, callouses: our bodies are always in flux, no matter what we do or don't do. HRT is just another way to redecorate this ever-evolving flesh sack we call home. It won't take me to a stable destination, and nor do I want it to. The destination is trans, and I'm here now. *Living the questions*, as I promised myself three years ago.

For now, the Androforte sits on my desk, its hexagon logo winking at me, a reminder that I hold the reins. It's my body, my life, I'm trans now and forever, and I can do that exactly how I wish.

ACKNOWLEDGEMENTS

I ALWAYS READ THE ACKNOWLEDGEMENTS first, because I'm a nosy voyeur. If you're anything like me, this is your first destination within these covers. Welcome.

As they say, it takes a village. Even though I wrote much of this book in physical isolation, while living alone during Melbourne's interminable 2020 lockdowns, the list of humans who made it possible is long indeed.

First and foremost, thank you to Clare Wright: colleague, comrade, podcast co-host, mentor, friend, confidante and all-round guardian angel. This book would not exist without you. You've been there right from the start and held my hand every step of the way. I am forever grateful for your big brain and even bigger heart.

To my stalwart agent Jacinta di Mase. Thanks for taking a punt on an emerging writer and championing my story. You are a consummate professional and a delight to work with.

It has been an enormous privilege to work with the team at Allen & Unwin, who were enthused about this book from the start. Jane Palfreyman: I've been watching your legend grow for years and I'm still pinching myself that you're my publisher. Your faith in my writing means the world. Samantha Kent and Vanessa Pellatt edited this manuscript with razor-sharp eyes and generous hearts. Thank you.

I'm grateful to *Australian Book Review* editor Peter Rose and the team behind the Calibre Essay Prize. Winning this prize in 2020 transformed my life and opened countless doors; thank you to everyone who supports literary awards. *Archer Magazine* has also been a great advocate of my work—thanks to editor Lucy Watson and publisher Amy Middleton for making an outrageously gorgeous home for queer writing.

Friends, allies and chosen family have been essential companions on this journey. Thanks to you all, most especially Clancy Reid, Sally Stuart, Liz Errol, Susan Papazian, Kristine Ziwica (and family Isla, Esme and Richard), Ben Huf, Kyle Harvey, Gemma Cafarella, and the inimitable Hysterians: Alexandra Roginski, Alexis Bergantz and Alessandro Antonello. Special thanks to friend and fellow trans writer Sam Elkin, who has been an unfailingly wise (and hilarious) sounding board. You're a stellar human and I'm so glad we met.

I'm indebted to the solidarity, critique and intellectual labours of other trans and gender diverse writers, including Bobuq Sayed, Nevo Zisin, Alison Evans, Kaya Wilson, Oliver Reeson, Alex Gallagher, Sandy O'Sullivan, Hayden Moon, Maddee Clark, Andy Kaladelfos, Quinn Eades, Priya Kunjan, Nat Hollis, Roz Bellamy, Rae White, Amy Thomas, Kin Francis, Jinghua Qian, Ellen van Neerven, Bonnie Reid, Sam Elkin, Joe Latham, and everyone in the Spilling the T collective. You've each done so much to develop my thinking and I'm in awe of your individual and collective excellence. Thanks to Hannah McCann for sharing her expertise in queer theory, and to Noah Riseman for advising on trans history and reviewing relevant parts of the manuscript.

Thanks also to the extended community of writers, academics, critics, activists and queers on Twitter and Instagram—I am ever enriched by your kindness, wit and whip-smart commentary. At the ABC Jacinta Parsons, Barbara Heggen, Raf Epstein and Jessica Lukjanow have all been wonderful supporters.

A highlight of this project was the fortnight I spent at Varuna: The National Writers' House. I am hugely grateful for the Residential Fellowship that allowed me to retreat into my writing cave amid the stunning Blue Mountains. Thank you to Veechi Stuart, Amy Sambrooke, Vera Costella and chef extraordinaire Sheila Atkinson, as well as the talented co-resident writers who offered feedback on my work: Louisa Lim, Nat Hollis, Angela O'Keefe, Jennifer Castles, Karen West, Tracy Sorensen, Emily Brugman and Auna Jornayvaz.

I am fortunate to work for an academic institution that held space for my transition and supported my trans writing and activism. Thank you to all at La Trobe University, especially Nick Bisley, Simon Evans and Kat Ellinghaus—the best bosses one could hope for—as well as my colleagues in the History program: Katie Holmes, Tim Minchin, Clare Wright, Roland Burke, Tim Jones, Claudia Haake, Jennifer Jones, Emma Robertson, Ruth Gamble, Liz Conor, Sianan Healy, Jordy Silverstein, Ruth Ford, Adrian Jones and Ralph Newark. I'm forever buoyed by the smarts and solidarity of (past and present) History postgrads, especially Averyl Gaylor, Holly Wilson, Jack Fahey, Jackie Hopkins, Portia Dilena, Nikita Vanderbyl, Jessica Horton, Kasey Sinclair, Rachel Goldlust and Natasha Joyce. Elsewhere at La Trobe, Lauren Gawne, Quinn Eades, Clare O'Hanlon, Matt Smith, Tasha Weir, Wade Kelly, Lawrie Zion, Carol D'Cruz, Fiona Kelly, Emma Russell and Kelly Gardiner have all been superlative comrades. Thanks also to the larger community of Australian historians (especially teams ANU and Sydney) who welcomed my transition with nary the bat of an eyelid.

To my father, brother and extended family: thank you for your love over the years. Thanks to my animal family: Arabella, Delphi and Ruthie (and honorary family Winnie and Harry) for teaching me about love untethered from gender, and offering the comfort of your wet noses and soft fur.

Lastly, to Robyn Lansdowne, my mother and so much more, who first gave me the gift of books, feminism and love. You are the foundation upon which everything else becomes possible. Thank you for the endless conversations about writing, memory, bodies and gender, as well as the priceless succour of your support. You are my favourite person to think with and it is an honour to learn and grow alongside you.

FURTHER READING, WATCHING AND LISTENING

NON-FICTION

Eddie Ayres, *Danger Music*, Allen & Unwin, 2017
Caspar Baldwin, *Not Just a Tomboy: A Trans Masculine Memoir*, Jessica Kingsley Publishers, 2019
Meg-John Barker and Alex Iantaffi, *Life Isn't Binary: On Being Both, Beyond, and In-Between*, Jessica Kingsley Publishers, 2019
Alex Bertie, *Trans Mission: My Quest to a Beard*, Wren & Rook, 2017
Angela Chen, *Ace: What Asexuality Reveals about Desire, Society and the Meaning of Sex*, Random House, 2020
Eli Clare, *Brilliant Imperfection: Grappling with Cure*, Duke University Press, 2017
Ivan Coyote, *Rebent Sinner*, Arsenal Pulp Press, 2019
Ivan Coyote, *Tomboy Survival Guide*, Arsenal Pulp Press, 2016
Ivan E. Coyote and Rae Spoon, *Gender Failure*, Arsenal Pulp Press, 2014
Cyrus Grace Dunham, *A Year Without a Name*, Little, Brown, 2019
Leslie Feinberg, *Transgender Warriors: Making History from Joan of Arc to Dennis Rodman*, Beacon Press, 1997
Leslie Feinberg, *Trans Liberation: Beyond Pink or Blue*, Beacon Press, 1999
Leslie Feinberg, *Stone Butch Blues*, Alyson Books, 2003
T. Fleischmann, *Time Is the Thing a Body Moves Through*, Coffee House Press, 2019
Jack Halberstam, *Trans*: A Quick and Quirky Account of Gender Variability*, University of California Press, 2018
Jack Halberstam, *Female Masculinity*, 20th anniversary edition, Duke University Press, 2018

Dino Hodge (ed), *Colouring the Rainbow: Blak Queer and Trans Perspectives*, Wakefield Press, 2015

Sarah Krasnostein, *The Trauma Cleaner: One Woman's Extraordinary Life in Death, Decay & Disaster*, Text, 2017

Ben Law (ed), *Growing Up Queer in Australia*, Black Inc, 2019

C.N. Lester, *Trans Like Me: A Journey for All of Us*, Little, Brown, 2019

Amos Mac and Rocco Kayiatos (eds), *Original Plumbing: The Best of Ten Years of Trans Male Culture*, Feminist Press, 2019

Maeve Marsden (ed), *Queerstories: Reflections on lives well lived from some of Australia's finest LGBTQIA+ writers*, Hachette, 2018

Thomas Page McBee, *Man Alive: A True Story of Violence, Forgiveness and Becoming a Man*, City Lights, 2014

Thomas Page McBee, *Amateur: A True Story About What Makes a Man*, Canongate, 2018

Janet Mock, *Redefining Realness: My Path to Womanhood, Identity, Love & So Much More*, Atria Books, 2014

Janet Mock, *Surpassing Certainty: What My Twenties Taught Me*, Atria Books, 2018

Maggie Nelson, *The Argonauts*, Graywolf Press, 2015

Daniel Mallory Ortberg, *Something That May Shock and Discredit You*, Scribe, 2020

Rebekah Robertson, *About a Girl*, Penguin, 2019

Juno Roche, *Trans Power: Own Your Gender*, Jessica Kingsley Publishers, 2019

Vivek Shraya, *I'm Afraid of Men*, Penguin, 2018

Arlene Stein, *Unbound: Transgender Men and the Remaking of Identity*, Random House, 2019

Susan Stryker, *Transgender History: The Roots of Today's Revolution*, 2nd edition, Seal Press, 2017

Lou Sullivan, *We Both Laughed in Pleasure: The Selected Diaries of Lou Sullivan 1961–1991*, Nightboat Books, 2020

Kai Cheng Thom, *I Hope We Choose Love: A Trans Girl's Notes from the End of the World*, Arsenal Pulp Press, 2019

Jacob Tobia, *Sissy*, Penguin, 2019

Alok-Vaid Menon, *Beyond the Gender Binary*, Penguin, 2020

Jonathan Van Ness, *Over the Top*, Simon & Schuster, 2019

Kaya Wilson, *As Beautiful as Any Other: A memoir of my body*, Picador, 2021

Nevo Zisin, *The Pronoun Lowdown: Demystifying and celebrating gender diversity*, Smith Street Books, 2021

Nevo Zisin, *Finding Nevo: How I Confused Everyone*, Walker Books, 2017

FICTION

Imogen Binnie, *Nevada*, Topside Press, 2013

Tom Cho, *Look Who's Morphing*, Giramondo, 2009

Akwaeke Emezi, *The Death of Vivek Oji*, Penguin, 2020
Akwaeke Emezi, *Freshwater*, Faber & Faber, 2018
Laurie Frankel, *This Is How It Always Is*, Flatiron, 2017
Andrea Lawlor, *Paul Takes the Form of a Mortal Girl*, Pan Macmillan, 2020
Torrey Peters, *Detransition, Baby*, Serpent's Tail, 2021
Jordy Rosenberg, *Confessions of the Fox*, Atlantic, 2019
Elliot Wake, *Bad Boy*, Atria Books, 2017

YOUNG ADULT

Michael Earp (ed), *Kindred: 12 Queer #LoveOzYA Stories*, Walker Books, 2019
Akwaeke Emezi, *Pet*, Penguin, 2019
Alison Evans, *Euphoria Kids*, Echo Publishing, 2020
Alison Evans, *Highway Bodies*, Echo Publishing, 2019
Alison Evans, *Ida*, Echo Publishing, 2017

GRAPHIC

Archie Bongiovanni and Tristan Jimerson, *A Quick & Easy Guide to They/Them Pronouns*, Oni Press, 2018
Fury, *I Don't Understand How Emotions Work: A Graphic Memoir*, Fury, 2018
Maia Kobabe, *Gender Queer: A Memoir*, Lion Forge, 2019

POETRY

Alex Gallagher, *Parenthetical Bodies*, Subbed In, 2017
Ellen van Neerven, *Throat*, University of Queensland Press, 2020
Rae White, *Milk Teeth*, University of Queensland Press, 2018

PODCASTS

Call Me By My Name, 2018–2019
Gender Reveal, 2018
NB: My Non-binary Life, BBC Radio, 2019
Queerstories, 2017–
Queery with Cameron Esposito, 2017–
Transdemic, 2020
Transgender Warriors, JOY 94.9 FM, 2019–2020

FILMS

52 Tuesdays, 2013
Adam, 2019
A Fantastic Woman, 2017
Boys Don't Cry, 1999
Girl, 2018
Tangerine, 2015
Tomboy, 2011

DOCUMENTARIES

(A)sexual, 2011
Born to Be, 2019
Disclosure, 2020
Man Made, 2018
Paris is Burning, 1990
Seahorse, 2019
The Death and Life of Marsha P. Johnson, 2017
Transhood, 2020

TV SERIES

Euphoria, 2019–
Feel Good, 2020–2021
First Day, 2020
Gentleman Jack, 2019–
I Am Cait, 2015–2016
Orange is the New Black, 2013–2019
POSE, 2018–2021
Tales of the City, 2019
The L Word: Generation Q, 2019–
Transparent, 2014–2019
Vida, 2018–2020
We Are Who We Are, 2020
Work in Progress, 2019–

ONLINE RESOURCES

Minus18, minus18.org.au
QLife, qlife.org.au
Switchboard Victoria, switchboard.org.au
Trans Hub, transhub.org.au
Transgender Victoria, tgv.org.au

LIST OF SOURCES

LIVE THE QUESTIONS

Rainer Maria Rilke, *Letters to a Young Poet*, W.W. Norton, 1962

Maggie Nelson, *The Argonauts*, Graywolf Press, 2015

Archer Magazine, no. 4: The Ageing Issue, 2015, https://archermagazine.
bigcartel.com/product/pre-order-archer-magazine-4-june-2015

Barry Reay, *Trans America: A Counter-History*, Polity, 2020

Susan Stryker, *Transgender History: The Roots of Today's Revolution*, 2nd
edition, Seal Press, 2017

Imogen Binnie, *Nevada*, Topside Press, 2013

READING THE MESS BACKWARDS

Maggie Nelson, *The Argonauts*, Graywolf Press, 2015

D. Callander, J. Wiggins, S. Rosenberg, V.J. Cornelisse, E. Duck-Chong,
M. Holt, M. Pony, E. Vlahakis, J. MacGibbon, T. Cook, *The 2018
Australian Trans and Gender Diverse Sexual Health Survey: Report
of Findings*, The Kirby Institute, 2019, www.tgdsexualhealth.com/s/
ATGD-Sexual-Health-Survey-Report_v7.pdf

YOUR DIAGNOSIS IS 58

World Professional Association for Transgender Health, *Standards of Care
for the Health of Transsexual, Transgender, and Gender Nonconforming
People* [7th Version, 2012], www.wpath.org/publications/soc

Eli Clare, *Brilliant Imperfection: Grappling with Cure*, Duke University Press, 2017

M.F. Rodríguez, M.M. Granda, V. González, 'Gender Incongruence is No Longer a Mental Disorder', *Journal of Mental Health & Clinical Psychology*, 2, no. 5 (2018): 6–8

Kenneth J. Zucker, 'The DSM Diagnostic Criteria for Gender Identity Disorder in Children', *Archives of Sexual Behavior*, 39 (2010): 477–98

American Psychiatric Association, DSM-5 Fact Sheets, Updated Disorders: Gender Dysphoria, 2013, www.psychiatry.org/File%20Library/Psychiatrists/Practice/DSM/APA_DSM-5-Gender-Dysphoria.pdf

MISADVENTURES IN MENSWEAR

Leslie Feinberg, *Stone Butch Blues*, Alyson Books, 2003

Noah Riseman, 'Searching for Trans Possibilities in Australia, 1910–39', *Journal of Australian Studies*, 44, no. 1 (2020): 33–47

'He's the Perfect Young Girl', *The Truth*, 28 June 1942, p. 17

'Youth Tells Why He Masquerades as Girl', *The Truth*, 21 June 1942, p. 24

'Affectionate Cavorting in Newtown Street too Much for Cop', *The Truth*, 9 January 1944, p. 11

J. Halberstam, *In a Queer Time and Place: Transgender Bodies, Subcultural Lives*, NYU Press, 2005

Elizabeth Freeman, *Time Binds: Queer Temporalities, Queer Histories*, Duke University Press, 2010

TRAPPED IN A BODY

Thomas Page McBee, *Amateur: A True Story About What Makes a Man*, Canongate, 2018

Eli Clare, *Brilliant Imperfection: Grappling with Cure*, Duke University Press, 2017

Alex Gallagher, *Parenthetical Bodies*, Subbed In, 2017

Alok Vaid-Menon, *Beyond the Gender Binary*, Penguin, 2020

Margaret Robinson, 'Two-Spirit Identity in a Time of Gender Fluidity', *Journal of Homosexuality*, 67, no. 12 (2020): 1675–1690

Amao Leota Lu, 'Fa'afafine: All Hail the Queen', *Archer Magazine*, 5 September 2019

Janet Gyatso, 'One Plus One Makes Three: Buddhist Gender, Monasticism, and the Law of the Non-excluded Middle', *History of Religions*, 43, no. 2 (2003): 89–115

Madi Day, 'Indigenist Origins: Institutionalizing Indigenous Queer and Trans Studies in Australia', *TSQ: Transgender Studies Quarterly*, 7, no. 3 (2020): 367–73

Troy-Anthony Baylis, 'Introduction: Looking into the Mirror', in *Colouring the Rainbow: Blak Queer and Trans Perspectives*, edited by Dino Hodge, Wakefield Press, 2015

Hayden Moon, 'Brotherboys and Sistergirls: We Need to Decolonise Our Attitude Towards Gender in This Country', *Junkee*, 20 July 2020

Sandy O'Sullivan, 'As queer Indigenous people we know a thing or two about days of action—IDAHOBIT', *IndigenousX*, 17 May 2019

Kate Manne, *Entitled: How Male Privilege Hurts Women*, Penguin, 2020

Kate Manne, *Down Girl: The Logic of Misogyny*, Oxford University Press, 2017

Ben Beaumont-Thomas, 'Sam Smith excluded from gendered categories at 2021 Brit awards', *The Guardian*, 13 March 2021

Jack Halberstam, *Female Masculinity*, 20th anniversary edition, Duke University Press, 2018

Brian Barnett, 'Anti-Trans "Bathroom Bills" Are Based On Lies. Here's The Research To Show It', *HuffPost*, 11 September 2018

K.A. Rimes, N. Goodship, G. Ussher, D. Baker & E. West, 'Non-binary and binary transgender youth: Comparison of mental health, self-harm, suicidality, substance use and victimization experiences', *International Journal of Transgenderism*, 20, no. 2–3 (2019): 230–240

A.S. Cheung, S.Y. Leemaqz, J.P. Wong, D. Chew, O. Ooi, S. Zwickl, P. Cundill, N. Silberstein, P. Locke, R. Grayson, J.D. Zajac, K.C. Pang, 'Non-Binary and Binary Gender Identity in Australian Trans and Gender Diverse Individuals', *Archives of Sexual Behavior*, 49 (2020): 2673–2681

J. Harrison, J. Grant, J.L. Herman, 'A Gender Not Listed Here: Genderqueers, Gender Rebels, and OtherWise in the National Transgender Discrimination Survey', *LGBTQ Policy Journal at the Harvard Kennedy School*, 2, no. 1 (2012): 13–24

'Confessions', Cub Sport, written by Tim Nelson, published by Sony/ATV, 2020

Robin Dembroff, 'Why Be Nonbinary?', *Aeon*, 30 October 2018

Robin Dembroff, 'Beyond Binary: Genderqueer as Critical Gender Kind', *Philosophers' Imprint*, 20, no. 9 (2020)

ALL ABOUT YVES

Alexis Bergantz, *French Connection: Australia's cosmopolitan ambition*, NewSouth, 2021

Zadie Smith, *Intimations: Six Essays*, Penguin, 2020

All About Eve, 1950, directed by Joseph L. Mankiewicz, 20th Century Fox

THE X FILES

S.E. James, J.L. Herman, S. Rankin, M. Keisling, L. Mottet, & M. Anafi, *The Report of the 2015 U.S. Transgender Survey*, National Center for Transgender Equality, 2016

C.L. Quinan and Nina Bresser, 'Gender at the Border: Global Responses to Gender-Diverse Subjectivities and Nonbinary Registration Practices', *Global Perspectives 1*, no. 1 (2020)

Katie Rogers, 'T.S.A. Defends Treatment of Transgender Air Traveler', *The New York Times*, 22 September 2015

Sydney Bauer, 'Trans travellers face "invasive" airport security at Thanksgiving', Openly News, 28 November 2019

'X Marks the Spot for Intersex Alex', *The West Australian*, 11 January 2003

'Sex and gender diverse passport applications', Australian Passport Office, www.passports.gov.au/getting-passport-how-it-works/documents-you-need/sex-and-gender-diverse-passport-applicants

Grace Elletson, 'How Should Professors Cite Their Transgender Colleagues' Work Produced Under Past Identities?', *The Chronicle of Higher Education*, 12 July 2019

SCREEN TIME

Disclosure, 2020

'New Research Shows Overwhelming Support among Australians on Trans Equality', press release, Equality Australia, 18 January 2021, https://equalityaustralia.org.au/overwhelming-support-on-trans-equality/

Katy Steinmetz, 'The Transgender Tipping Point', *Time*, 29 May 2014: https://time.com/135480/transgender-tipping-point/

Anne Boyer, *The Undying: A Meditation on Modern Illness*, Penguin, 2019

Derrick Clifton, 'At Least 350 Transgender People Have Been Killed Globally in 2020', *Them*, 11 November 2020

Stevie Zhang, 'Trans University Students Say They Feel Unsafe Over a Professor's "Transphobic" Website', *Junkee*, 19 March 2021

Joshua Badge and Alex Garcia Marrugo, 'Here's Proof that Trans People are the New Target of *The Australian's* War on Queer People', *Junkee*, 18 December 2019

Priya Krishnakumar, 'This record-breaking year for anti-transgender legislation would affect minors the most', CNN, 15 April 2021

Noah Riseman, 'Transgender Histories seminar', Melbourne Feminist History group, 8 October 2020, www.youtube.com/watch?v=1SiRCpw_jdY

Ruth Ford, 'Speculating on scrapbooks, sex and desire: Issues in lesbian history', *Australian Historical Studies*, 27, no. 106 (1996): 111–126

Noah Riseman, Shirleene Robinson and Graham Willett, *Serving in Silence? Australian LGBT Servicemen and Women*, NewSouth, 2018

Caspar Baldwin, *Not Just a Tomboy: A Trans Masculine Memoir*, Jessica Kingsley Publishers, 2019

Alison Evans, 'Word School', Queerstories, 25 July 2018

Alison Evans, *Euphoria Kids*, Echo Publishing, 2020

EVERYDAY ARMOUR

Scout Boxall, 'Everyday Armour', Queerstories, 7 May 2019

E-J Scott, 'Trans masculinity on the record', Wellcome Collection, 25 February 2020, https://wellcomecollection.org/articles/XjFY1hQAACMAKesE

S. Peitzmeier, I. Gardner, J. Weinand, A. Corbet & K. Acevedo, 'Health impact of chest binding among transgender adults: a community-engaged, cross-sectional study', *Culture, Health & Sexuality*, 19, no.1 (2017): 64–75

THEY

Gretchen McCulloch, 'A Linguist on the Story of Gendered Pronouns', *The Toast*, 2 June 2014

Lingthusiasm podcast, episode 2, 'Pronouns. Little words, big jobs', 14 December 2016, https://lingthusiasm.com/post/154520062361/lingthusiasm-episode-2-pronouns-little-words

'The singular, gender-neutral "they" added to the Associated Press Stylebook', *The Washington Post*, 28 March 2017

'2019 Word of the Year is "(My) Pronouns," Word of the Decade is Singular "They" as Voted by American Dialect Society', press release, American Dialect Society, 3 January 2020, www.americandialect.org/wp-content/uploads/2019-Word-of-the-Year-PRESS-RELEASE.pdf

'Merriam-Webster's Words of the Year 2019', www.merriam-webster.com/words-at-play/word-of-the-year-2019-they/quid-pro-quo

BLOOD WILL TELL

Trans Pathways Summary, Telethon Kids Institute, www.telethonkids.org.au/globalassets/media/documents/brain-behaviour/trans-pathways-summary.pdf

Seahorse, 2019

WOMEN'S SPACES

Brazen Hussies, directed by Catherine Dwyer, 2020

Cameron Awkward-Rich, 'Trans, Feminism: Or, Reading Like a Depressed Transsexual', *Signs*, 42, no. 4 (2017): 819–41

D. Callander, J. Wiggins, S. Rosenberg, V.J. Cornelisse, E. Duck-Chong, M. Holt, M. Pony, E. Vlahakis, J. MacGibbon, T. Cook, *The 2018 Australian Trans and Gender Diverse Sexual Health Survey: Report of Findings*, The Kirby Institute, 2019, www.tgdsexualhealth.com/s/ATGD-Sexual-Health-Survey-Report_v7.pdf

Clare Wright, *You Daughters of Freedom: Australians Who Won the Vote and Inspired the World*, Text, 2019

Jinghua Qian, 'Walking Away, Backwards; Or Women-Lite in Women's Lit', Feminist Writers Festival, 2020, https://feministwritersfestival.com/leaving/

Alex Gallagher, *Parenthetical Bodies*, Subbed In, 2017

Robin Dembroff, 'Why Be Nonbinary?', *Aeon*, 30 October 2018

WHAT'S SEX GOT TO DO WITH IT?

Barry Reay, *Trans America: A Counter-History*, Polity, 2020

Leslie Feinberg, *Transgender Warriors: Making History from Joan of Arc to Dennis Rodman*, Beacon Press, 1997

Stephen A. Russell, 'Presidential thoughts: Eileen Myles on gender, sexuality and the bathroom wars,' SBS Online, 2 May 2018

Abigail Meinen, 'I am Legion: An interview with Eileen Myles', *Sampsonia Way*, 22 June 2018

Anne Boyer, *The Undying: A Meditation on Modern Illness*, Penguin, 2019

Lou Sullivan, *We Both Laughed in Pleasure: The Selected Diaries of Lou Sullivan 1961–1991*, Nightboat Books, 2020

'Grindr Users Talk About Transphobia', Kindr episode 3, 2 June 2018, www.youtube.com/watch?v=vLrEtSd3ttE

Karen L. Blair and Rhea Ashley Hoskin, 'Transgender exclusion from the world of dating: Patterns of acceptance and rejection of hypothetical trans dating partners as a function of sexual and gender identity', *Journal of Social and Personal Relationships*, 36, no. 7 (2019): 2074–95

Brandon Taylor, 'On Being Queer and Happily Single—Except When I'm Not', *Them*, 9 December 2017

Cameron Awkward-Rich, 'A Prude's Manifesto', Button Poetry, 16 January 2014, www.youtube.com/watch?v=nInAqWF0tt4

Ela Przybylo, *Asexual Erotics: Intimate Readings of Compulsory Sexuality*, Ohio State University Press, 2019

Angela Chen, *Ace: What Asexuality Reveals about Desire, Society and the Meaning of Sex*, Random House, 2020

Gala Vanting, 'Playboy (Step)Mommy', Queerstories, 16 May 2019

Brook Pessin-Whedbee, *Who Are You? The Kid's Guide to Gender Diversity*, Jessica Kingsley Publishers, 2017

CALLING PURPLE GREEN

Alexander Humphries and Ellen Coulter, 'Tasmania makes gender optional on birth certificates after Liberal crosses floor', ABC News, 10 April 2019

Yves Rees, 'Who's Afraid of Transgender Cricket?', *Overland*, 22 August 2019

Joshua Badge and Alex Garcia Marrugo, 'Here's Proof that Trans People
    are the New Target of *The Australian's* War on Queer People', *Junkee*,
    18 December 2019
Amy Thomas, Hannah McCann and Geraldine Fela, 'Long Live the Gender
    Whisperers', *Overland*, 15 October 2018
Amy Thomas and Hannah McCann, 'Marriage equality: yes, it's about
    gender', *Overland*, 7 September 2017
Amy Thomas, Hannah McCann and Geraldine Fela, '"In this house we
    believe in fairness and kindness": Post-liberation politics in Australia's
    same-sex marriage postal survey', *Sexualities*, 23, no. 4 (2020): 475–496
Alex Gallagher, 'Is it really a win for queer rights if we exclude our most
    vulnerable to achieve it?', *The Guardian*, 6 September 2017
Laila Lalami, '"Bothsideism" is poisoning America', *The Nation*, 17 December
    2019
'How Transgender People Experience the Media', Trans Media Watch,
    April 2010, https://transmediawatch.org/wp-content/uploads/2020/09/
    How-Transgender-People-Experience-the-Media.pdf
'The British Press and the Transgender Community', Trans Media
    Watch, December 2011, https://transmediawatch.org/wp-content/
    uploads/2020/09/Publishable-Trans-Media-Watch-Submission.pdf
'Additional Submission to the Leveson Inquiry', Trans Media Watch, February
    2012, https://transmediawatch.org/wp-content/uploads/2020/09/
    Additional-Trans-Media-Watch-Submission-Public.pdf
Faisal Ahmed and Angela Lucas-Herald, 'What are puberty blockers, and how
    do they work?', *The Conversation*, 10 December 2020
Brian Barnett, 'Anti-Trans "Bathroom Bills" Are Based On Lies. Here's The
    Research To Show It', *HuffPost*, 11 September 2018
'Personal Safety Survey, Australia, 2016', ABS cat. No. 4906.0, Australian
    Bureau of Statistics, 2017, www.abs.gov.au/ausstats/abs@.nsf/mf/4906.0
Ryan Storr, 'Elite sport is becoming a platform to target the trans community',
    The Conversation, 15 March 2019
Toni Morrison, 'You've got some dragons to slay', PSU Black Studies Center
    public dialog, 1975, https://soundcloud.com/portland-state-library/
    youve-got-some-dragons-to-slay-toni-morrison-psu-black-studies-center-
    public-dialog-1975
Yves Rees, 'Debate on transgender "issue" has one thing missing', *The Age*,
    7 December 2020
'*The Age* removes transgender opinion piece as editor offers apology', *Out In
    Perth*, 14 December 2020
Carolyn Cage, 'Bridget Flack was Days from Receiving Mental Health Care
    Before Disappearance,' *HuffPost*, 11 December 2020
Jessi Lewis, 'Remembering Bridget Flack', *Star Observer*, 23 December 2020
Trans Pathways Summary, Telethon Kids Institute, www.telethonkids.org.au/
    globalassets/media/documents/brain--behaviour/trans-pathways-summary.pdf

National LGBTI Health Alliance, 'Snapshot of Mental Health and Suicide Prevention Statistics for LGBTI People', July 2016, https://d3n8a8pro7vhmx.cloudfront.net/lgbtihealth/pages/549/attachments/original/1595492232/2016_SNAPSHOT-Mental-Health_%281%29.pdf?1595492232

D. Callander, J. Wiggins, S. Rosenberg, V.J. Cornelisse, E. Duck-Chong, M. Holt, M. Pony, E. Vlahakis, J. MacGibbon, T. Cook, *The 2018 Australian Trans and Gender Diverse Sexual Health Survey: Report of Findings*, The Kirby Institute, 2019, www.tgdsexualhealth.com/s/ATGD-Sexual-Health-Survey-Report_v7.pdf

Audre Lorde, *Sister Outsider: Essays and Speeches*, Crossing Press, 1984

'New Research Shows Overwhelming Support among Australians on Trans Equality', press release, Equality Australia, 18 January 2021 https://equalityaustralia.org.au/overwhelming-support-on-trans-equality/

IN THE TIME OF CORONA

'Development of trans and gender diverse services in Victoria: Final report', Department of Health and Human Services, June 2018, https://www2.health.vic.gov.au/about/publications/researchandreports/development-trans-gender-diverse-services-victoria-final-report

S. Zwickl, L.M. Angus, A.W.F. Qi, A. Ginger, K. Eshin, T. Cook, S.Y. Leemaqz, E. Dowers, J.D. Zajac & A.S. Cheung, 'The impact of the first three months of the COVID-19 pandemic on the Australian trans community', *International Journal of Transgender Health* (2021): DOI: 10.1080/26895269.2021.1890659

'Transgender Mental Health and Suicide Risk During the Covid-19 Pandemic', Trans Medical Research Group, University of Melbourne, https://mhcc.org.au/wp-content/uploads/2020/06/CMHDARN-Trans-MH-Suicide-COVID-19-Findings-Trans-Medical-Research-Group.pdf

Eileen Myles, *Afterglow: A Dog Memoir*, Grove Press, 2017

Judith Butler, *Gender Trouble*, Routledge, 1990

Benjamin Riley, 'With queer spaces closed due to Covid, I feel more disconnected than ever from who I am', *The Guardian*, 19 October 2020

'Living Trans During C19', ACON Forum, 6 May 2020, https://youtube.com/watch?v=3cSTEDMv1g4

BLONDIE

Roz Bellamy, 'On physical queer identifiers and "passing" as straight', *SBS Online*, 20 September 2017

Roz Bellamy, 'My Helmet', *Going Down Swinging*, February 2016

Richard Dyer, *White*, Routledge, 2017

Rebecca M. Herzig, *Plucked: A History of Hair Removal*, New York University Press, 2015

Pat Jalland, *Australian Ways of Death: A Social and Cultural History, 1840–1918*, Oxford University Press, 2002

Jayne Persian, *Beautiful Balts: From Displaced Persons to New Australians*, NewSouth, 2017

Noah Riseman, Shirleene Robinson and Graham Willett, *Serving in Silence? Australian LGBT Servicemen and Women*, NewSouth, 2018

Vivek Shraya, *I'm Afraid of Men*, Penguin, 2018

Amanda Third and Diane Negra, 'Does the rug match the carpet? Race, gender, and the redheaded woman', in *The Irish in Us: Irishness, Performativity, and Popular Culture*, Duke University Press, 2006

Susan J. Vincent, *Hair: An Illustrated History*, Bloomsbury, 2018

Australian Human Rights Commission, 'Face the Facts: Lesbian, Gay, Bisexual, Trans and Intersex People', 2014.

Trans Murder Monitoring project, transrespect.org

BPM

Sophie Alexander, 'Exercise-mad British pensioner found to have world's slowest EVER heartrate', *Express*, 15 May 2014

DESTINATION TRANS

Juno Roche, *Trans Power: Own Your Gender*, Jessica Kingsley Publishers, 2019

NB: My Non-binary Life, BBC Radio, 2019, episode 8

'Development of trans and gender diverse services in Victoria: Final report,' Department of Health and Human Services, June 2018, https://www2.health.vic.gov.au/about/publications/researchandreports/development-trans-gender-diverse-services-victoria-final-report

Jeffrey M. Jones, 'LGBT Identification Rises to 5.6% in Latest U.S. Estimate', Gallup, 24 February 2021

'Change the Story: A shared framework for the primary prevention of violence against women and their children in Australia', Our Watch, 2015, https://media-cdn.ourwatch.org.au/wp-content/uploads/sites/2/2019/05/21025429/Change-the-story-framework-prevent-violence-women-children-AA-new.pdf

'Challenging gender stereotypes in the early years: the power of parents', Our Watch, 2018, https://media-cdn.ourwatch.org.au/wp-content/uploads/sites/2/2019/11/06031050/Our-Watch-Parenting-and-Early-Years.pdf